WINS, LOSSES, AND LESSONS

ALSO BY LOU HOLTZ

Winning Every Day:

The Game Plan for Success

WINS, LOSSES, AND LESSONS

AN AUTOBIOGRAPHY

LOU HOLTZ

 HarperLargePrint
An Imprint of HarperCollinsPublishers
www.harpercollins.com

WINS, LOSSES, AND LESSONS. Copyright © 2006 by Lou Holtz. All rights reserved. Printed in the United States of America. No part of this book may be used or reproduced in any manner whatsoever without written permission except in the case of brief quotations embodied in critical articles and reviews. For information address HarperCollins Publishers, 10 East 53rd Street, New York, NY 10022.

HarperLargePrint
An Imprint of HarperCollins Publishers
10 East 53rd Street
New York, NY 10022.

ISBN: 0-06-123295-5

Printed in the U.S.A.

10 9 8 7 6 5 4 3 2

To every person who has faced adversity, whether in their personal, business, or social life, and responded positively to it. I admire the person who says, "Everyday someone does something great, today that someone will be me."

CONTENTS

Introduction   ix

1   It's Not What You Have,
    It's Who You Have   1

2   Success Is a Choice You Make   29

3   First Impressions
    Have Lasting Results   57

4   A Day Without Learning
    Is a Day Without Living   75

5   Setbacks Don't Define
    Your Goals, You Do   101

6   Greatness Starts with Belief
    and Total Commitment   123

7   Leading Is Easy When
    People Want to Be Led   153

8 A Halfhearted Commitment Is
   Worse Than No Commitment at All   179

9 What Behavior Are You
   Willing to Accept?   207

10 Bad Things Sometimes Happen
   for a Good Reason   245

11 Getting Rid of Excuses   283

12 Success Is a Matter of Faith   323

13 Perfection Is Possible If
   You Accept Nothing Less   349

14 All You Can Do Is
   All You Can Do   379

15 Everyone Needs Something
   to Look Forward To   401

   Epilogue   427

   Acknowledgments   437

   Appendix   443

INTRODUCTION

Celebrating Notre Dame's victory over Per-
due, 52–7, September 24, 1988. No individual or team can perform under pressure without preparation. **(Courtesy of Dr. Freddy
Achecar)**

Three seconds left in the game, and I'm on the sidelines watching as our kicker, Daniel Weaver, paces the field, collects his thoughts, and waits through what seems like an endless series of time-outs. Daniel needs to kick the ball 42 yards through the uprights, not a particularly long kick given the steady Florida wind at his back, but for him, and for our team, there is no bigger play. If the field goal is good, our South Carolina Gamecocks will win their second consecutive bowl game for the first time in 108 years. It will also be our second victory in as many years at the Outback Bowl over Ohio State, a team we beat 24–7 the previous New Year's Day. But more important, this play represents the culmination of three years of hard work, heartache, dedication, and belief in ourselves when it seemed that no one else believed in us. If good, Daniel's kick will cap the second greatest turnaround in the history of Division I college football. Our team, which had gone 0–11 two years before, will finish the year ranked in the top twenty in the country for the second consecutive season, something never before accomplished at South Carolina.

Regardless of the outcome, I'm really proud of these players, coaches, administrators, and fans. Our athletes played their hearts out all year long, and now stand on the threshold of accomplishing something they will carry with them for the rest of their lives. Of course, I'm not in a position to share my reflections. The game is tied at 28. Daniel's kick will be the final play of regulation. If the ball hits the upright, or hooks outside, or if our holder bobbles the snap, or if one of Ohio State's fine defensive linemen breaks through and blocks the kick, the game will go into overtime. This is the last thing I want, because the Ohio State team is brimming with confidence after having fought its way back from a huge deficit. I don't want our team thinking that I am considering this. I'm fully confident in our kicking team. Daniel Weaver is a fine kicker, Eric Kimrey is a fine holder, and our protection has been solid all year.

It's an odd time, but during the first time-out, I think about something the great golfer Ben Hogan once said. Hogan, who was famed for his Trojan work ethic, said, "Playing a tournament is almost an anticlimax. Tournaments are won and lost in preparation. Playing them is just going through the motions." I would never describe a football game as "going through the motions," although I've read those very words after some of our losses, but Hogan's point about preparation is correct. No individual or team, whether in sports, business, the church, or the family, can perform under pressure without preparation. I'm confident about this field goal because our kicking team has practiced this scenario hundreds of times. Daniel Weaver has been preparing for this since he was twelve years old.

I'm sure someone upstairs in the television booth is talking about the "pressure" Daniel is feeling. That's the whole reason Ohio State has called this time-out. Coach Jim Tressel is giving our team a little extra time to ponder the situation. I've done the same thing to opponents under similar circumstances. But this pause in play doesn't concern me. When I was coaching at Notre Dame, Tony LaRussa, who was then managing the Oakland A's, once told our team, "Pressure comes when someone calls on you to perform a task for which you are unprepared." I know we're prepared. This play is simply another repetition, an opportunity to execute what we've practiced all year long.

Still, you have to think ahead. If we miss, we still have a chance to win if we can keep the team focused. The hope would then be to prevail in overtime. Then again, as General Tommy Franks says, "Hope is not a strategy."

By all rights we shouldn't be in this situation. We dominated the first three quarters, leading 14–0 at halftime and scoring twice more in the third quarter to take a 28–0 lead. It was as fine a performance as our team had had since I took the head-coaching job at South Carolina. Now, the score is tied at 28. Our offense has failed to put a single point on the board in the fourth quarter, while Ohio State, led by quarterback Steve Bellisari, has come roaring back, predominantly on the strength of his passing.

Bellisari put the Buckeyes on the board at the end of the third quarter with a 2-yard run for a touchdown. Four minutes later he threw a 16-yard touchdown pass to cut our lead in half. After our offense was unable to do anything, Bellisari drove the ball deep into our territory before losing the snap and fumbling on our eighteen. We returned the favor by fumbling on the first play from scrimmage and giving the ball right back to them. Three plays later, they ran in for another score to draw within a touchdown. At that point I looked up and saw that we had five minutes to go, plenty of time.

Our quarterback, senior Phil Petty, had played great all afternoon, but the Ohio State defense stiffened, and we had to punt with just under four minutes on the clock. Bellisari then pecked through our defense, completing six out of six passes, the final one for 9 yards and a touchdown to tie the score. He has been aided by the fact that we lost two fine defensive backs in the second half due to injuries.

Those are the particulars of how we got here, but they don't tell the whole story. I'm sure plenty of "experts" around the country are jabbering about how Ohio State has the "momentum." Sure, they haven't given up, but neither have we. I always get hot when I hear some expert going on and on about momentum shifting this way or that in a game. Momentum is nothing more than attitude. Three hours ago, this game was tied 0–0. It stayed that way through much of the first quarter. Now that it's tied again at 28, why would anyone say we're worse off than we were when the game started? What's the difference between a 0–0 score and being tied at 28?

I'll tell you: the only difference is attitude. If every player on our team believes he is going to beat the man across from him on the next play, and the play after that, and the play after that, we're in no worse shape now than we were throughout most of the first quarter. Sure, I'd like to be leading by a couple of touchdowns, but I'm not about to fall for the folly that we're on the wrong side of some nebulous shift in momentum. I've said many times that how you respond to challenges in the second half determines what you become after the game, whether you are a winner or a loser. I would be hard-pressed to find any losers on the football field this afternoon, on either side.

I put my hands on my knees as the referee blows the whistle and puts the ball in play. The clock will start when the ball is snapped. Daniel goes through his preparation—three steps back and two to the side—visualizing the kick, swaying his arms back and forth to relax himself, and then focusing on the spot where the holder will place the ball. Each man on the line knows his assignment. Our holder raises his hands to catch the snap; the center glances between his legs for one last visual cue, just as he has hundreds of times in practice.

The snap is away. Ohio State defenders surge against our offensive line. A couple of their speedy safeties try to swing in from the outside, while one of their corners leaps so high that if he were on a basketball court he could take a quarter off the top of the backboard. The holder takes the snap and puts the ball down perfectly, laces facing the middle of the uprights. Daniel takes two quick steps forward, eyes focused on the ball, and hits the kick.

I can tell that he makes contact a little low on the ball, not his best effort.

It's on the way.

The human brain is an amazing and wonderful thing, capable of conceiving split atoms, harmonic symphonies, poetry, and prose. While the kick is in the air, I wish my thoughts could run on fast-forward. Images of my uncle Lou Tychonievich, who was my first coach, my best friend, and one of the most influential role models in my life, flash through my mind. Uncle Lou has been gone five years, but I can still see his smiling face. I also think about my father, and my uncles Leo, Bill, Walt, and John, all the men who took a young, small, irascible kid and molded him into the man on the sidelines. My mind sees Wade Watts, the high school football coach in East Liverpool, Ohio, who thought enough of his second-string blocking back to tell the boy's parents that he should go to college and be a coach someday. And I see my mother, a strong and deeply spiritual woman who took a night job at the hospital so that her only son could become the first member of the family to darken the doors of a university. I see the thousands of players I've coached in my forty years on the sidelines, most of whom never played a down of football after college, but many of whom went on to achieve great things in life: Doug DiOrio, a walk-on who only played a couple of plays, but who is now a successful physician; Reggie Ho, a five-foot-four-inch placekicker who is now a surgeon at Johns Hopkins; Flash Gordon, a former Notre Dame player who now runs a camp for underprivileged boys. I think about Woody Hayes, the most demanding boss I ever had, and a man I will always admire. It seems fitting that we're playing Ohio State, where the spirit of Coach Hayes still paces the sidelines. It seems like yesterday when I was a young assistant for the national championship Buckeyes led by Coach Hayes. Could it really have been thirty-five years ago? Those memories race through my brain as the ball arcs and spins toward the crossbar. This one is going to be close.

From my angle, I can't tell if the ball makes it over the crossbar. I look at the referee standing beneath the left upright. He hesitates, then runs forward. Is it good? Do we win? Or are we playing more football?

The arms go up, and everything turns to chaos. Thank God they didn't paint the goalposts or this one wouldn't have made it. Jeremiah Garrison, one of our linebackers, almost runs over me as he leaps out onto the field in celebration. The kick is good. I look out and see our kicking team swarming Daniel Weaver. Team members embrace me. They hug one another. They dance. They celebrate.

They deserve it.

I meet Coach Tressel at midfield. We shake hands, and I say, "Great job, Coach. Your team showed a lot of heart."

He thanks me and returns the compliment. I can see that he's disappointed by the loss, but his team has no reason to hang their heads. If they had given up when they were down by four touchdowns, then they might have reason to lose sleep. But those athletes showed the kind of courage, confidence, and determination that would make any coach proud. Sure, they came up a little short today, but this is the kind of game, win or lose, where players and coaches can walk away knowing that they gave it all they had. I can't know at this moment that Ohio State is a year away from a national championship, but I do know that Coach Tressel's team is on the cusp of greatness.

We are fortunate to walk away with the win. I don't know what would have happened if Daniel's kick had come up short. All I know is that our team continues to exemplify one of my favorite quotes by the great philosopher Ayn Rand, who said, "The ladder of success is best climbed by stepping on the rungs of opportunity."

That quote typifies this team. Every athlete on the field hauled himself to this point by grabbing the rungs of opportunity. The quote also says a lot about my life. I've been blessed to come into contact with people who cared enough about me to steer me in the right direction, and show me rungs of opportunity I never could have imagined without them. I pray that the story of my life will provide rungs of opportunity for those who read or hear it, so that I may leave this earth having done for others what many others so graciously did for me.

Coaching gives one a chance to be successful as well as significant. The difference between those two is that when you die, your success comes to an end. When you are significant, you continue to help others be successful long after you are gone. Significance lasts many lifetimes. That is why people teach, why people lead, and why people coach. As I leave the field of play, I enjoy the feeling of being a winning coach. But more important, I hope that I have been a person of significance in the lives of these young men.

1

IT'S NOT WHAT YOU HAVE, IT'S WHO YOU HAVE

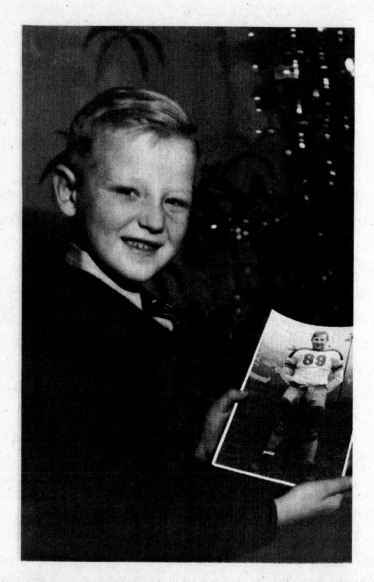

Christmas, 1944: I'm holding a photograph of my dear uncle Lou, who played football for East Liverpool High School and would be my first coach at Saint Aloysius.

When I die and people realize that I will not be resurrected in three days, they will forget me. That is the way it should be. For reasons known only to God, I was asked to write an autobiography. Most people who knew me growing up didn't think I would ever read a book, let alone write one. Anyway, here goes:

I was born January 6, 1937, eight years after Wall Street crashed, and two years before John Steinbeck published **The Grapes of Wrath,** his Pulitzer Prize–winning novel about the plight of a family during the Great Depression. How bad was it? Well, we weren't Okies, in the sense that we weren't from Oklahoma, but in every other respect the Holtzes of West Virginia could easily have been mistaken for the Joads of the dust bowl South.

Like many children of that era, I was born at home. Hospitals were expensive, and Dr. McGraw, our local physician, made house calls, so there was never a question about where the labor and delivery would take place. My parents, Andrew and Anne Marie, rented a two-room cellar in Follansbee, West Virginia, a small steel mill town in the northernmost sliver of the state between Ohio and Pennsylvania. That's where God saw fit for me to join this world and where I lived the early years of my life. Not that where we lived mattered much: the majority of the people in western Pennsylvania, eastern Ohio, and West Virginia survived in spartan conditions similar to our own.

My father's father, Leo Holtz, had moved to Follansbee from Rossiter, Pennsylvania, about five miles from Punxsutawney, to work at Wheeling Steel. Grandpa Holtz had been a coal miner in Rossiter, where he lived in company housing and was paid in company scrip that could be redeemed only at the company store, a situation so akin to indentured servitude that it was later outlawed. It took a lot of courage for him to pick up the family and move, but if you've ever been inside a coal mine, you can understand his motivation.

My grandmother, Jenny Holtz, was a deeply spiritual woman who attended mass every day of her life. She also lost her first two children at birth, both boys she had named Andrew. When my father came along she named him Andrew as well. It must have given the Rossiter records office fits—all those birth and death certificates with the same name—but somehow my dad made it, and grew up the oldest living Holtz child. He had two sisters, Mary and Evelyn, and two brothers, my uncles Leo and John.

My father stayed in Follansbee after he married my mom, even though the work was sparse. Dad picked up odd jobs here and there, working on the railroad, driving a truck for a while, and a bus for a period. We never went without food, but like most people in town we lived on the bare minimum. I always knew I'd had plenty to eat because when I asked for more my father would say, "No, you've had plenty."

Our cellar home had a kitchen and a combination bedroom and half bath, which meant we had a sink next to the bed. We had no refrigerator, no shower or tub, and no privacy. My parents shared the bedroom with my sister and me. We bathed in the sink when we could, ate outside when the weather permitted, and slept in whatever configuration kept us warm and comfortable. We didn't have a closet, because we didn't need one. I owned one pair of overalls and one flannel shirt, an outfit I wore every day. My mother washed it on the weekends, and my father always said, "Be careful playing. If you rip a hole in your butt it will heal. A hole in those pants won't." I wish my father had listened to his own warnings. When I was in grade school, Dad spilled paint on my only shirt. Up to that point, nobody had known that I wore the same clothes every day. Other kids just assumed I owned four or five identical outfits and had no sense of style. But with paint on my shirt it became obvious that I never changed clothes.

We needed a raise to be considered poor. Every day we awoke to hardship, and every night we fell asleep thankful for one more day of sustenance. At age nine, I got a paper route. Sixty-six papers had to be delivered to sixty-six families every day. I also had to collect thirty cents a week from each customer. I owed the paper twenty cents per customer per week, and got to keep the rest. When I didn't collect, the balance came out of my profit. My average income was six dollars a week.

Every member of the family did what he or she could to help make ends meet, same as all the other families in our area. No one I ever knew used the words "disposable" and "income" in the same sentence. At age five, I got my first Coke. It was so good that I wanted it to last. Chances were pretty good that it might be three or four years before I would get another one. So after a few sips, I put the bottle in the windowsill (we didn't have an icebox, much less a refrigerator). Unfortunately, the next morning the soda was flat and stale and had to be thrown away. As a five-year-old, I suddenly understood that you should enjoy life's blessings, no matter how small, when you can, because they won't last forever.

Yes, we were poor, but we always had one another. Unlike some of today's young people, I never suffered from depression, never needed therapy, never contemplated injuring myself or others, and never fretted over all the things I didn't have. I was a happy, normal kid because I knew God and my family loved me. That was all that mattered. Today, we live in an age and a place that make the lost city of El Dorado look like a slum, but too many people's riches leave them empty. They buy more and more things, attend more parties, eat at more fine restaurants, lease all the right cars, and max out credit cards in the hopes of filling some void. Unfortunately, material goods are never a substitute for a family's love. I never had that problem. We never had any material goods, but I had lots of people who loved me.

My mother's parents, Louis and Carey Tychonievich, both hailed from Chernobyl in the Ukraine. They had come over as young adults, arriving in America with little more than the clothes on their backs and dreams as big as the country they now called home. My mother was the oldest child. She had three younger brothers, Bill, Walt, and Lou. So for a while, I was the only grandson for two sets of grandparents, and the only nephew for five uncles. To the extent that they could, my uncles and my grandparents spoiled me rotten, taking me to the park to play catch when we could scrounge up a ball, teaching me how to tell a joke, and how to laugh at a good one told. They introduced me to sports, putting me on their laps as the sounds of Ohio State and Notre Dame football games crackled from the family radio. They gave me my first nickname, "Champ," a name that followed me throughout my early school years, and left a lasting impression as I matured into a young adult. I was always small, always a little shy, and always the youngest kid in every group, so it was a great help for me to have strong male role models to look up to. My uncle Lou, who was closest to me in age, became my best friend, someone who made me forget about the pressures and hardships of everyday life.

I didn't realize it at the time, but during those formative years I practiced what I would later learn was my "WIN" strategy for life. WIN is an acronym for "What's important now?" the question I have always asked myself when facing tough decisions. No matter what situation you are in, you should constantly ask yourself, "What's important now?" If you have a test in the morning, but your buddies have tickets to a late-night concert, "What's important now?" If your team has an important game on Saturday and you need plenty of rest, but your roommate asks you to go clubbing, "What's important now?" In some instances, the answers are easy. If my car is in a ditch, what I'm having for dinner tonight isn't important. If my wife comes home with a bad report from her doctor, the score I shot on the golf course tumbles down the importance list. When I was a young child and my father was out of work for a week, leaving no food in the house, the question

"What's important now?" had an easy answer: get out, work, hustle, and do whatever it took to survive. The WIN strategy is as applicable in times of prosperity as it is during a depression.

You couldn't survive in our time and not learn somehow to focus on what was really important in life. People's priorities were different two or three generations ago. Not a news cycle goes by today when someone isn't in front of a camera or behind a microphone complaining about a violation of his or her rights. Spill coffee in your lap? Sue the restaurant that served you. Want to prance around your high school in a headdress, disrupting the learning environment? Plenty of lawyers are ready to take your case—free expression and all. These were not issues fifty or sixty years ago. People my age and older weren't concerned about their rights and privileges: we were conscious of our obligations and responsibilities. I learned early that I had an obligation to contribute to the family, and any income I earned would go straight into the family budget. Sure, it might not have been "fair" for a nine-year-old to carry that kind of burden, but that was simply the way life was. If you contributed nothing to society, you were not entitled to the rewards. Work hard and you earned certain perks. Do nothing and you got nothing. I learned that before I could write my name (and trust me, L-O-U wasn't that tough). The nebulous concept of "rights" never entered my mind until much later, and any thought that I might actually have rights didn't dawn on me until young adulthood.

I also learned about the importance of duty, and about committing to things larger than self. Americans from the Great Depression are called "the Greatest Generation" because of their sacrifices—their quiet but strong commitment to doing right no matter what the cost. My father and uncles were a part of that Greatest Generation. Not long after Pearl Harbor, the men in my family volunteered for service. Within a year, they had all marched silently away to war.

We all supported the war effort. When Dad left for the Navy, my mother, sister, and I moved to East Liverpool, Ohio, to live with my grandparents Tychonievich and my uncle Lou (who was fourteen years old at the time). My grandparents were happy to have us, but I wasn't thrilled to be there, because of the friends I had left in Follansbee. Fortunately, my uncle Lou was like an older brother to me. He taught me to catch a football and baseball. He was there to answer the burning questions on every boy's mind—"So, is Betty Boop supposed to make you tingle like this?" He took me to the corner store for a soda whenever we could scrounge a few coins. Lou was also a high school football player. This was my first exposure to organized football, and I loved every second of it, mostly because Uncle Lou was an excellent tight end. It was fun to cheer for a relative, especially someone like Lou.

My grandfather was too old-fashioned to be much of a cheerer, although he was a huge football fan. He would listen to Notre Dame every time a game aired, which was often. Knute Rockne had seen to that. During his time as coach, Rockne not only convinced the university to build a sixty-thousand-seat football stadium for a college with only three thousand students, he also lobbied to have Notre Dame football games broadcast on radio stations across the country. Grandpa tuned into those games as if the Lord had commanded it, in part because he was Catholic, and in part because Notre Dame went four years without losing a football game. It was fun following a winner. I didn't understand everything I heard, but I listened to every play. I also learned to read so that I could wade through the sports pages, following the games that interested me by reading reporters' summaries. I heard stories from my grandpa about the Four Horsemen, Notre Dame's legendary backfield of Harry Stuhldreher, Jim Crowley, Don Miller, and Elmer Layden, and the 1924 national championship season, and I heard lectures about how every good Catholic had to support Notre Dame.

Uncle Lou would antagonize his father by trying to turn me into an Ohio State or Illinois fan, and I did, indeed, pull hard for both of those teams. Lou also put me up to no good around the house. During the height of the war, he pulled me aside and said, "Next time your grandpa comments on something in the paper, I want you to say, 'Oh, that's just propaganda.'"

"What's propaganda mean?" I asked.

"Nothing," he said. "Your grandpa will think it's funny."

Sure enough, after dinner that night Grandpa read the paper and made some gruff comment on either the rubber drive or the sugar ration, I can't remember which. On cue, I piped up and said, "Oh, that's just propaganda."

I barely saw the back of his hand before it caught me in the temple. Propaganda entered our lexicon during World War II, in part because the Nazis were so good at it. I had no idea what the word meant, but for my grandfather at least, that was no excuse. The next thing I knew I was on my behind in the middle of the floor with Grandpa standing over me, and Uncle Lou in the corner holding his mouth to keep from laughing.

"I thought you said he'd think it was funny."

"No. I meant **I** would find it funny."

Oh.

My grandfather wasn't humorless, but he had a hard edge to him. I never saw him answer the telephone. Even sitting next to the phone, he would yell for my grandmother to answer it. I also saw him harrumph around the kitchen and grumble his discontent when my grandmother forgot to put cream in his coffee. He was a good husband, but he was definitely old-fashioned. What I couldn't comprehend at such a young age was the kind of stress he had to be under. Two of his sons and his son-in-law were overseas fighting for the survival of Western civilization. In hindsight, we all could have cut him a little slack.

The biggest argument I remember from that time took place in the spring of 1945 when Uncle Lou, then a junior in high school, came home with enlistment papers. Because of his age, he needed my grandfather to sign a waver. Grandpa wasn't thrilled by that idea. After several loud and lengthy discussions, my grandfather finally acquiesced and signed the paperwork for my uncle Lou to enter the service. Three months later, the war ended. Lou, like most late entrants, was sent home. My father and uncles weren't far behind him.

None of my relatives ever talked about the war. No one regaled me with stories from the front. There were no feature articles written about their overseas exploits, and no one in our house questioned them. They could have been file clerks or latrine diggers for all I knew. It wasn't until decades later, years after my father's death, that I learned how my dad spent his time in the Navy.

I was coaching at Notre Dame when a call came out of the blue from someone in Naval Veterans Affairs. He wanted to know if my father had indeed been in the Navy during World War II. I told him that my dad had been in the Pacific on a small landing craft called an LCI, slightly smaller than the more popular LST, but that he never talked about it. I had learned earlier that my uncle Walt, who also never spoke of the war, had been on the front lines during the Battle of the Bulge, and that my uncle Bill, again, mute on the subject of his service, had seen combat in Belgium. I knew this only because I had lived with Walt and Bill's parents during the war. Dad had never uttered a peep about his days in the Navy, and he had already passed away, so I didn't expect much from this conversation. The fellow ran a short blurb in a veterans' newspaper asking, "Did anyone serve with an Andrew Holtz on an LCI?"

A month or so later I get a call from a man in Colorado Springs who said, "Coach, I think I served in the Navy with your father." He described him, and it sounded right. Dad was the only guy I knew from Follansbee who had moved his wife and two children to East Liverpool while he went off to serve on an LCI. The man sent photos confirming that he had, indeed, served with my father.

He also sent a journal he had kept during the war. Keeping detailed notes was a flagrant violation of military protocol at the time, which is why there are so few first-person real-time accounts from the war. The man had broken the rules by keeping a journal, but I was sure glad he had. In his writings I learned that my father had been at the battle for Saipan. He had also been at Midway, the turning point of the war in the Pacific. I learned that my dad and his boat mates had worried constantly about the kamikaze pilots, and had always been on the lookout for incoming Zeros. I also found out that when the war ended, Dad was preparing for the invasion of Japan. I sat behind my desk, stunned by what I was reading. My father had been a part of some of the most epic military battles in history, and I never knew it.

With the permission of the author, I made copies of the journal and gave them to my sisters Shirley, two years my elder, and Vicky, who came along when I was ten years old. They had a hard time believing it, too, but in hindsight, none of us should have been surprised. Service was just something Dad's generation did. You didn't brag about it, or even talk about it. You did your job, and you came home. Chest beating was for those who weren't there.

This sparked my lasting distaste for excessive celebrations and "look at me" exploits, whether by athletes, politicians, or businesspeople. If one of our players scored a touchdown, I wanted him to walk away as if it were no big deal. "You want it to look like you're used to being in the end zone,"

I would always say. But my message was much broader. What I was really telling those players was that true heroes walk the walk with quiet confidence. They do the job, and then let the job they've done speak for itself. I hope that message stuck with my players the way that it stuck with me.

Dad chose to keep the family in Ohio once he came home. No job waited for him in Follansbee, and East Liverpool, while not huge, was a bigger town with more opportunities. After a few more odd jobs, he finally landed steady work as the local bus driver. My sister and I were in school by then—I started the first grade at age five to help the nuns at Saint Anthony's fill a first-grade class the year Dad left for service, and was in the fifth grade by the time he returned—so uprooting us didn't make a lot of sense. That's how I came to hail from East Liverpool, a town on the banks of the Ohio River, except for the springtime when it could be found **in** the river.

We had floods, a few snowstorms, and summers so hot you could break a sweat in a swimming pool. I was a typical midwestern boy. I loved the St. Louis Cardinals—Harry Brecheem on the mound, Joe Garagiola behind the plate, Marty Marion at short, Red Schoendienst at second, Whitey Kurowski at third, and Nippy Jones at first, with Terry Moore, Enos Slaughter, and Stan Musial in the outfield. I listened to the games in the hot summer evenings after a good swim down at Beaver Creek. I also hung out at Dairy Land Corner and watched the crowds file in and out of the horse track. I worked a paper route, covering the east side of town where the roughnecks lived, hauling papers straight up what seemed like a north face of the Eiger. Thursday's paper was thirty-two pages, and hauling a bundle up that hill was like pulling a plow through quicksand. Saturday's edition was only eighteen pages (it's amazing what you remember fifty years after the fact).

I went to my first college football game in 1946 when my uncle Leo took me to see the Pittsburgh Panthers play the University of Illinois. The star of the game was an Illinois running back named Buddy Young, who on the second play from scrimmage rambled 67 yards for a touchdown. From that moment forward, I loved Illinois, following their progress as closely as my grandfather followed Notre Dame's.

Of course it was hard not to be a Notre Dame fan in those days. From 1946 through 1949 they played some pretty good football. Coach Frank Leahy was a revered figure in our home, one I would learn to respect even more after I got into coaching. Moose Krause, a Notre Dame legend whose work with and for the university spanned five decades, would spend hours telling me stories about Coach Leahy. I never wanted the stories to end, and would often prompt Moose with more questions. Leahy had seven undefeated seasons in fourteen years, a pretty stout record even by Notre Dame standards. As a kid, I settled down by the radio to hear most of those victories.

I also became a football player myself, an eighty-pound wonder boy who made up for his lack of size by being slow and weak. My gridiron debut came at the ripe old age of nine when I was in the fifth grade. Saint Aloysius decided to field a team for seventh- and eighth-graders. I was allowed to play as a fifth-grader because my uncle Lou was the coach, one of many career moves my favorite uncle undertook after his brief stint in the service. After Lou returned home, he realized that the government would pay him twenty dollars a week for fifty-two weeks as long as he applied for a job a week. So he applied for the president's job at Crucible Steel, for taster in a pie factory, and for elevator operator in a one-story building. How he ended up coaching football for Saint Aloysius is still a mystery, but I couldn't have been more excited to play for him.

Of course, my "playing" that first year was purely academic. No matter the opponent I was the smallest and youngest on either sideline by a healthy margin. That didn't dampen my enthusiasm. I followed Uncle Lou every step he took on the sidelines. "Put me in, Uncle Lou," I said. "I'm ready. I can do it. Come on, put me in." Finally, as we were playing Immaculate Conception from Wellsville, Uncle Lou gave in to my begging. He grabbed my shoulder pads and told me to get in at safety. I can't imagine what the opposing coach thought as he saw this tiny kid trotting out onto the field. He must have told his team that if they could just get their halfback through the line, they had an easy touchdown. On the first play with me in the defensive backfield, the halfback came barreling past our linebackers and headed straight at me.

I froze. Everything I'd practiced, everything my uncle had tried to teach me, every drill I'd worked on, flew out of my brain and was replaced by paralyzing fear. The halfback looked seven feet tall and as fast as a Pontiac as he tore at me with reckless abandon. I made a small attempt at tackling him, but most of my effort was spent getting out of his way. I would later tell Uncle Lou that my helmet fell down over my eyes, which was true to an extent. Saint Al's didn't have helmets small enough to fit me, if they were even made at that time. The truth was, I wasn't interested in hitting the guy.

When I came back to the sidelines, I saw something in my uncle Lou's eyes I had never seen before. He was hurt and disappointed, wounded that I would give up on a play. My teammates felt the same way. Not many of them said so out loud, but they didn't have to. I knew that I had disappointed them, and they knew that I knew. All the excuses in the world wouldn't negate the fact that I had turned away from my responsibilities. In hindsight I had no business being on the field. I was nine years old playing against kids who shaved in the morning and had five o'clock shadows by kickoff. But that was no excuse for my failure to honor the commitment I had made to my coaches and teammates.

I realized that day, and it has stuck with me for the rest of my playing days and well into my coaching career, that the mental anguish you feel from letting down your coaches and teammates far exceeds any physical pain that might be inflicted on the football field. I promised myself at that moment that I would never give up on a play again. It didn't matter if the guy across from me outweighed me by two hundred pounds (which wasn't out of the realm of possibility), I was not going to turn my back on my responsibilities. I might get pounded or squashed, but I was not going to let my coaches and teammates down by quitting.

I remember playing Midland Grade School later that same year, and thinking the kids on that team must have gone to eighth grade on the GI Bill. I played an exceptional game and must have had twenty tackles. They were bigger, stronger, and quicker than I was, which was a situation I would encounter throughout my playing career.

People would later ask me what it was like to play linebacker at Kent State even though I weighed less than 160 pounds. I always said, "I don't know, I've never weighed two hundred pounds." What's it like to be stupid? I don't know. I've never been smart. All I ever knew how to do was take what God had given me, utilize my strengths, and minimize my weaknesses.

If the coaches wanted me to block a big defender in a specific direction, but he weighed fifty pounds more than I, had hair on his chest, breathed through his nose, and didn't like people who tried to block him, I wanted to sign a nonaggression pact with him—you don't hit me, and I won't hit you. When that didn't work, I learned to block the big guys whatever direction they wanted to be blocked. The backs had to learn to run off my blocks. Knowing this served me well when I entered coaching. If someone was incapable of blocking a defender in a specific direction—a common occurrence in Division I college football, where linebackers often outweigh fullbacks by twenty or thirty pounds—then the blocker should stick a body on the defender. It's the runner's job to read the blocks, and adjust accordingly. To ask someone to do something he is incapable of doing doesn't make him a better player: it makes you look like a bad coach.

I played for my uncle Lou longer than any other coach I had, three whole years from the fifth through seventh grades. His full-time job at Montgomery Ward became too demanding after that. During those years, my skills improved, and Saint Al's went undefeated one year, but the gap between my size and the size of the kids on the other side of the ball only grew larger. As a freshman in high school, I didn't quite weigh a hundred pounds. I was a young, scrawny kid who spoke with a pronounced lisp, just the kind of fellow who was ripe for ridicule in high school. Fortunately, I had learned to look at things from a humorous point of view, and this disarmed people quickly. Since I wasn't a threat to anyone, I wasn't bullied much, though kids did make fun of me. I learned to live with it, the insults only serving to strengthen my resolve to succeed. The love of my family and the confidence they showed in me—especially my uncles—kept my self-esteem above average.

I was not a good student, but I received a good education, not only academically but also in the intangibles everyone must have to succeed. Doing the right thing was ingrained into my thinking by the nuns and by my family. Did I do the right thing all the time? No, but those decisions always carried consequences. The nuns would punish me when I failed to do the right thing in school, and my family would take care of my mistakes at home. I never told my family when I was punished at school, because I knew that the punishment would be doubled. Running home and saying, "My teacher hit me, call the ACLU" wasn't an option. I'm afraid we've lost some of that "do the right thing" attitude in our culture and in our families. The most important thing a youngster can be taught yesterday, today, and tomorrow is respect for authority. Respect your parents, your elders, your teachers, law enforcement, the military, and show respect for other people's property. In my day this was taught at home and reinforced at schools.

Throughout high school, I worked jobs around school and sports, which didn't leave a lot of time for socializing. I never had a date in high school. When my classmates were going to the prom, I was still playing with trucks in the sand. Eventually, I made many good friends, and seven lifetime friends whom I still see half a century later at a gathering we have once a year. Two of the original gang of eight have passed away, and I was glad to have had the chance to tell them how much I appreciated their friendship. Relationships evaporate because people don't stay in touch. My friends and I have refused to let that happen. My buddies were smart, clever, and full of wit. I was the dull one in the group, and the worst student by far. If it wasn't for people like them there wouldn't have been a top half of the class, since I set the standard for what the lower half should look like. Of our group of eight great friends from senior year of high school, one is a lawyer, one has a Ph.D. in mathematics, one is a pharmacist, one is an engineer, one is a college professor, one became a radio executive, and one worked his way into an executive position at Daimler Chrysler. Oh, and one became a coach: the six of us who are left still laugh about that unlikely career choice.

We laughed a lot as kids as well. King Solomon said, "A kind word turneth away wrath," and Jimmy Durante said, "If they're laughing, they ain't gonna shoot you." Both those adages worked for me. I fine-tuned my wit at an early age, learning to use it to make friends and also to make larger points. Right before an important high school final exam, the tension in the room was so thick I didn't think anybody would do very well. After the teacher passed out the test, she pointed an accusatory finger around the room and said, "If I even suspect you of cheating, I'll dock ten percent off your grade immediately."

I promptly opened my desk and took out my textbook.

"Lou Holtz, what do you think you're doing?"

I said, "Ninety sounds pretty good to me."

From a football standpoint, my playing career was uneventful. I never did anything outstanding, but I tried to be a good teammate. I played blocking back in the single wing, the old-style offense with no quarterback, two lead blockers, and half a dozen running plays to either side of the line. It worked pretty well. We went 8–2 my sophomore year and 9–0–1 my junior year. I did nothing spectacular either of those seasons, but I did learn a lot by subconsciously studying my coaches. You can learn a lot by observing as well as by performing. When I was in the huddle, I knew everybody else's assignment as well as the technique everyone needed to employ. For someone who couldn't distinguish between a noun and a verb and who didn't know Dionysus from Dion, this impressed my coaches. The big difference was that I wanted to learn football. What I have since discovered is that learning can take place only when you have a desire to learn. Our coaches had such an enthusiasm to teach, it was only natural for me to want to learn. Great coaches and teachers—like those I had whom you never heard of, with names like Glenda Dunlap and Lou Vendetti—exemplify this attitude.

My aptitude for learning football caught the eye of my head coach, Wade Watts. Coach Watts accepted the head-coaching job at Canton McKinley High School after my junior year when we had gone undefeated. Before he left for his new job, Coach Watts asked for a meeting with my parents. This distressed me a bit. I couldn't imagine what

I'd done to earn a coach-parent conference, but I was always doing something stupid, so getting in trouble was not a star-in-the-east kind of event.

Imagine my surprise when Coach told my parents, "I think Lou ought to go to college and someday become a coach."

My mom and dad were too stunned to say anything at first. Mom had been the valedictorian of her graduating class in high school, but Dad had quit school in the third grade to go to work. Nobody in our family had ever thought about college. College was for the gifted, the select few, but certainly not for me.

After an awkward moment, my folks asked Coach Watts to repeat himself. "Lou should go to college, and become a coach," he said.

This came as a shock to my parents. Dad had seen me play one football game—a loss to Alliance, Ohio, where I had been the one-game team captain and he had driven the team charter bus— and Mom had always prayed that I would just graduate from high school. She had never seen me play in a single athletic contest. Still, Mom had insisted that I take college preparatory courses in high school, even though I had no intention of going to college. I had three years of Latin—Latin One, and Latin Two, twice. Going to college was about as important to me as visiting Botswana, and being a coach never entered my mind. I wasn't a very good athlete, or a very mature student. But I did have a natural inclination to teach. I knew my assignments on the football field, but I also knew everyone else's. There were many times during practice and on the sidelines during games when I would tell other players what to do and how to do it even though they had the physical skills to execute their assignments a lot better than I did.

Coach Watts saw this trait in me and decided I should be a coach. My parents decided that Coach Watts was right: I should go to college.

I said, "No."

They said, "Yes."

So we compromised the way we always compromised in our house. I went to college.

As poor as we were, I had the richest upbringing a young man could ever want because of the love of those around me. I learned at an early age that it's not **what** you have but **who** you have that counts. I had family, coaches, teachers, and friends who cared about me, and who took a strong interest in raising me well. Without those people, all the riches in the world would have meant nothing. Their love was all the wealth I needed.

2

SUCCESS IS A CHOICE
YOU MAKE

College, the men I played for, and the friends I made helped shape the path of my career. **(Courtesy of Kent State University)**

Before Coach Watts told me and my parents that I should go to college and become a coach, my only aspirations in life were a car, a girl, five dollars, and a job in a steel mill. I had never had any of these, so they all sounded great to me. Years later Coach Watts said, "Lou, when I told your folks you should get into coaching, I meant in a high school. I wasn't talking about Notre Dame." In my senior year at East Liverpool High, I figured I was better suited to run a lathe than run a defense.

Years later Coach Watts took a job in California, where he eventually retired. My first year coaching at Notre Dame, I got a call from his wife, who said, "Coach Watts isn't doing well, and it would sure boost his spirits if you would call him." Not only did I call, I invited him to the Notre Dame–Southern Cal game in Anaheim. "Come ride the bus with us," I said. I put him in my wife's seat, and we won the game 38–37. The next year, I called again and said, "Coach, you've never seen a game at Notre Dame. Why don't you come to the Southern Cal game here?" He did, and stood on the sidelines with our team.

The next year, I had him back out to L.A. when we played Southern Cal. Coach Watts and I kept that tradition going for eleven years. He died two months after I retired from Notre Dame. After his death, his wife told me that the Notre Dame–Southern Cal game kept him alive longer than anyone expected. "He lived for that weekend," she said.

I could never have guessed how things would turn out when Coach Watts told my folks I should go to college. Even though Mom and Dad were firm in their resolve when telling me that I would, indeed, be attending an institution of higher learning, their decision couldn't have been easy. As much as they wanted me to further my education, our family budget barely covered the basics. Tuition, board, and books were extras we simply couldn't afford. So my mother went to work as a nurse's aide at East Liverpool City Hospital on the 11 P.M. to 7 A.M. shift so she would be home during the day with my younger sister, Vicky, age ten. My older sister, Shirley, worked as a nurse at the hospital, so she was able to help Mom get the job.

Neither of my siblings bore any hard feelings when I went away to school. Shirley couldn't have been happier for me, as we had only one bathroom, and Vicky loved the fact that her big brother was in college. Mom did what she had to do to make it all happen. I was able to attend

Kent State because of the sacrifices of others. I consider this often. Anytime I get the urge to pat myself on the back for something, I think about what the members of my family did to give me a chance at a better life.

Everyone has someone to thank for what he or she has, and every time you see a successful person, you should think about the people in that person's life who made sacrifices for his or her success. No achievement, great or small, comes without sacrifice. My father and the millions who fought with him in World War II sacrificed life, limb, and treasure to ensure that our country remained free. The same can be said for soldiers and sailors from generations before and generations after. On the home front, coaches and teachers today work harder than ever to provide opportunities to students who may or may not remember their names. And parents struggle and sacrifice to make life better for their children just as they did two generations ago. In my case, my mother gave up her nights (and most of her sleep) in order for me to attend college. For that I will always say, "Thank you, Mom, and I love you dearly."

Even with Mom working, I was able to get into college only because my father was a resident of Ohio. State law required state-sponsored schools to admit residents for one quarter. If you paid your tuition and passed your classes, you got to stay. If you failed, you went home. Schools made the first quarter as tough as possible on incoming freshmen in order to distinguish those who were serious from those who were just biding time and enjoying a few months away from home.

We chose Kent State because it had an opening, and because the campus was close enough to East Liverpool that I could hitchhike back and forth between school and home. I paid for my first semester with $175 that I had saved up in the hopes of buying a 1949 Chevrolet. Dad told me that the money could be better spent on tuition and books. I disagreed, but my opinion in the matter carried little weight. The car money went into the college fund, and I put up my thumb on the side of the road. "Thumbing," as we called it in those days, was the way a lot of kids got around. If I couldn't catch a ride in East Liverpool with someone heading straight to Akron, I would hitch up on Route 45 with a trucker going to Salem, where I would then catch another ride up Route 14 to Kent. It was a different time then. Riding with strangers was not just an acceptable mode of transportation, it was expected. If you had a car, you helped out those who didn't. If you didn't have a car, you put out your thumb and relied on the benevolence of others. I never had a problem catching a lift, especially after I enrolled. Unbeknownst to me, my mother had signed me up for ROTC, which didn't thrill me at first. Then

I realized that a kid in a uniform had no trouble getting a ride.

Once I arrived at school, transportation became the least of my worries. I wanted to do well academically, but given my history in the classroom, I wasn't sure that my "want" was going to cut it. Then I had what I would later realize was a life-changing experience. In the summer before I was to leave for Kent State, while walking through the Wellington Neighborhood Grocery, I heard a couple of my mother's friends talking one aisle over.

Mrs. Hoback said, "I can't believe Anne Marie Holtz is wasting her money sending that boy, Lou, to college."

Mrs. Toft then said, "I know what you mean. She took a night job and everything. It's such a waste."

They didn't know I'd overheard them, since I was one aisle over, but those comments cut me deeply and burned inside me throughout my freshman year. I knew that my mother was sacrificing for me, but to have her friends, **the people in my town,** think that I was not worth the effort, that I was bound to fail, turned my wounded feelings into something quite different. My "want" to do well became a fiery determination. I would do whatever it took to pass, especially as a freshman, a year when the adjustment to college life can take its toll.

This was a turning point for me for several reasons: I could have felt sorry for myself after the criticism. I could have said, "Those women are probably right. I've got no business going to school. I shouldn't waste my mother's time and money." I could have used the comments as an excuse the first time I encountered a tough class or a hard-nosed professor, or the first time I struggled through a difficult test. After all, I wasn't supposed to be there anyway. But I didn't go that route. Sure, the criticism stung, but I internalized it, made it a challenge, a competition with those who thought I couldn't make it, even though they had no idea I was competing against them. Although I didn't know it at the time, I owe those two women a lot of thanks. My objective was to prove them wrong by passing, staying in school, and getting my degree.

It wasn't easy. I struggled in my first year at Kent State, primarily because I didn't have a strong academic foundation or good study habits. My concentration waned at times, but I had several friends who helped and encouraged me on a daily basis. Plus I was determined not to fail. And at the end of the day, commitment and determination triumph every time.

So many times people are afraid of competition, and they shouldn't be. We all have talents and abilities that reside deep within. Competition brings those talents out. Fear of failure keeps them repressed. I have always loved competing. At Notre Dame I used to have "friendly" golf games with Dick Rosenthal, our athletic director; Father Beauchamp, vice president of the university; and our sports information director, Roger Valdiserri. These were all kind men, friends whom I would have done anything for, but those "friendly" matches could become remarkably unfriendly if they were close. One day I made a hole in one (my third), and the only comment out of the group was "We press," the golf equivalent of doubling down a bet. One of the best shots I'd ever hit in my life, and all they could say was "We press." Now, that's competitive!

I wasn't in much of a thankful mood my first year. I spent most of my time with my nose in a book. I was also hampered by some health problems. With three weeks remaining in the first semester, I came down with strep throat, a very treatable ailment if you go to the doctor. For financial reasons, I didn't seek medical attention, and when I got home at the end of the semester, my temperature was 105 and rising. I fell unconscious and don't remember much about the next four weeks. My condition was touch and go for the better part of a month, as were my grades. Fortunately, I had a group of understanding professors who allowed me to make up work. They didn't coddle me—I still had to do the work—but they gave me a chance, which was all I wanted.

In terms of factual information that I learned, about the only thing I remember from my freshman year was that Ohio and Michigan are the only two states in the USA ever to call out the militias and go to war with each other. The dispute was over possession of Toledo. History doesn't record who won, but we have to assume Michigan prevailed, since I can't believe we went to war to **keep** Toledo. Besides that trivial tidbit, I can't tell you one thing I learned in my first year of college. But the self-discipline, preparation, and study habits, and learning what it means to be a good teacher and a good student, are critical attributes that have stuck with me for fifty years. Not a day goes by that I don't use the preparation and teaching tools I learned as a freshman at Kent State. For example, I learned that in order to keep up, I had to read ahead. If I waited to be told to read an assignment, I was already behind. Wait twice and I would never catch up. Because I wasn't a particularly fast reader, and since I hadn't developed great study habits in high school, I learned to anticipate assignments and read ahead to stay one step in front of the rest of the class.

Even more important, I learned early on that if you help other people get what they want, you get what you want. Life is not a zero-sum game:

just because you win, someone else doesn't necessarily have to lose. My good friend Zig Ziglar, one of the greatest motivational speakers of all time, has been pounding home this message for more than twenty years, but it was a principle that came naturally to me. If I wanted to make good grades, I needed to satisfy my professors. In order to do that, I had to show enthusiasm, excitement, and interest in their classes and in them. I had to make each professor believe that his class was not only the most important, but the **only** class that piqued my interest. Then I had to show diligence and a willingness to work hard. This wasn't brain surgery or nuclear physics: people take an interest in those who are interested in them. It's human nature. The same relationship exists between a coach and his players. Those players who hang on the coach's every word, who go out of their way to show enthusiasm and commitment to the coach's philosophy, and who work hard every day are the ones who earn the coach's respect and praise. Those who go through the motions and show contempt or complacency for the coach's teachings, even though they might be talented players, rarely do well.

College was not real complicated for me. I had to make good choices in picking my classes, and in picking my professors. Then I had to work hard to make those professors happy. If they were happy with me, I was going to be happy with them.

I also learned what it takes to be a great teacher, because I had some great ones. My history professor Dr. Kaplan, for example, was so knowledgeable and enthusiastic that he inspired me to become a history major. In that first year I realized that to be a good teacher you had to (1) know your subject inside and out, (2) be able to present what you know in a cohesive and interesting way so that your audience understands what you're talking about, and (3) have enthusiasm for teaching.

Every good professor I've known has embodied all three of these traits, and every bad one has fallen short in one or more. I knew that if I was going to become an effective coach, I had to embrace the principles of good teaching. What I didn't know was how soon I would get to test my abilities.

After my freshman year at Kent State, I went back home and slept on the porch of my parents' two-bedroom house in East Liverpool. Things had picked up financially for us, which meant we were no longer living in someone else's cellar. Dad had steady work as a bus driver, and he and Mom were able to buy a modest home for thirty-two hundred dollars. My sisters shared one of the bedrooms, and my parents took the other, which left me sleeping on the porch in the summer and on the floor in the living room in the winter. Still, we had a kitchen and a bathroom, which was an upgrade from our old place in Follansbee.

While I was home that first summer, I ran into Coach Frank Smouse, who had coached at East Liverpool High when I was a senior. Frank had taken a head-coaching job at Ravenna High, just a few miles northeast of Kent. When he found out I was an incoming sophomore at Kent State, he said, "Why don't you come over and coach our freshman team at Ravenna?" Coaching high school in those days didn't require a teaching certificate or even a college degree. Most people who coached freshman squads weren't teachers or in any way employed by the school district. They were just football enthusiasts, much like the recreational league and Pop Warner coaches of today. I accepted Frank's offer, and spent the fall of my sophomore year hitchhiking back and forth between Kent and Ravenna every weekday afternoon.

I made every mistake in the book that year. First, I was scared to death. I showed up at Ravenna as an eighteen-year-old who had always been small and a little shy. I also had a speech impediment, something that I've worked on for most of my life, but which is still apparent if you listen closely when I speak. Coaching athletes who were two, three, no more than four years younger, who were almost all bigger than I, and who spoke more clearly than I did wasn't what I would call a perfect tutoring environment.

Fortunately, I had some great athletes. We ran the single wing, which was the offense we had run at East Liverpool when I played in high school, and our tailback, Joel Daunic, was talented enough to mask a lot of coaching mistakes. Joel went on to play at Dartmouth, where he had an excellent college career. He was easy to coach. Others weren't as talented or as receptive to my suggestions. I learned a lot about motivation, communication, and focus in my foray into coaching.

More than once, I jumped into the middle of a scrimmage without pads to demonstrate a blocking or tackling technique. I know this shocked a lot of players, but I was passionate about doing things the proper way. If I got down in the middle of a pile with no pads, there was no reason that kids who were much bigger than I couldn't do the same when fully outfitted. I told them, "If you're going to do something, do it to the best of your ability. If not, don't waste your time or mine." Those are words I repeated throughout my coaching career. How good those players were was not important to me. What was important was the effort they showed. I wasn't a great player, which meant I had to put forth 100 percent on every play just to equal those athletes who were more physically gifted than I. Overcoming my own physical shortcomings made me a better coach because I knew what it was like to give everything you had on every play. I still can't understand people who fail not because they aren't physically or mentally up to the task, but because they simply don't put forth the effort to succeed. If you aren't going to be the best you can be, why try?

I also learned that no matter what age or size or shape a coach comes in, he has to know what he's talking about, he has to communicate that knowledge to his team, and he has to inspire them to do things they might not otherwise believe they can do. All I did was try to emulate the great teachers and coaches who had taught me. I must have done a reasonably good job impersonating them. Our freshman team went undefeated that fall.

Winning every game impressed Coach Smouse. Within the year, he had taken a job as an assistant coach at Kent State, and he approached me with a different offer. "Lou, you should go out for football next fall," he said. "You need to play at the college level. That will help you become a better coach."

I was excited to try out for the team, but most people felt I would not be successful. I loved football and everything that went with it. I felt it was a privilege to be able to play for Kent State. I was 165 pounds and the smallest player on the team. I was a junior, a little late in my collegiate career to be going out for a sport, but I wasn't going to graduate in four years anyway. When my mother filled out my initial registration form, she and I didn't realize that ROTC and physical education didn't count as full credits. Because I took both, my stint at Kent State would take four and a half years. This didn't sit well with my grandparents, who had difficulty understanding how you could go to school for four years, pass every course, and still not graduate. The only good news was that my commitment to ROTC meant I would be in school for five falls, which meant I had three years of eligibility left for football.

I used them as wisely as I could. Some friends thought I might embarrass myself, but my attitude was that you couldn't embarrass yourself if you gave your best effort. I believed I could succeed on the football field, just as I had in the classroom. Nothing was more important than belief in myself. The previous summer I'd been taught a valuable lesson about taking on new challenges, one I've tried to teach to every athlete I've coached. My seven best friends and I were swimming in the Ohio River, as we were prone to do on hot summer days, when one of our group came up with the bright idea that we should swim all the way across the river, about a mile at that point. Whoever finished last would walk back across the bridge, get the car, and pick everybody else up.

"I'm not going," Nevitt Stockdale said.

"What do you mean you're not going?" I asked.

"I can't swim that far."

"You can make it," I told Nevitt. "And if you can't, I'll save you."

"You would do that for me?"

"Of course. You've got my word."

I was motivated to have Nevitt join us because he was the only one I knew I could beat. In a race not to finish last, having one guy you can beat is a plus.

Everything went according to plan for the first three-quarters of a mile. Nevitt kept up, but showed no signs of beating me to the finish. I didn't worry about who was winning. All I cared about was not being last.

Then, out of the blue, Nevitt said: "I can't make it."

"You can do it," I said.

"No, I can't. Save me, Lou."

I'd promised him I would save him, given him my word of honor. All our other friends had already made it across and were sunning themselves on the riverbank. Only Nevitt and I remained in the water. So I did the only thing I could do: I left him there to drown and continued swimming toward the opposite shore.

Nevitt thrashed about for a minute or two before doing the only thing he thought he could do to save his life: he turned around and swam back to where we'd started. He ended up swimming a mile and a half because he didn't believe he could swim a mile.

I didn't know if I could play college football, but I wasn't going to swim a mile and a half
because I wasn't sure if I could swim a mile. I
went out for the team, promised myself not to
make any excuses, and gave it everything I had.

I played inside and outside linebacker in what
turned out to be an uneventful college football
career. However, I earned the respect of my teammates and coaches, which was more important to
me than any on-field accomplishments. One of
my teammates, Sugar Ball King, a six-four, 260-
pound lineman from Cleveland, befriended me, so
very few people gave me any trouble. With friends
like Sugar Ball at my side, I suffered few insults.
(Sugar Ball would die at age twenty-six. Later I
would learn from Don King, the famous boxing
promoter, that Sugar Ball was his brother.)

Because of my effort and attitude, I did a lot
of things as well as my teammates, even those
who had far more natural talent. I worked as hard
as anyone on the fundamentals, and I did whatever it took to learn the game. I also realized that
sometimes success doesn't require talent or natural ability. Showing up on time, studying harder,
and doing all the little things the coaches asked
of me went a long way toward leveling the playing
field for a scrawny, slow kid.

Of course there were times I did things I'm
not proud of. On Parents' Day, the only time

my mother came to see me play, we took on Miami of Ohio, and when I got into the game, I was promptly ejected. It was one of those classic "retaliation" scenarios. One of their players shoved me, so I shoved him back. He hit me, and I hit back. We were both promptly thrown out. It was stupid, and it never happened again, but my mother never saw me play another down.

By then I had joined the Delta Upsilon fraternity, a group of outstanding young men, many of whom I am still close to today. I didn't officially "rush." Some of the brothers asked me to dinner one night, so we ate, and then I followed the group out to a sorority house, where they serenaded the girls. Afterward, a smaller group headed down to an area we called Water Street Skid Row, a block of town made up of nothing but bars. We ended up at Rathskeller's, one of the liveliest local bars. I went too, although I didn't drink.

I did, however, enjoy the company of my fraternity brothers. That first night at Rathskeller's one of the brothers spread the word that it was his birthday, and before I could blink, several girls came by and kissed him. That sealed the deal for me. I had never been on a date. Never went to the prom. Never parked, or kissed, or did any of the things teenage boys dreamed of doing. A fraternity seemed like the logical place to become socially acceptable. I pledged immediately. It was a great decision. I am proud of the fact that before graduating, I set a fraternity record for getting invited to seven of the eight different sorority formals.

In between dates, I worked as a janitor at a place called Mullins, thanks to my head coach, Trevor Rees, and I made $29.50 a month for being in ROTC. That, plus football, being active in the fraternity, and holding my grade point average around the 3.0 range kept me busy and happy. My confidence grew daily.

Then I got a call from my mom and dad. They said I needed to come home right away. I hitch-hiked back to East Liverpool not knowing what they wanted. Mom and Dad didn't request my presence for trivial matters, so it had to be something big and urgent. When I got home the entire family was gathered in the living room. Mom took charge of the meeting, and announced that she and Dad would be separating.

At first the word didn't register. Separate? Separate what? A second later I realized she was talking about divorce, only she didn't say "divorce," since such a word was verboten in a staunch Catholic household such as ours.

"We will be living apart from now on," she said. "We've discussed it, and that's just the way it has to be."

I was dumbfounded, but in hindsight I should have seen it coming. My father had never had any material things throughout his life. Then, suddenly, Mr. C. A. Smith, the owner of several businesses in town, including the Rock Springs Amusement Park and the bus company Dad had worked for, died. His heirs didn't want to run a bus company, and the city had no desire to get into public transportation, so the bus company appeared destined to shut down. It looked like my father would be out of a job again.

There was only one catch: Saint Aloysius chartered Mr. Smith's buses to shuttle Catholic kids to and from school. When the demise of the bus company became imminent, the fathers at Saint Al's asked my dad if he would put together a couple of buses and run a charter for the school. He agreed. When the city got word of this deal, they approached Dad about running the bus company for the town. Dad knew the profitable routes, so as long as the city didn't force him to run anywhere that he couldn't make money, he agreed to that deal as well. Within a couple of months, he went from being a bus driver to owning the East Liverpool bus company.

The deal didn't make Dad rich, but he had more money than he'd ever dreamed possible. Plus, he became a "businessman," someone the townspeople knew and respected. This was heady stuff for a poor steel-mill kid from West Virginia who never went past the third grade. Suddenly,

Dad started staying out late. He spent money in ways and in places that he shouldn't, and he began accepting the attention of other female companions. He had fallen into the classic success trap: he thought his newfound wealth and fame had made him simultaneously invincible and invisible. As happens to many successful people, my father thought he could go anywhere and do anything without any ramifications. He could do anything because he could afford it, and nobody would see him because he wanted it that way. My father was a good man and I loved him. He had a lot of great qualities, but the ability to handle success was not one of them.

Throughout my career, I've warned athletes and students of the intoxicating power of success. In life you have to handle tough times—everybody has hard decisions, tough choices that he or she has to make—but you also have to be equally prepared to handle success. This is particularly true with athletics. I can't tell you how many outstanding student-athletes have shown up to play for me without enough money to buy a bus ticket home. They struggle and scrape their way through school, working hard in the classroom and even harder on the field. Then, for those fortunate few who are drafted into the NFL, the world changes overnight. Deals are thrown at them like confetti. Good-looking women want to come back to their rooms. Hundreds of people want to be their friends. It's a surreal experience, especially for a man in his early twenties. It takes a lot of courage and maturity to handle that kind of instant success, especially if you've come from the lower end of the economic scale. Some handle it very well, and unfortunately, others don't. I know. I saw it firsthand with my father.

My parents' separation devastated me. I left the house and thumbed my way back to school, determined to pay my own way through school from that moment forward. I wouldn't take another dime of Dad's money, which was tainted as far as I was concerned. I was also afraid Dad's fortunes wouldn't last. You can't run a successful business, manage and motivate a staff, and keep up with the thousands of details if you aren't completely focused. At the time, I guessed that Dad's days as an East Liverpool transportation magnate were numbered.

Sadly, my fears turned out to be well founded. Mismanagement and poor planning drove Dad's business into bankruptcy. And while he and my mother never divorced, they never reconciled either. My dad was a good man who handled the deepest depths of the Great Depression with great resolve. He handled the kamikazes and the horrors of places like Midway and Saipan without uttering a single complaint. But success proved to be too much for him, just as it has for many other people.

Dad's fall made quite an impression on me, and since then I've tried to impress upon every athlete I've ever coached the importance of being able to handle success.

I threw myself into the college experience for the final year and a half I was there. My play, such that it was, earned me a partial scholarship, and the jobs I managed to keep along with my ROTC pay kept me solvent. I lived in the fraternity house and dated a beautiful and talented young girl named Edie (whom I would "pin" in my senior year), and I played football without doing anything outstanding, but with more success than anyone expected. I remember one night in our fraternity house during the Truth Session, a meeting in which brothers could say whatever they wanted but nothing could be answered, two of my teammates and fraternity brothers, Tony Zampino and Mario Pissanelli, two friends for whom I had great respect, told the rest of the brothers how they had thought I was crazy for going out for football. "We didn't think Lou would last a week," they said. Then they added that I had earned their respect by making the team. This meant more to me than they ever knew.

Their respect lasted a lot longer than my playing career. The spring of my fourth year, with one season of eligibility left, I injured my knee in spring practice and had to be taken to Akron

Hospital. The news wasn't good. Torn knee cartilage, while still a serious injury, is like a hangnail today compared to what it was back then. I've coached athletes who have had arthroscopic surgery and been back on the field on crutches in two days, and back in the weight room in six weeks. The incision on my knee made me think the surgeon had sneezed with the scalpel in his hand. Not only was I out for the summer, but my leg did not respond, and I came to camp walking like Chester on **Gunsmoke**. In my mind I would be ready. All it would take was a little loosening up. But it didn't take long to realize that I couldn't go. Six months later, the leg was fine (I've never had a moment's trouble from it since), but the season was over, and my playing career quietly came to a close.

Of course I was disappointed. Nobody wants his playing career to end with an injury. Fortunately, the coaching staff at Kent State—head coach Trevor Rees, who had played tight end at Ohio State; Rick Forzano, who would later become head coach at Navy and the Detroit Lions; Don McCafferty, who would replace Don Shula as the head coach of the Baltimore Colts in 1970; and Frank Smouse, who went on to become a superscout for the Cincinnati Bengals—knew what I hoped to do with my life. They helped me out by offering me a job to help Moose Paskert coach the freshman team at Kent State during my final few months in school. I jumped at the chance.

John Konstantinos, a fraternity brother and teammate of mine, also helped coach the freshmen. John had run out of eligibility before graduation in part because of a little ruse the coaching staff pulled on him when he transferred to Kent. During his first year with the team, I asked him: "John, what's your major?"

He said, "I'm going to graduate next year in engineering."

"Really," I said. "I can't wait to see that ceremony."

"Why?"

"Because we don't have an engineering school," I said.

Since Coach Forzano had conveniently forgotten to mention that majoring in engineering was not an option, John changed his major to math and spent the extra two quarters it took him to graduate coaching the freshman team with me.

Freshmen weren't eligible to play varsity at that time, so our main job was to keep the players happy and eligible, and teach them how to block and tackle. We played only a few games, but we practiced five days a week. In addition, every Saturday, John and I would drive to another campus and scout the varsity's opponent for the following week. The coaching staff seemed impressed by our work, and Kent State went 7–2 that year.

College opened up new worlds for me. And the people I met at Kent State, the men I played for, and the friends I made provided me with opportunities that I would never have dreamed possible, opportunities that went far beyond my degree, cutting the path that would later become the road of my professional career.

Everyone's life is a compilation of the people he meets, the things he does, and the decisions he makes. I was blessed with a wonderful family who did what it took to make sure I had opportunities no one else in our family had ever had. And I was fortunate enough to have coaches and teachers who took an interest in my future; who saw something more than a small young man with big glasses and a lisp; who helped me learn how to learn; and who gave me a foothold on the first rungs of the ladder of success.

Life provides all of us with a series of choices. The choices we make determine how successful we are. When you acknowledge that you and only you are responsible and accountable for the choices you make, and when you refuse to blame others for the choices you have made, you have in your hands the blueprint for success. When you allow others to choose your path so that you can then blame someone else when things don't go your way, you are fooling no one and cheating no one but yourself. When you accept the fact that you are in your present condition, good or bad, because of the choices you have made, you will then find yourself capable of changing your situation by making better choices.

No one but you determines your success in life. Making the right choices paves your way.

3

FIRST IMPRESSIONS HAVE LASTING RESULTS

My Kent State graduation portrait. I considered making a career out of the Army, but I
knew that my true calling was on the football
field.

I didn't have to worry about my first job out of college. ROTC came with a six-month commitment to the Army, so I wasn't scrambling for interviews my senior year, worrying about being unemployed and unable to pay the rent. Having a military obligation was quite liberating. I didn't love ROTC, but I felt that everyone had an obligation to serve his or her country. Plus, the leadership skills, discipline, sense of purpose, and focus on accomplishing the mission at all costs proved invaluable to me when I got into coaching. I didn't like marching, but the discipline and everyone being in step were impressive.

This was during a time when the country was not at war, but when our preparedness was at an all-time high. Korea had ended in a stalemate, and troops remained poised on both sides of the thirty-eighth parallel. Churchill's "Iron Curtain" speech still rang in our ears, especially as we watched Soviet tanks roll through Budapest and saw Germans being shot as they tried to cross into West Berlin. Cuba's revolution was still fresh in everyone's mind, and within three years we would be on the brink of war because the Soviets had parked missiles ninety miles from Miami. It was an unstable time to be entering the service. I would be accepting my commission when no American troops were engaged in active combat—we were three years away from sending armed advisers to Vietnam—but our bravest soldiers still manned posts at flash points all around the world.

I left school with a clear vision of what the next year of my life would entail. Unfortunately, I also left with a heavy heart. My first real girlfriend, Edie, broke up with me shortly before graduation. I celebrated by going on a nine-day drinking binge, my first and last such excursion. Despite many temptations, including some outright bribes from my fraternity brothers, I kept my promise to my mother that I would never drink while I was away at school. But as soon as graduation ceremonies were over, I set about drowning my sorrows in hole-in-the-wall juke joints in and around Akron. It was an immature and ridiculous act, but for more than a week I was drunk more hours than I was sober.

My tenth morning of waking up feeling like the New York Giants' backfield had run over my head and left clumps of sod in my mouth, I sat up, rubbed my aching eyes, and said to myself: "What on earth are you doing? Are you going to let someone else, someone who doesn't care about you, affect your life like this?" The answer was obvious. You can't let someone else determine your happiness. Only you can be responsible for your feelings. My choice was either to make the best of the situation I was in, or to wallow in self-pity and stay drunk the rest of my life. I would never again let anyone else set the parameters of my happiness. If you control nothing else in your life, you do control your feelings. You can choose to face your circumstances, no matter how cheerful or bleak, with happiness or with despondency. No one can take that choice away from you. I chose to move on with a positive spirit. From that day forward, I never had more than a social drink or an occasional glass of wine with dinner. I was fortunate in that I associated alcohol with heartbreak and depression, two things of which I wanted no part.

I recount that incident as proof that God's plan for life takes many varied and interesting turns, and everything within that plan happens for a reason. When Edie broke up with me, I felt as low as a human could feel.

Back home in East Liverpool, I had a week to kill before reporting for duty at Fort Benning, Georgia, so one Sunday evening my friends Gary Calvert and Jack Goodwin and I decided to go to New York for a few days. We pooled our money, drove to the city, stayed at the Piccadilly Hotel, saw **My Fair Lady** and **The Music Man,** and thoroughly enjoyed ourselves. I've been back to

New York thousands of times since then—I even worked there for a while, which I'll get to later—but I never had a better experience in the city than during that spring week in 1959 with my friends.

On our way home from New York, Jack Goodwin wanted to stop in Pittsburgh to see some girls. I wasn't at all interested in stopping, but Jack was behind the wheel, so he overruled me and we paid a visit to the girls.

Among them was Beth Barcus, who was an X-ray technician at Saint Francis Hospital. Beth was from East Liverpool and had moved to Pittsburgh to live with two of her friends. When I saw Beth, I was taken by how beautiful and bright she was. I had known her in high school, but I had never given her a second look—then again, I hadn't paid a lot of attention to any girl in those days. This girl was vibrant, intelligent, with a great personality and sense of humor. Her father and mother, both solid, hardworking people, had recently opened a neighborhood grocery store that would eventually become very successful. Beth was the oldest of three girls. Her sister Brenda was two years younger than she, and her sister Janna was twenty years her junior. I learned all of this during our brief visit. I also learned that she would be going home to East Liverpool the following day, so I asked her out on a date, and she accepted.

I had only a three-day window before I was to report to Fort Benning, so Beth and I went out all three of those days. My last day, we caught an early movie before my midnight flight out of Pittsburgh. After the movie we talked for a while, which set me about an hour behind schedule. I got home around 10:30 P.M., and with the Pittsburgh airport a good hour's drive from our house, we were cutting it close. My mom cried and my dad yelled at me the entire trip.

My father was not amused. Having been in public transportation for much of his adult life, Dad understood that the plane was going to leave on time whether or not I was on board. I have since figured this out for myself. An airplane is, indeed, easier to catch while it is on the ground than it is once it's in the air.

I ran to the gate, but my bags were too heavy. They had to be checked. This wasn't a problem. Sure, they could store my suitcase. Plenty of time.

Then the gate attendant asked for my orders, which I had to show in order to board the plane. My eyes got wide. I said: "They're in the bottom of my suitcase."

"Which suitcase?" she asked.

"The one you just stored."

Now I was sure I was going to miss my flight, which meant I would start my military career by being AWOL. Fortunately, I retrieved the case and dug through my belongings until I found my orders seconds before the cabin door closed. I can still hear my dad yelling for me to hurry as I bade them good-bye.

I never wrote my parents while I was in the service. I figured that their abrupt good-bye at the Pittsburgh airport meant that they didn't care. This was very immature of me. But I figured that not communicating with them was a good way to voice my disapproval. I now realize that your children can never love you as much as you love your children. I felt that I was the one who suffered, because I didn't get a single letter in my first five weeks of officer training. My parents didn't write me, because I didn't write them. They didn't have an address, and didn't work very hard to find one. I was angry with them, and they were upset at me.

The guys in my platoon took pity on me and sent my name and address to every junk mail vendor they could find. By the sixth week, I went from receiving no mail to getting more letters than anyone. Unfortunately, all of it was junk. I was a confirmed winner of more major prizes than I could count, and every beachfront resort on the East Coast wanted to give me a toaster if I would only take their no-obligation tour. Beth never wrote, even though I sent her a few letters. After a while, I quit writing.

If my lack of contact with the outside world wasn't bad enough, I got to spend the summer in the Chattahoochee Valley between Columbus, Georgia, and Phenix City, Alabama, where the temperature and relative humidity were both in the high nineties on a daily basis. My last week at Fort Benning was spent crawling along the ground in the rain during field exercises. The morning we came out of the field, we had inspection. Because I tried to save money from my uniform allowance, I had only two uniforms. Before heading out for exercises, I had instructed the base dry cleaner to pick up my spare uniform and clean it while I was away. He let me down, though, and the uniform was still in my locker, dirty and wrinkled, when I got in at 2 A.M. Fortunately, I had plenty of friends in my company, good people who helped me out. One of them was Mark Huber, who was the same size as me and loaned me a uniform for the 6 A.M. inspection. Everything worked out, but I remember thinking, "I'll remember this night for the rest of my life, because I think this is as low as I can go." I felt as though no one cared if I lived or died, which—although not true by any stretch—was a helpless feeling. I've used the memory of that night many times in my life since. Anytime I feel helpless or hopeless, I think about how I felt that last night at Fort Benning, and how persistence and perseverance helped me through that difficult time.

The next week I was transferred to Fort Knox, Kentucky, after a short furlough. I drove to Fort Knox a day before I had to report, checked into a hotel, got a good night's sleep, showered, shaved, put on my freshly pressed dress uniform the next morning, and drove five minutes to the CO's office to report. This wouldn't have been a big deal, but I was one of a half dozen men who were reporting for duty that morning. The others hadn't come in early. Instead, they'd driven all night. When they arrived, they were wrinkled, disheveled, and in desperate need of a shave. I looked like an **Esquire** model by comparison.

The base commander was so impressed by my appearance that he struck up a conversation. He asked me where I'd gone to school and what I wanted to do. We talked about football, and I told him that after completing my service I wanted to be a teacher and a coach. Before the day was over, he asked if I would be interested in teaching Military Justice, Code of Conduct, and Punitive Articles classes. I accepted on the spot. I had assumed I would be assigned a job, but I would never have guessed that I would be offered a position as an instructor.

That incident taught me that first impressions are invaluable, so make yours a good one. The CO singled me out because of my appearance. I wasn't any taller or better looking that day, but I was freshly groomed and pressed. That little extra attention to how I looked made a big difference. For the rest of my stint at Fort Knox, I was one of the most popular Military Justice instructors, probably because I tried to keep the class funny and interesting, and one of the most enthusiastic instructors on the shooting and grenade range. I can still remember shouting the orders: "Ready on the left; ready on the right; ready on the firing line; flags up; flags waved; seven seconds to commence firing; cease fire; lock and clear all weapons; proceed downrange." It was a great job, one I might not have gotten had I not dressed well on that first day.

I spent the next fifty years teaching this to every athlete I coached. Every team I ever coached wore coats and ties on and off the buses on game days. Anybody who had a shirttail out of place made that mistake only once. I was unyielding when it came to enforcing the team dress and appearance code. If you meet a hundred people a day, a thousand people will make a judgment about you based on your appearance. Your neighbors will make judgments about you based on how your lawn and house look, and people who see you in passing will judge you based on how clean you keep your car. It's not always fair, but it has always been true: appearances matter, so make yours a good one.

So good was my tenure at Fort Knox that I actually considered making a career out of the Army. I really loved the fact that you shined your shoes for a purpose. Every job was important, and every soldier was expected to give nothing less than his best in every circumstance. There is a higher calling when you are a member of the armed services. You learn that there are things more important than yourself and your career, things worth sacrificing, fighting, and even dying for. That clarity appealed to me. When my six months were up, I thought long and hard about accepting a regular Army commission, and even had the paperwork delivered to my quarters. But I knew that my true calling was on the football field. Coach Watts had seen it in high school, and Coach Rees had seen it in college. I was a teacher and a coach, whether I was in an Army uniform or the uniform of a high school or college team. My future was in the classroom and on the field. The only question was, where would I end up plying my trade?

If I thought I would hop out of the Army and have a handful of coaching offers, I was sadly mistaken. I couldn't get a job as an equipment manager. So I moved back home and worked at East Liverpool City Hospital scrubbing operating-room floors. To call that job unglamorous would be underselling it in a big way. Scrubbing blood off tile was not my first career choice. In fact, it was a big step backward from my job at Fort Knox. The only bright spot was the fact that Beth had moved back to East Liverpool and worked at the hospital as an X-ray technician. We rekindled our friendship and started seeing each other again.

I worked in the hospital for several months, dating Beth and doing everything I could to launch my coaching and teaching career. The midwestern landscape was dotted with my résumé. I don't know of a school superintendent in Ohio, Pennsylvania, West Virginia, or Michigan who hadn't seen or heard from Lou Holtz, aspiring history teacher and football coach.

During that time, I stayed in touch with my college coaches, including our head coach, Trevor Rees. When Coach Rees realized that I was floundering in my job search, he called one of his old shipmates from the Navy, a fellow named Forest Evashevski, who was the head coach at the University of Iowa. I wasn't privy to the conversation, but from what I gather it went something like this:

Coach Rees: "Forest, you need to hire Lou Holtz."

Coach Evashevski: "Lou who?"

Coach Rees: "Lou Holtz, the kid who used to play linebacker for us who coached our freshman team a couple of years ago.

Good guy, and somebody who's going to be a decent coach someday."

Coach Evashevski: "Well, that's a ringing endorsement, but I don't have a job right now."

Coach Rees: "Then let him come in as a graduate assistant."

Coach Evashevski: "I don't have any graduate assistants."

Coach Rees: "All the more reason to bring Lou on."

Coach Evashevski: "I don't know."

Coach Rees: "Good, I'll tell him you're going to work something out."

At the same time this conversation was going on, I finally broke through on the high school front. Coach Earl Biedermann at Conneaut High School offered me a job as an assistant coach. So I went from scrubbing hospital floors with no prospects of a coaching job to having two job offers at the same time.

Under any other circumstance I would immediately have accepted Coach Evashevski's offer and been on the first bus to Iowa City. But Beth had accepted my proposal to be married. So I decided to go to Conneaut, where I would spend the rest of my life as a high school history teacher and football coach. If I worked really hard, I might even be hired as the head coach at one of the larger high schools in Ohio, but that was a few years away. Right now, I was ready to settle down and get my life and career in gear.

Then, out of the blue, Beth told me she didn't feel ready to get married, and, in fact, she wanted to see other people. This was July 8, 1960, at 9 P.M. I wasn't about to pull another nine-day binge as I had when Edie left me, but I wasn't going to hang around Ohio and think about Beth every day either. By 10 P.M., I had called Coach Beidermann and turned down his offer, and then my old pal Nevitt Stockdale and I got into my 1952 Ford Fairlane and headed to Iowa. A few hours into the trip Nevitt cheered me up by saying, "Lou, you and Beth have a love-hate relationship: you love her, and she hates you."

Nevitt and I drove all night to get there. I'd never seen so much corn in my life. The only thing I remember about the trip, other than being exhausted, heartbroken, and angry at what had happened but excited about the job opportunity that lay ahead, was the stop we made for breakfast. It was at a side-of-the-road diner in the middle of nowhere, about an hour outside Iowa City. I sat down, ordered a cup of coffee, and said to the waitress, "Can I just have a bowl of cornflakes, please?"

"Sorry," she said, "we don't have cornflakes."

I looked out the window and guessed that the cornfields had to stretch for at least a hundred miles in every direction. "No cornflakes, huh?"

"No, sorry."

"That's sort of like running out of ice in Iceland, isn't it?"

"No," she said. "We didn't run out of cornflakes. We don't ever have any."

"Oh," I said. "Now it makes sense."

Two hours later, Nevitt and I rolled onto the campus at the University of Iowa, and I met Coach Evashevski. He was more than a little surprised to see me. "I thought you were going to coach high school football in Ohio," he said.

"No, sir, Coach, I'm here to work for you," I told him as confidently as I could. And that's exactly what I did. After going through all the details of enrolling in graduate school and renting a room, I drove back to East Liverpool, packed my belongings, and went to Iowa as the football program's only graduate assistant coach.

The significance of that first job, and the circumstances surrounding it, didn't become apparent to me until much later in life. I went to Iowa because Beth had broken up with me. If not for what I assumed to be a bad thing—the breakup of a romantic relationship—I would never have accepted the job. Who knows what direction my life would have taken? I probably would have spent the rest of my life coaching high school football in Ohio. Not that this would have been a bad thing, but no one would ever have heard of Lou Holtz, and you certainly wouldn't be reading this book. What I thought was a terrible setback turned out to be one of the greatest things that ever happened to me.

Thankfully, I had people like Coach Rees, who still cared enough about one of his former players to place a call to an old Navy buddy, and friends like Nevitt, who stayed up all night to drive with me to Iowa. As the sisters at Saint Al's always used to say: "The Lord looks after animals, small children, and idiots." I don't know which of those categories I fell into at the time, but the Good Lord and good friends were certainly looking out for me.

I could never have guessed what a wonderful decision I had made. I arrived at Iowa with just enough money to set up in a rented room and survive until I received my first stipend. I knew absolutely no one in the entire state of Iowa, but I was working in college football, the career that would take me places that I never dreamed possible.

4

A DAY WITHOUT LEARNING IS A DAY WITHOUT LIVING

July 22, 1961: Marrying Beth was the smartest thing I've ever done in my life.

Learning is an incremental process. No matter what the subject, you must first learn the fundamentals, putting in long hours to master the basics. You have to be able to add, subtract, multiply, and divide before you can move on to quantum physics. An art student doesn't sit down behind the canvas on the first day of class and say, "Show me how Rembrandt did it," and a first-year writing student can't expect to pen a Pulitzer Prize–winning novel in one sitting. Only after you've mastered the fundamentals can you take the next step, and the next, and the next, progressing until you have reached your goal. All talented individuals develop their talents over long periods of time, and I was no different.

At Iowa I was the lowest staff member on the totem pole, which was just fine with me. I was fortunate to be immersed in a college football program that ran like a finely tuned piece of industrial machinery. Coach Evashevski had been there a long time, and had been ultrasuccessful. He had a very knowledgeable staff that took time to teach me the intricacies of coaching. Jerry Burns, Archie Kodros, Bob Flora, Hap

Happel, and Olin Treadway were great. Everything I wanted to know about coaching was right in front of me. All I had to do was work my tail off to learn it.

As the only graduate assistant, I did anything and everything the coaching staff needed. I was the football version of a gym rat: working between sixty and a hundred hours a week, constantly hanging out in the football office, shuffling film back and forth between coaches, getting in the middle of blocking and tackling demonstrations, running a thousand errands, and helping coach the freshman team. On game day I was assigned to the press box to assist Jerry Burns. If it was gofer work, I was the guy. And I was thrilled to do it. I would have done the laundry if Coach Evashevski had wanted me to. Remember, I'd just come from mopping blood off the floors at East Liverpool City Hospital, and now I was learning about coaching at the feet of one of the best in the business.

I also took graduate courses to earn an M.A. degree, which kept me busy. I had gotten my undergraduate degree in history, but was getting my master's in physical education, in part because the athletic administration office and the physical ed department were in the same building, and the university had me teaching physical education to handicapped children—kids with spina bifida, muscular dystrophy, and other physical challenges. Dr. Red Marx was my superior. What a great man. At first I was apprehensive because I'd never been exposed to people, especially children, with such conditions. It didn't take long for me to realize that they were just like any other children emotionally, and it took even less time for them to have a profound impact on me. I became angry at myself for the whining and self-pity I'd displayed at various times in my life. Sure, I'd gone through some tough times, but I wasn't confined to a wheelchair! I could sit upright and eat on my own! Working with those children made me realize how lucky most of us are. It also shortened my patience for people who complain about trivial slights. No matter how bad someone has it, there are others who have it worse. Remembering that makes life a lot easier, and allows you to take pleasure in the blessings you have been given.

I couldn't have been happier, especially when Iowa went 9–1 with an unknown graduate assistant named Lou Holtz on the sidelines. When we beat Notre Dame in South Bend, we ended our season ranked second in the nation.

My personal life was also on track. Through nothing more than dogged tenacity and an unwillingness to take no for an answer, I eventually convinced Beth to reconsider my marriage proposal. After she initially broke off our engagement, I figured I had two options: let her go out with other people and forget about me, or refuse to give up, stay focused and dedicated, and continue to believe in myself and in our future together. I chose the latter.

Persistence is, in my mind, the quality that is most critical to success and happiness. Nothing takes the place of persistence. Talent won't; nothing is more common than unsuccessful men with talent. Genius won't do it; unrewarded genius is almost a proverb. Education will not; the world is full of educated derelicts. Persistence alone is omnipotent. Everybody of my generation knows that Babe Ruth hit 714 home runs. I am one of the few who also know that he struck out more than thirteen hundred times. I wasn't going to give up on Beth until she ran me off with a stick, because I knew that the key to any successful relationship was persistence. If I remained diligent, things might work out; if I quit, our relationship would be over. We continued to date when I was back home, and I either rekindled the spark of love or wore her resistance down to a nub. Either way, she finally acquiesced. We would be married in the summer of 1961.

I thought I had my life on track. I was working in the field I loved, for a coach I admired and respected. The woman I wanted to marry had said yes to my second proposal. And I was due to earn my master's from the University of Iowa. What could possibly go wrong?

I found out after our last game of the season. As we were flying back on one of two small charters from South Bend after beating Notre Dame, Coach Evashevski announced that he would be retiring. Jerry Burns would be taking over as head coach at Iowa. I was sad to hear that Coach Evi was leaving, because my position was year to year. I had hoped he would retain me for the following season or get another college to do so. After all, I was an all-purpose gofer. I wasn't indispensable by any means—I didn't know much, and I knew that everybody could be replaced—but Iowa didn't have anybody on the staff who took care of all the little things I did. I felt secure that I would stay on at Iowa.

Coach Burns liked me and appreciated all the things I did for the program. I knew this because he told me so as he was firing me. It turned out Coach Burns didn't want any married graduate assistants on his staff. He figured a graduate assistant should be an all-purpose, do-everything, on-call-at-all-times football fanatic, just the kind of person I had been for Coach Evashevski. But Coach Burns felt that a married man, especially a newlywed, had obligations at home. Hanging out at the football office at midnight on Friday would create problems at home. At the time I didn't believe Beth would have minded, but I also understood Coach Burns's logic. He didn't need any young wives calling his coaches and saying, "When are you coming home?"

I wish I had been detached (and mature) enough to find humor in the irony of my situation. The dogged persistence that had brought Beth and me back together had just cost me my job. I couldn't laugh. I wanted to cry. But first I had to get out and get to work.

Coach Rees heard what had happened and offered me an assistant-coaching job at Kent State. This was a great break, and one I promptly accepted. Unfortunately, the athletic director at Kent State did not approve of the hire, telling Coach Rees that he should choose someone who had attended a different school. This didn't make sense to me then, and it still doesn't to this day. Coach Rees couldn't believe it, either. So I was still stuck without a job.

Fortunately, Coach Burns didn't leave me twisting in the wind. One of my final jobs at Iowa was to entertain visiting coaches during spring practice on the same weekend. Bobby Bowden visited Iowa, as did Bud Grant, who would later coach the Minnesota Vikings, and Milt Drewer, the head coach and athletic director at the College of William and Mary in Virginia. Bud and Bobby weren't looking to hire a young, green assistant. Coach Drewer was. Thanks to some cajoling by Coach Burns and other members of the staff, Milt Drewer offered me a job as offensive and defensive backfield coach at William and Mary. I accepted the offer.

I had never been to historic Williamsburg, Virginia, but then, I'd never been to Iowa City before showing up to work for Coach Evashevski. Sure, I was anxious—change, no matter what the form, has never been something I've relished—but I was also excited about this new opportunity. That excitement increased when I visited the campus. Williamsburg was one of the most beautiful places I'd ever seen. Entering the town was like going through a time warp back to colonial Virginia, and the campus was like Mount Vernon and Monticello rolled into one. I loved the school from the first moment I saw it.

I couldn't wait to move to Williamsburg so we could start our life together as a family. But first I had to finish my dissertation and orals for my master's degree at Iowa. And Beth and I had to get married. Both of those things happened in a four-day stretch in July of 1961.

The most important decisions a man makes in his life are what kind of relationship he has with God, whom he marries, where he lives, what he does for a career, and what kind of example he sets for others. Of those, the relationship with God is, by far, the most important. But the second most important is marrying the right person. If you marry the wrong person, you can be a millionaire living on Maui and you'll still be miserable. Marry the right person, and you can find happiness cleaning septic tanks in Cleveland.

Marrying Beth was the smartest thing I've ever done in my life. I tell anyone who will listen that for forty-four years I've been married to my trophy wife, someone with whom I've been able to share everything and without whom I would never have amounted to anything. Coaching is the kind of profession where you buy your houses based solely on how fast you can resell them when you're fired. In forty years we moved twelve times, or an average of one move every forty months. Time-share salesmen and drifters move more often than coaches, but not by much. It's a gypsy life, one that tests even the strongest of relationships. I was lucky. Beth made every move we made easier. She supported me, worked with me, and turned every place we lived into a loving home. A house is an address; a home is an environment. Whenever we moved, Beth and I moved a home.

Our first move as a couple was a quick one. Beth and I spent our honeymoon in our first house. We were married on July 22, 1961. On July 18, I had driven to Iowa City for my oral examinations and to get my dissertation approved. That was a two-day process, which put me under tremendous pressure to get back to East Liverpool for our wedding rehearsal. I arrived back home a few hours before the rehearsal, and received some distressing news.

"Your father will be taking our wedding pictures," Beth said.

Since I had left the wedding planning up to Beth, she had an understandably negative reaction when I said, "You've got to be kidding."

She wasn't. My father had not only volunteered to be our official wedding photographer, he had refused to take no for an answer. Dad loved photography, and had all the right cameras, films, and lenses for any job. There was only one problem: He couldn't take a decent photo if his life depended on it. His was the only house in East Liverpool that had more cameras than photos.

"Dad can't take our pictures," I said.

Beth nodded and said, "Fine. You can fire him."

"But I didn't hire him."

"Neither did I, and he's your father."

So, I did the only thing I could: I ignored the problem and let my father take our wedding photos. As a result, the only surviving photo of our wedding came from a guest who happened to bring a Polaroid camera.

I look at the grainy shot now, and I can't help but smile. It is a constant reminder that it's important to be truthful with yourself and with others no matter whose feelings you might offend. If you want the best from others, you have to hire the best people, define what it is you want from them, and come to a common agreement on the terms and conditions of your relationship. If I'm ordering chicken noodle soup in a restaurant, I expect it hot, and I want it to come with a cracker or two. If that doesn't happen, I will be truthful in voicing my displeasure. I'm not going to eat cold soup to keep from hurting someone's feelings. I don't advocate being a jerk. You can voice your displeasure in a positive manner so that you aren't critical of a person, but of his or her actions. However, by compromising your quality expectations, you not only lower your own personal bar, you do a disservice to the person whose feelings you are afraid of hurting.

Throughout my coaching career, I've had to tell people hard truths about things more important than wedding photographs. I've had to fire assistant coaches who were longtime friends because their performance was not up to the standards we agreed were important, and I've had to bench players who were great people who simply did not get the job done. Not to fire or bench those people would have meant accepting mediocrity in order to preserve peace and harmony. Not only would that have been unfair to our teams, it would have been a terrible disservice to the person I fired or benched. My son Skip played for me at Notre Dame, and coached under me at South Carolina. When he fouled up on the field, which was seldom, I let him know it. It's always better to face the truth, no matter how uncomfortable, than to continue coddling a lie.

I should have told my father, "Dad, I love you, but we would rather have you enjoying our wedding from a pew in the front row. We'll hire a professional photographer." He might have been hurt for a minute or two, but it would have been better for everyone if I'd let him know the truth. I haven't repeated that mistake very often, and I've counseled many others to avoid making it as well.

Unfortunately, telling people what they need to hear is hard, so most people choose not to do it. To pull one example from popular culture, look at the number one television show in the country, **American Idol,** the latest in a long line of televised talent shows. When I was young it was **Ted Mack's Original Amateur Hour,** a show that discovered such stars as Pat Boone and Gladys Knight. I rarely watched and never had a desire to be on that show because I knew I couldn't sing. If I hadn't known, I had plenty of responsible, loving adults who would have told me the truth: "Lou, you've got a few talents, but singing is not among them." Today, the line of less-than-skilled singers auditioning for **American Idol** is as staggering as it is sad. Simon Cowell, one of the judges on the show, has gained a reputation as being the "mean old bad guy" because he tells people the truth: some of them simply can't sing. The fact that they've never been told this for fear of hurting their feelings is a troubling commentary on what we value today. The truth is too often suppressed in deference to feelings. That's a tragedy, one I have worked for more than forty years to avoid.

Immediately following our wedding reception, Beth and I hopped in the car and drove east. It was so hot we both wore Bermuda shorts and rolled down every window. The plan was to stop somewhere in Pennsylvania or western Virginia and spend our wedding night in as nice a hotel as we could afford (which wasn't much). Then we would get up and drive to Williamsburg the next morning. William and Mary was hosting the Virginia high school coaches' clinic that year, and I had to be back on campus Monday morning to be host and tour guide for our main speakers, Bo Schembechler and Woody Hayes. It wasn't much of a honeymoon, but it was all we wanted and all we could afford.

Unfortunately, our wedding day, July 22, 1961, was the Saturday on which the centennial of the first Battle of Bull Run was being commemorated. You'd think a history major would have known the centennial date for one of the most famous battles of the Civil War, but I had no idea why the roads were packed and the hotels full. When we stopped about 10 P.M. at what appeared to be a nice eastern Pennsylvania hotel, the desk clerk actually laughed at me.

"You won't find any rooms tonight," he said. "They're reenacting the battle for the centennial. We've got two hundred thousand people participating. There's not a vacant room between Breezewood and Williamsburg."

So I drove all night while Beth slept in the front seat with her feet propped up on the dash. Then we spent our honeymoon entertaining the Schembechlers, which was as good a week as we could have wanted. They, too, had been married the previous weekend and were spending their honeymoon at the same coaching clinic, so we were able to go out with them and share some quality time together.

At least we were in a great area. William and Mary was one of the best places I've ever worked. I was as happy a backfield coach there as I've been at any other time in my career. Not only were we in a town we loved, at a school that was as beautiful and friendly as any in the country, we also had a nicer home than any assistant coach I've ever known. Because Coach Drewer had built a home in Williamsburg, the faculty house for the head football coach was empty. Beth and I moved in, made ourselves at home, and promptly joined a bridge club. We didn't make much money, but we didn't need much. I had more time to spend with Beth, and we made our first friends together as a married couple. Mont Linkenauger, the team trainer, and Dr. George Oliver, our team physician, became lifelong friends. It was a wonderful time, one that I was never able to replicate in any other job I accepted.

William and Mary was quite a bit different from Iowa. In addition to the quaintly southern and pleasingly formal campus, the folks at William and Mary weren't as passionate and intense about their football as the fans at Iowa had been. A two-loss season at Iowa was viewed as devastating. Two losses at William and Mary and you'd be offered a lifetime coaching contract. It was the perfect environment for a young, inexperienced backfield coach to start his college coaching career. If I had stayed in that post for seven or eight years, my career might have been much different. Fortunately for me, adversity wasn't far away.

After three years as Milt Drewer's backfield coach, I had settled into a comfortable routine, one I was not anxious to change. Beth had given birth to our first daughter, Luanne, and we were both happy with our lives. But change in life is inevitable. Successful people adapt to change, even thrive on it, while those who dread and resist change have trouble. Like many people, I wasn't a big fan of change, but when change came, I did everything in my power to capitalize on it. That was the case in the early months of 1964 when Coach Drewer resigned as head football coach at

William and Mary to become president of Claritin Trust, one of the largest banks in the region. He would later become chairman, and retire as one of the most successful bankers in Virginia.

The head-coaching job was open, and I was one of the first to be approached about becoming the head coach. I was twenty-six years old with a grand total of three years' experience as an assistant coach. Why the athletic director and president of William and Mary would not want me as their head coach was beyond me. In hindsight, it's amazing that I made it to the final two in the selection process. I wasn't ready to be a head coach. Not even close. If I had been hired, I would have failed, and who knows where my career would have gone. As it was, the selection came down to Marv Levy, who had just been fired from the University of California and would later coach the Buffalo Bills to four Super Bowl appearances, and me.

I was surprised when they hired Marv. What could they have been thinking? He was only an experienced college coach who would only go on to become one of the most successful NFL coaches of all time, but, gosh, I was already a fixture on campus, and I wanted the job! That was the logic of a twenty-six-year-old. A more seasoned Lou Holtz would have realized what a blessing it was when Marv got the job instead of me. At the time, I felt hurt and slighted.

Losing the head-coaching job to Marv forced me out of my comfort zone. I had to find another coaching job, and I had to do an even better job than I'd done at William and Mary to prove to everyone that I was head-coaching material. This was not a move I would have made if Coach Drewer hadn't resigned. I would have been quite content to live in our nice house, go to my nice job, play bridge with our nice friends, hit a few golf balls in the summer, and play patty-cake with Luanne. But change came into our lives just as surely as a sunrise, and I was shaken into action as a result.

I received a few assistant-coaching offers. When I found out that my old position coach from Kent State, Rick Forzano, had become the head coach at the University of Connecticut, I felt sure he would offer me a job as an assistant. He did.

We had a great staff and did a good job at UConn, but the lifestyle wasn't as conducive to family life as we might have liked. Storrs, Connecticut, wasn't Williamsburg, Virginia. Houses in the nice parts of town were out of our price range, and the bad parts of town were places you wouldn't wish on an enemy. Plus, it snows a lot more in Connecticut than it does in Virginia. Despite our hearty midwestern upbringing, neither Beth nor I care much for cold weather. This comes as a great surprise to some people, especially since two of my last three coaching jobs were in Minnesota and South Bend, Indiana, neither of which would be classified as "tropical." But I've always been averse to cold weather, and Beth, who had given birth to our second child, Skip, and was pregnant with our third child, Kevin, would have preferred to go through her final trimester in something other than tundra conditions.

I went through some gut-wrenching times in my two seasons at Connecticut. Not that the job was bad: Rick Forzano was a fantastic coach, and a great friend who did everything he could for us. But I was feeling like I was on a treadmill. I was twenty-eight years old, a father of two, a fine assistant coach with very little money, and seemingly going nowhere. So Beth and I sat down at the kitchen table and asked ourselves three simple questions:

1. Did we really want to stay in coaching? It's a hard profession, and during the apprenticeship, the hours are long, the pay is at or below the poverty line, and job security extends no further than your next win or loss. Was this what we wanted to do as a family?

2. Should we go to law school? I framed this question as a "we" because the sacrifices of such a decision would fall on us as a

family. Law school is often tougher on the family members than it is on the student.

3. Should we get a doctorate in history and teach college? This was certainly an option we strongly considered. I have always loved teaching. Of all the choices we considered outside of coaching, this one had the greatest chance of success.

We prayed a lot, talked a lot, and wrote a lot of things down. Out of that discussion came our creed for what's important in choosing a profession: First, you have to do something that you love. Work isn't work when you love what you do. If you dread going to the office in the morning and can't wait for the workday to end, you need to seriously rethink your career choice. Second, you need to find something you do well. You might love to play golf, but if you shoot 100 every time you play, you're not very good, and you're going to starve to death playing golf for a living. Finally, you have to find somebody who will pay you. You might love something, and be very good at it, but if no one is willing to pay you for doing it, you don't have a career. I love eating Snickers bars, and I'm very good at it. Unfortunately, I've yet to find anyone who is willing to pay me to eat Snickers bars, so that aspect of my life doesn't qualify as a profession.

After going over our list and doing a lot of soul-searching, Beth and I decided to stick with coaching for five more years. By that time I would be thirty-three years old. If things worked out, we would stay in coaching forever. If they didn't, I would still be young enough to make a career change.

Within a few weeks of our heart-to-heart family meeting, the Lord sent a signal about his plan for our lives. I got an out-of-the-blue offer from Coach Marvin Bass to go to the University of South Carolina as an assistant. I didn't know Marvin Bass, or anybody else at South Carolina. But Bud Carson, the school's defensive coordinator, had just been hired by Georgia Tech to replace the legendary Bobby Dodd, and I was offered Bud's old job in Columbia. While I didn't want to leave Rick Forzano, I thought South Carolina was a better opportunity. Plus, it was warm. This was a chance to move south again, and, with Beth pregnant, I viewed the offer as a sign that maybe coaching was the right road for us.

On an early April morning, two months after spending every penny of our savings for the down payment on a house, packing up the family, and moving to Columbia, I learned what a great sense of humor God has, especially when you think you've figured out His plan for your life. We hadn't unpacked all the boxes or hung all the pictures in our home when I woke up, picked up the paper, and saw a headline that read, "Marvin Bass Resigns."

I said, "I wonder if he's related to our coach?"

Later that morning I learned that the Marvin Bass in the headline was, indeed, the man who had brought me to South Carolina. And he had, indeed, resigned. Before the end of the day, South Carolina president Thomas F. Jones called a meeting of all the assistant coaches. None of us were sure if we would leave the meeting employed.

"I know this comes as a surprise to many of you," he said.

I didn't say "No kidding" out loud, but that was the universal sentiment in the room.

President Jones cleared his throat before saying: "I want everyone here to know that I intend to hire the best coach I can for this university. I also want you to know that if the coach I hire chooses not to keep any one of you, the university will keep you on for a reasonable amount of time."

I raised my hand.

"Yes, you have a question?" he said.

"I do. What's a reasonable amount of time?"

President Jones cocked his head and shrugged his shoulders as if such a niggling little detail was unimportant. "Oh, about a month," he said.

After the meeting I called Beth and said, "Don't unpack the rest of the boxes."

President Jones hired a fine coach named Paul Dietzel as athletic director. I didn't know him, and didn't know anyone who knew him. But he had a reputation for being fair, so I did my best to impress him when he came to campus to interview the assistants. I must have done a great job, because he fired me within the hour.

At least Coach Dietzel offered some words of encouragement. As I was leaving his office after receiving the bad news, he said, "Lou, just one more thing."

"Yes?" I said.

"Have you ever thought about going into a different profession?"

I put the résumés and feelers out as soon as I got home, but finding a coaching job in April is like finding a snowball in Miami. It's possible, but not likely. So we were stuck. I had no job. We'd spent all our savings buying our house. With Kevin being born, we now had three small children. And we were living in a town where we knew practically no one. Other than that, things were great.

I was twenty-eight years old and had already been through three assistant-coaching jobs in three different states. I'd been rejected for the only head-coaching job I'd applied for, and now I was a couple of months away from being out on the street with nothing. This was not how I had envisioned my life. I wondered if God was testing me, or if I had somehow rejected or misinterpreted His will. We prayed a lot, and turned to scripture for guidance. One passage jumped off the page. It came from the apostle Paul's letter to the Romans. In chapter 5, verses 3–4, Paul wrote: "We also rejoice in our sufferings, because we know that suffering produces perseverance; perseverance, character; and character, hope."

I didn't feel much like rejoicing in our plight, but I wasn't about to give up either. We had promised ourselves that we would give coaching five years, and after a great deal of discussion, Beth and I decided that we would stick to our plan. She got a job as an X-ray technician for a group of urologists, and I stayed home with the children, made phone calls, sent out résumés, but most important, tried to be a good father. I did everything I could to turn perseverance into character, and character into hope.

During this time, in between diaper changes and getting the Kool-Aid out of the refrigerator, I sat down and reflected on the goals I wanted to achieve in my life. I broke the list down into five categories:

1. Things I want to do as a husband and a father
2. Things I want to do religiously
3. Things I want to accomplish professionally
4. Things I want to do financially
5. Things I want to do for excitement (personally)

When I finished I had 108 items listed. In the "for excitement" column I wrote such things as "jump out of an airplane," "land on an aircraft carrier," "go out on a submarine," "appear on **The Tonight Show** with Johnny Carson," "go white-water rafting down the Snake River," "play the greatest golf courses in the world," "have dinner in the White House," "meet the Pope," "go on an African picture safari," and "run with the bulls in Spain with a slower person." Forty years later, I've completed all but two of the items from my original list.

I couldn't wait to show Beth the goals and priorities I'd set. When she came home that night, I proudly shared my lists with her. She read and nodded. Then she turned the paper over to see if something was on the back.

"What's the matter?" I asked.

"It looks like you've left something off."

"What?"

"Well, it is your list, but if it were me, at the top of the first page, in big letters, I'd write, 'Get a job!'"

Once again, my wife had successfully put things into perspective.

5

SETBACKS DON'T DEFINE YOUR GOALS, YOU DO

Woody Hayes was one of the greatest coaches in the country, but when the offer came in to work for him, the decision wasn't as easy as I'd thought.

Nothing focuses the mind like crisis. Throughout history, the most extraordinary acts of genius have often come in the depths of turmoil. The atom was split during the height of World War II, when American scientists were racing the Nazis on the nuclear front, and Neil Armstrong walked on the moon because of the breakneck space race NASA had with the Soviet Union. On a smaller scale, we've all seen football teams that struggle to get anything done for three and a half quarters only to mount miraculous game-winning drives at the end. It happens all the time. When your back is against the wall and you know you have only one chance to win or lose, your senses become keener and your performance elevates. As a coach you always try to get your players to give 100 percent on every play of every game, but I'm not naive enough to believe they did it. When we found ourselves behind or tied in the final minutes of a game, I could see our players dig deeper, focus more intently, and find something within themselves that pushed their performance up a notch. It's human nature.

When it's now or never, everyone tends to focus on "now."

I was no different. When I was unemployed and staying home with our small children, I focused with laserlike intensity on the goals I had for my family and me. Changing diapers while Beth went to work was not among those goals. Fortunately, I didn't remain a stay-at-home dad for very long. Two months after Paul Dietzel asked me if I'd ever considered another line of work, I got a call. Realizing that I wasn't leaving Columbia anytime soon, Coach Dietzel figured there was a need to have someone serve as an academic liaison for the football team. He made me an offer.

"If you'll take a pay cut, and be in charge of academics and the scout squad, I've got room for you on my staff."

"How big a pay cut?" I wanted to know.

"Three thousand dollars."

In today's coaching world that would be an easy call. When your base salary is a hundred thousand, a three-thousand-dollar pay cut is like swatting a fly. But in 1965 I was making only eleven thousand dollars. Three thousand dollars was 27 percent of my salary. The pay cut being offered would push me down to eight thousand a year. With three kids and a wife to support, this should have been a tougher decision than it was, but I accepted Coach Dietzel's offer.

Since there wasn't much money in coaching at any level at that time, financial considerations were always secondary. The month was June, and there were no job opportunities at that time of the year. If I had a coaching job, regardless of how insignificant, it would be much easier to secure a coaching job in January, when positions would be open. I also had something to prove. Coaching was my chosen profession, and I wanted Coach Dietzel and his assistants to see just how serious I was about making it. If that meant taking a temporary demotion, then that was what I would do.

Beth quit her job the day I went back to work. Neither of us ever considered anything else. We both believed that our job as parents was to raise our children in a loving, stable, and hands-on fashion, which, for us, meant having one parent at home. I understood the value of being there for kids, because I always had my mother, sister, grandparents, and uncles around when I was growing up. I never came home from school to an empty house, and I was never left in the care of someone not related to me. Child care and nannies are common today, and those sorts of arrangements work well for a lot of people, but not for us. We squeezed our already tight family budget a little tighter, and lived the next year on love, prayer, and eight thousand dollars.

At least I got to see a lot of great football teams that season—LSU, Alabama, Georgia, and Florida State to mention a few—just none of them in South Carolina. Because I was always scouting the opposition, I did not attend a single South Carolina game that year, which wasn't a terrible thing, since our team went 1–9.

Scouting gave me a chance to learn more about planning and preparation, and to observe some of the finest coaches in the country at work. I got to observe their offenses, defenses, and special teams and, equally important, had to determine why they ran the plays they did. It became obvious to me by scouting that there are a lot of ways to win and succeed. Coach Paul "Bear" Bryant at Alabama and Coach Charles McClendon at LSU were different, but the one thing all great teams had in common was that they blocked and tackled very well. They executed the fundamentals of the game. This made me all the more determined to be the best teacher of fundamentals in the country.

I also learned a lot from handling our players' academics. I wasn't aware of it at the time, but players don't care how much you know until they know how much you care. There is no more rewarding feeling that I have experienced as a coach than to help a player graduate.

Since my earliest days in coaching I've always said that in order to be a student-athlete, you first have to be a student. College athletics is more about college than about athletics, and I've always believed that every student-athlete must make academics his or her number one priority. It is a fact that few players go on and play profession-ally. Even if they do, the average stay in the NFL is 4.2 years. This means that even if you do play professionally, your football career is over at age twenty-seven, but your life is only one-third over. I made sure our athletes attended class, made it to study hall, and got tutoring if it was needed. If a player struggled in a class, I would often make a point of meeting with him twice a week to work through problems and chart his progress. Ath-letes knew they could come to me with questions about their academics, and I would do whatever I could to help them reach their classroom goals. But I refused ever to visit with a professor about a player's grades. I had a sign on my desk that said, "The time to worry is before you place your bet and not after they spin the wheel." In other words, get your grades.

That same philosophy stuck with me through-out my career. No matter where I coached, I always encouraged our players to excel academically. Sometimes I had to do very little—players like Flash Gordon and Frank Stams, two outstand-ing defensive ends at Notre Dame, always made their grades. Most top programs have a full-time academic counselor for football. Mike DeCicco

108 | LOU HOLTZ

at Notre Dame and Jason Pappas at USC are the best. There were plenty of times when I had to have a conference with a player on his attitude or put my hand on a player's shoulders and point him toward the library. Sometimes I had to threaten; other times I had to encourage; and on a few occasions I had to have serious sit-down heart-to-heart chats. But my objective was always the same: I wanted any student-athlete who played for us to be the best athlete, and the best student, he could possibly be.

What I never did, and what I never saw anyone who ever worked for me or with me do, was advise an athlete to take an "easy" or "crip" course just to get by. If "getting by" was all an athlete wanted to do, he needed to do it somewhere else. The same was true for the people around me. No one I ever worked for, with, or around ever asked a professor for a special grading favor, or requested that someone "go easy" on one of our guys. It was something we never considered, and something I would never have tolerated.

Now, if an athlete had struggled to make C's in high school biology, we might have advised him to ease into that premed major, but we never discouraged an athlete from aiming high academically. And I take personal offense when anyone says otherwise. I remember what it's like to be a poor student in high school and have everyone expect you to do poorly in college. I showed up at

Kent State with "Low Expectations" stamped on my forehead. But not only did I do well in school, I went on to earn a postgraduate degree. I know that if I could do it, every athlete I ever coached could do the same.

Like everyone, I've heard stories about grade inflation, and about athletes today who glide through school learning little or nothing. Heck, I've even been accused by some glib and ill-informed sportswriters of turning a blind eye to those same kinds of shenanigans. But I know coaches who have taught classes like "How to Line a Football Field" or "Fundamentals of Basketball," and athletes who have passed those classes with flying colors. If I had ever heard of anything like that going on in one of our programs, I would have fired any coach and suspended any player involved. I challenge you to find one athlete I have ever coached who will say I didn't emphasize honest academics.

In 1965 we didn't have those problems, because players were especially motivated to do whatever it took to pass and remain in school. President Johnson had just armed the advisers we had on the ground in a little Southeast Asian country called Vietnam. The draft was in full swing. Those students who stayed in school were given deferments. Those who flunked or dropped out went to 1-A status at their local draft boards. Avoiding the draft became a great, clarifying motivator to many students in that era, and academic performance across the board improved as a result. Once again, crisis sharpened focus, and students everywhere worked harder in the classroom as a result.

I didn't feel bad about pushing our athletes on the field or in the classroom. In fact, I would have been doing them a disservice if I hadn't pushed most of them further than they thought they could do. Humans aren't wired to push themselves beyond their comfort zone. We certainly didn't invent the easy chair and the remote control because we love suffering. But no one will question the fact that it makes us stronger and teaches us things about ourselves that we might otherwise have never known. Saint Peter commanded us to "rejoice" in our suffering, and not to "be surprised by the painful trial you are suffering, as though something strange were happening to you." It is a natural part of life, a part that, as long as it doesn't destroy you, builds character and helps you define your priorities.

A perfect example of this was the scout squad I coached. Many of those young men were walk-ons or partial-scholarship athletes who weren't expected ever to start a game at South Carolina. They weren't All-Americans, and most of them knew it. They worked hard, but no one expected much out of them. They didn't disappoint. Suffering wasn't high on their agenda, because they didn't see any reward in it. Until I arrived, nobody had set a standard for the practice squad. I told them that if we were going to do something, we would do it to the best of our ability.

At first they were shocked. What could that lunatic Coach Holtz be thinking? Why should the scout squad go through the pain, suffering, and sacrifice of those intense practice sessions when not one of the players would receive accolades on game day? My answer was simple: You work hard and suffer because it makes you a better man. If the rewards you seek are found in the praise and adulation of others, you are destined for disappointment, because the moment you drop one pass, or lose one game, the cheering stops and the praise goes away. Internal rewards, the ones you gain from pain, sweat, and tears, stick with you forever. They understood, and their attitude and their performance changed accordingly.

We had many memorable players on the scout squad, but one man in particular deserves recognition: Freddie Zeigler, a freshman walk-on wide receiver who was slow but really competitive. He went on to be an ACC All-Conference receiver for South Carolina.

People perform to the level expected of them. If you expect a child to pass algebra, he's going to do what it takes to pass, not an ounce more or less. If you expect B's, communicate those expectations, and talk about the consequences for failing to meet those goals, the student will make B's. But if you drive home an expectation of greatness, straight A's for example, communicate the rewards that will come from meeting that goal, and make known the dire consequences that will follow anything less than perfection, then your student will do whatever it takes to make perfect grades. If I had expected the scout squad to go through the motions and pump up the egos of our starters, that's exactly what they would have done. But because I demanded nothing short of greatness, the players elevated their performance far beyond anyone's expectations. This is the way I was coached and the only way I knew to coach.

In late November, Coach Dietzel decided to put together a game between South Carolina's outstanding freshman team (at that time, freshmen were not allowed to play varsity football, a rule that was changed in 1973) and the varsity scout squad. No one expected our guys to do much. Even though they had shown a lot of heart and a surprising amount of skill during the regular season, they were the nonstarters on a 1–9 football team. The freshmen had talent.

When our scout squad beat them badly, you would have thought it was for the national championship. The kids I coached were overjoyed. Only a handful of people saw the game; there were no cheerleaders, no bands, no sideline reporters, and no chants from the crowd, but the players couldn't have cared less. They had suffered, not for the cheers or the fleeting warmth of a temporary spotlight, but for themselves. They had been given a chance in a game situation against an opponent they weren't supposed to beat. Not only had they won that game, they had dominated.

Shortly afterward, Coach Dietzel reinstated my original salary, elevated George Terry, a man I loved, to assistant athletic director, and made me the defensive backfield coach. We had a better season the following year, going 5–5 on the strength of some outstanding sophomore athletes. But those five wins weren't nearly as impressive to me as the intersquad game my scout team won the previous spring. Those young men, although not the most talented I've ever coached, pushed themselves further than they ever thought possible, not for glory or fame, but for the self-satisfaction of knowing they could do it. I'm as proud of that group of men as any I've ever coached.

During the 1967 season, I told my friend Rick Forzano that if the opportunity ever presented itself, I would love to coach at Ohio State and work with Woody Hayes. This wasn't an earth-shattering revelation: Woody was one of the greatest coaches in the country, and, having grown up on the banks of the Ohio River, I placed Ohio State a couple of notches below heaven on the "want to go there" scale. Telling a friend I would like to work for Coach Hayes was like saying, "Gee, I'd like to win the lottery."

So I was somewhat surprised when Rick arranged for me to have lunch with Esco Sark-kinen. He had played at Ohio State, had been an All-American, and was one great person. We had a nice lunch (even though Esco showed up forty-five minutes late) where I reiterated my heartfelt desire to someday work for Coach Hayes at Ohio State. Since Coach Hayes wasn't in a position to hire anybody at the time, I assumed this was nothing more than nice lunchtime conversation.

Ohio State had a less-than-spectacular season that year, and the following winter, Coach Hayes decided to change his staff. Harry Stroebel, the offensive line coach, retired. I never thought about being part of that change. I was very happy at South Carolina, Beth enjoyed Columbia, the weather was nice, and the kids were toddling around our neighborhood, making friends and enjoying life. I wasn't averse to talking to someone about moving, but I certainly wasn't looking for a job.

In January 1968, I went to New York for the National Coaches' Convention. I was the recording secretary for the American Football Coaches Association, a position given to me by Coach Dietzel, who was president of the organization. Coach Dietzel was coaching in the Hula Bowl at the time, so he missed the meeting, but I went to record the minutes. The fact that I got to spend my birthday, January 6, on Broadway was a bonus.

Another bonus came the first day of the AFCA meeting when Bill Murray, a coach at Duke University who was executive director of the AFCA, asked me to stay for dinner and cocktails with the trustees of the board. I was thrilled. Here I was, a relatively unknown backfield coach from an ACC school that was far from a powerhouse, and I was being asked to dine with the best coaches in the game. It was quite an honor. I couldn't accept fast enough. When I came down for dinner, my excitement doubled. At my table sat Ben Schwartzwalder, coach at Syracuse University; Charles "Rip" Engle, head coach at Penn State; and Coach Woody Hayes, one of my modern-day idols in the game.

Typically, Coach Hayes dominated the conversation. I'd met him once before at the coaches' clinic we hosted at William and Mary the week after I got married, but he didn't remember me. When I introduced myself, I saw a quizzical look enter his eye. I wouldn't realize it until much later, but he was connecting my face with the name Esco Sarkkinen had given him as a possible candidate for defensive backfield coach at Ohio State. I figured Coach Hayes was just being polite when he started asking me about defensive backfield formations and how we covered certain pass patterns at South Carolina. I didn't know it, but I was being interviewed for a job.

Before my week in New York ended, on a trip where I'd figured to do little more than take notes and catch a show or two, I had two job offers, and a huge decision to make.

The first offer came from Bud Carson, the man I had moved to South Carolina to replace. Bud was the head coach at Georgia Tech, having replaced the legendary Bobby Dodd, the man for whom the Georgia Tech stadium is now named, and the first coach ever to take the Yellow Jackets to a national championship. Bud had inherited a world-class program with some fine athletes. I was flattered that he thought enough of me to ask me to join his staff.

That same day, my thirty-first birthday, I got a call in my hotel room from Coach Woody Hayes. "Lou, I'd like to talk to you about coaching our defensive backfield," he said. "When can you come to Ohio State?"

I stammered for a second or two before finally saying, "Coach, I'm flattered. I need to get back to South Carolina and talk about this with my wife. Can I call you next week?"

The subsequent pause couldn't have lasted more than three seconds, but it felt like an hour. "Make it quick," he finally said.

Not quite two years after sitting in my living room, unemployed, writing my list of 101 goals for life, I flew home from New York with two of the best job offers an assistant coach could want. The only problem was, I couldn't accept them both.

Beth and I prayed about the offers, as we did with every family decision. Time was short: Bud Carson and Woody Hayes had to fill their coaching rosters so they could get on with the business of signing incoming freshmen and preparing for the 1968 season. We asked God to give us an answer, and if it wasn't too much trouble, to do so quickly.

The Lord didn't call our home, and unfortunately, I wasn't very attuned to the way He answers prayers. So, I did what anybody in my position would do: I asked other coaches what they thought. The answers heavily favored going to Georgia Tech. For starters, the people whose opinions I solicited knew Bud Carson, and knew that I would fit in well with his coaching staff. "Woody Hayes is insane," I heard more than once. Paul Dietzel shared no love with Coach Hayes. As a matter of fact, he flew back early from Hawaii to talk me out of going to Ohio State to visit. "You don't want to go up there," he said. "It's cold. It's rough. The alumni and fans are as hard to please as any place in the country. Plus, you'd be working for a certifiable lunatic who's on a year-to-year contract."

This made sense. My heart was telling me that Ohio State was the right move, but my common sense and my bank account screamed for me to pack my bags and beat a trail to Atlanta. Bud had offered a salary of thirteen thousand dollars, plus the down payment on a home, plus moving expenses, plus a car allowance, plus a vacation in Florida every year for my family and me. (That final perk was an off-the-books bonus. I would recruit South Florida high schools for a couple of weeks, a perfectly legal and very nice incentive.) Coach Hayes had offered me a flat salary of thirteen thousand, no down payment, no car, no bonus, and no perks. It should have been an easy call.

Then word of my offers filtered back to East Liverpool, and my phone started ringing. The call that stands out the most came from my uncle Lou, who said: "You have got to go to Ohio State. There's no other choice. Why would you ever consider going anywhere else?" Other relatives were equally insistent. If I wanted a warm reception at the Thanksgiving dinner table, I had better say yes to Coach Hayes and get to Ohio State as quickly as possible.

Given how quickly Bud and Coach Hayes needed answers, I could visit only one school. I already had a hotel reservation in Atlanta. But on the Sunday night before I was to leave, I changed my plans and flew to Columbus, Ohio. I spent two days with Coach Hayes where he talked, I listened; he asked questions, and I answered. Even though he had formally offered me the coaching position, it was as intense a trip as I had ever taken. Coach Hayes had a way of keeping you on your toes at all times, even when he was trying to convince you to come work for him. During one of our lunches, after I'd already been grilled on everything from defending the bootleg sweep to what kind of car I drove, Coach Hayes stared through the back of my eyes and said, "What about spices?"

My brain went into overdrive. Spices. Spices. Was this some new formation I'd missed?

When I didn't answer immediately, he picked up the salt and pepper shakers. "Spices. You want spices on your chicken?"

"No thanks, Coach," I said. "The chicken's fine."

After two full days of exhausting discussions, I realized that I hadn't been allowed to talk to a single assistant coach. That bothered me. If I was going to be a member of the coaching staff, I should at least meet and speak to the men I would be working alongside. But when I broached the subject, Coach Hayes said, "Don't worry about it. You'll be working for me, not them."

This set off every alarm in my brain. If all the negative things I'd heard about Coach Hayes were untrue, why wouldn't he let me talk to one of his assistants? "Coach," I said, "I really feel that it's crucial that I talk to an assistant."

For five or six seconds I was treated to another of his laser-beam death stares. He finally said, "All right. You can meet with Tiger Ellison."

Tiger was the freshman coach and a former college teammate of Coach Hayes's at Denison University. He was also one of the nicest guys I'd ever met. He made me feel completely at ease as we chatted about the program. When I asked him what it was like to work for Coach Hayes, he laughed and said, "A little like being back in the military."

I could handle that. I had loved my stint in the service.

"He's tough, demanding, aggressive, but overall he's a good guy. He's also a great leader."

That was all I needed to hear. When I got home, I told Beth, "I think I can work for Woody Hayes. If Tiger Ellison can work for him, I can work for him."

Because of an Ohio State policy, the athletic board and the athletic director, Dick Larkins (who hailed from East Liverpool although I did not know him), had to approve of Coach Hayes's decision to hire me. That wouldn't happen for a couple of weeks, during which time I technically had not been hired. For those fourteen days, I went into the office like an idiot because of habit. The staff constantly tried to talk me out of going to Ohio State. "Hayes is insane, and you're insane for thinking you can work for him!" Coach Dietzel again told me. They all wanted me either to stay at South Carolina or to take the job at Georgia Tech. Finally, after a week of hearing what a horrible mistake I'd made, and how I would forever regret not taking the Georgia Tech job, I decided to tell Coach Hayes that I wasn't coming.

I tracked him down at the home of Tom Campagna Jr., a player he was recruiting. I happened to know the young man's father (we were also trying to convince him to come to South Carolina), so I felt comfortable calling Coach Hayes at their home. "Coach," I blurted out. "I've decided not to come to Ohio State."

His breathing got louder and faster until he sounded like a panting animal. Then he let loose in classic Woody Hayes style, setting what had to be a new world record for four-letter words in a two-minute period. These were not whispered obscenities. If the mother of the house had been anywhere nearby, Coach Hayes could have forgotten about signing her son. I came within two seconds of hanging up on him. After a couple of minutes of this unbelievable rant, I told myself I should hang up on him, but I decided that because I had changed my mind, I owed it to him to let him swear. I can honestly say that while he was yelling and swearing, I said to myself, "Lou Holtz, you made the right choice by calling him and saying no."

When his breathing returned to normal, he said, "Okay. All right. You're not coming. That's fine. But let me tell you one thing, something that's going to stick with you for the rest of your life: Whatever it was inside you that made you want to come to Ohio State in the first place, that little voice that told you to say yes when I offered you the job, that reason, that voice, is still there. It might be silent right now, but it's still there. The reason you wanted to come work for me is still inside you. It may be dormant, but it's not going away."

He was right, and I knew it. "Coach," I said. "A minute ago I was two seconds away from hanging up on you. Now, I'm wondering…if the job's still available, I think I'd like to change my mind and accept."

He paused again, and I thought I'd blown it for good. Indecision was not something Woody Hayes took lightly, and I had to look like the wishy-washiest guy in the world. After a couple of seconds, I heard him sigh.

"Board meets tomorrow," he said. "I'll see you up here the day after that."

6

GREATNESS STARTS
WITH BELIEF AND TOTAL
COMMITMENT

The Ohio State coaching staff in Vegas after the 1968 National Championships. We all went on to great careers. **(Las Vegas News Bureau) Top to bottom:** George Chaump (head coach, U.S. Naval Academy); Rudy Hubbard (head coach, Florida A&M); Earle Bruce (head coach, Ohio State); Lou McCullough (athletic director, Iowa State); me; Bill Mallory (head coach, Universities of Colorado and Indiana); and Hugh Hindman (athletic director, Ohio State).

My first day at Ohio State it snowed eight inches and the temperature never got above twenty degrees. With the wind, which blew the snow sideways at about fifteen miles an hour, the effective temperature was somewhere between zero and minus ten. Beth had given me a new winter coat as a belated birthday present when she learned that we were moving to Columbus, and it didn't come a moment too soon. After two winters in South Carolina, where a bad day meant wearing khakis and a sweater, my cold-weather wardrobe had dwindled to nothing. As I stepped out the door for my first day of work, coat snugly buttoned to its collar, my lungs all but shut down from shock at the bitter cold air.

This wasn't the only shock of the day. At the dining hall where new assistant coaches ate breakfast alongside students, I left my coat on the back of my chair as I went to refill my coffee cup. When I returned, the new coat—the only coat I owned heavier than a windbreaker—had been stolen. I searched the dining hall and interrogated a few students, but to no avail. The coldest day of the year, I headed to my first staff meeting in a thin cotton shirt and Ohio State baseball cap. At least Coach Hayes wouldn't accuse me of being soft. Stupid, maybe, but not soft.

The staff meeting at St. John Arena was the first gathering of all the new coaches, including a fellow named Hugh Hindman, who would go on to become an athletic director; Earle Bruce, who later became the head coach at Ohio State; George Chaump, who became the head coach at the Naval Academy; Bill Mallory, who went on to Indiana University; Rudy Hubbard, who would become the head coach at Florida A&M; Lou McCullough, who would go on to be the athletic director at Iowa State; and me. I arrived a few minutes early, cold, but excited. This was a great staff. I got tingles thinking about the coaching potential we had sitting in that room.

Then Coach Hayes arrived. We heard him before we saw him. The tone of his voice sounded foul. I was smoking a pipe, something I'd been doing since I was twenty-six, when Beth bought me one (I've never smoked cigarettes or cigars in my life). He looked at me, pointed, and said, "What are you doing smoking a pipe? You couldn't work for Paul Brown. He says anyone who smokes a pipe is lazy and complacent."

I knew that Coach Hayes didn't like Paul Brown. Some of the alums had said Brown should have been hired at Ohio State. So I said, "Coach, that's why you're smarter than Paul Brown. You don't believe that nonsense."

He looked at me for a few seconds without saying a word. I think my sharp comeback surprised him. Anyway, he never said anything more about my pipe.

In that first meeting, the staff and I broke up a physical fight between Coach Hayes and an assistant coach over a student's academics. Coach Hayes believed that the assistant was not spending enough time with this particular athlete on his schoolwork. The assistant respectfully disagreed, and Coach Hayes went after him, grabbing him by the shirt and starting a tussle. The man had what counselors today would term "anger-management issues." I just knew I'd never seen a head coach be so volatile in his first meeting of the season. All the other coaches leaped in and broke up the skirmish before it got out of hand. I jumped to my feet a little slower than the others. If anything, I wanted to be ready in case I needed to run for the door.

Breaking up the fight was just for starters. Later Coach Hayes got mad over something else and picked up the projector and hurled it through the glass door that led to the hallway. Fighting another coach must not have appealed to him, so he vented his anger by ruining an expensive film projector and breaking a glass door.

From that moment forward, by an edict from the athletic director, all film projectors in St. John Arena were chained to the tables.

Then he went on with the meeting as if nothing had happened. As a matter of fact he gave us a history lesson, and I could tell there was something special about Coach Hayes. As I stretched my aching legs and exited the room with my head down, the only thought rumbling like a train through my mind was, "Oh my God, Lou, what have you gotten yourself into?"

Then I heard one of the coaches behind me singing a popular Bobby Russell song: "God didn't make the little green apples/and it don't rain in Indianapolis/in the summertime." I turned and saw our troubadour, Tiger Ellison, the man who had assured me that Coach Hayes was "overall a good guy, and a great leader."

"Tiger, how can you be singing?" I said.

"I just open my mouth and the melody comes out."

"Well that's wonderful, but didn't you see what just happened in there?"

He laughed and put a hand on my shoulder. "Don't worry about it, son. You'll get used to it."

Oh no! He'd just said I would get used to fistfights and flying projectors!

"Tiger, I thought you said Coach Hayes was a good guy, a great leader?"

He chuckled again. "Hey, Attila the Hun was a great leader. Doesn't mean you'd have him over for dinner."

That's when I realized I'd been snookered. Coach Hayes had kept me away from every assistant coach except Tiger Ellison because Tiger had never said an unkind word about anybody in his life. The guy even found a way to compliment Attila the Hun! Coach Hayes knew this, so he let Tiger be the recruiting spokesman.

Through the spring and summer I learned a lot more about Coach Hayes. I found him to be everything everyone had said: demanding, tough, but exceptionally smart and well read. Sure, he had a volatile temper: you never knew what was going to happen when he was around. But he was also a brilliant tactician. After a while I realized that many of his tantrums were calculated to make a point. He wanted people to think he was more volatile than he was, so that all those around him would do their best for fear of a potential eruption. Today, I believe that next to Father Theodore Hesburgh, president of Notre Dame for thirty-five years, Coach Hayes was the most remarkable person I've ever known.

Coach Hayes had the incredible knack of knowing everyone's strengths and weaknesses, and he did not hesitate to expose both. If your image of yourself exceeded his image of you, he was going to knock you down until you realized the error of your egotistical ways. But if you were down, if you were really, truly in need, he was the first person to put his hands on your shoulders and lift you up. After I coached for Woody, he never again went through my hometown of East Liverpool without stopping and calling my mother to find out how she was doing.

I also learned a lot about building winning teams from him. Practices were like being back in basic training, except that in the Army you stopped drilling occasionally. Coach Hayes's practices were nonstop drills from the moment we hit the field until the moment he blew the whistle. During spring practice, I saw him spend an entire day talking and coaching about a play like the fullback off tackle.

He knew every one of his players' tendencies, and he knew how the opposition was going to exploit those tendencies to its advantage. Jack Tatum, our sophomore defensive back who went on to become one of the most fearsome players in the history of the NFL, had a tendency to over-read and overpursue, which made him susceptible to well-executed play-actions, counter plays, bootlegs, and reverses. Coach Hayes knew this, and when we scrimmaged against each other, he would run misdirection plays again and again. When Jack bit on the fake or overpursued, Coach

Hayes would yell, "That is what Michigan will do to you."

Sometimes I thought he went over the line in his browbeating criticisms. At least he was an equal-opportunity yeller. He was tough on everyone—coaches, stars, and third teamers. He wanted everyone to be the best he could be. He also demanded that players accept his high standards.

When our All-American tackles Rufus Mayes and Dave Foley didn't line up in the stance he wanted, Coach Hayes would scream like a charging Apache. He knew how much weight each player should have on his hands and how much should be on his feet when he got into his stance, and he would kick his All-Americans in the rump if their spine angles were slightly off, cheating in one direction or another. He was also a stickler for the position of a player's head when he came to the line. If you looked to your left and then stunted in that direction, he would slap the left side of your helmet until you never looked that way again. The detail he demanded could be maddening, especially when you considered that the average athlete on our team, even though young, had been playing football more than half of his life.

Coach Hayes believed in pounding home the fundamentals. Usually half of our practice was devoted to individual teaching of blocking and tackling, which, in addition to winning the one-on-one battles at the line of scrimmage, were his obsessions. But make no mistake: the coaches and players learned to love and respect Woody as much as you respect your parents. Of course, all the coaches would tell Woody stories, but when we became head coaches, we all coached just like him.

Woody Hayes affirmed my belief that humans are capable of far more than they realize, and that each individual's performance is predicated on what's expected of him. Ohio State started twelve sophomores in 1968. This was when freshmen weren't eligible. No one knew what to expect from a team that young. Michigan and Purdue were both ranked higher at the beginning of the year, and after the disappointing 1967 season, a lot of experts bet on Ohio State finishing with at least three or four losses, respectable, but uninspiring. Conventional wisdom had Purdue winning the conference, and maybe the national championship. The only team that could stand in their way was the University of Southern California, or "Tailback U" as it was known in those days. They had a fine young running back named O. J. Simpson who was setting all kinds of records. Most polls had Purdue and USC as the top-ranked teams in the country. Coach Hayes not only refused to believe the polls, he refused to let any of us settle for being second or third best. He told us not only that we were going to beat Purdue and Michigan, but that we had better **dominate** them. There would be no second best on his watch. If we wanted to avoid the Wrath of Woody, athletes and coaches alike had better exceed every expectation.

I think we won most of our games that season because we were tougher, more disciplined, more confident, and better fundamentally than the opposition. That proved to be a huge psychological advantage for our players. A lot of opposing tailbacks came to the line a little apprehensive when facing the likes of Mark Stier, Jack Tatum, and Jim Stillwagon. Our players were competitors, and losing was not an option. As a result, they wanted not only to win on the scoreboard, but to beat our opposition physically. Woody believed in the brush tackle. He believed in brushing the ball carrier's chest up against his spine.

Our first game of the season, and my first at Ohio State, was against Southern Methodist University. Up to that point I'd never been as nervous about a game in my life. I'd studied every film I could find on SMU and memorized the scouting reports, but in the season opener you know very little about your opponent, and even less about how your athletes will perform. We were as prepared as we could be, but game day is about executing under pressure: some teams step up and get the job done, and others, no matter how well prepared, don't.

Fortunately, we were the former. Chuck Hixson, SMU's fine quarterback, threw seventy-six times, an unprecedented air attack in the sixties, and completed forty of those passes for 420 yards, an NCAA record. But of those thirty-six passes he didn't complete, we intercepted the ball six times. We also shut down the run, allowing only 50 yards on the ground the entire game. On offense, our sophomore quarterback, Rex Kern, played like a four-year starter. He threw for 145 yards and orchestrated another 227 on the ground thanks to some explosive running by our fullback, Jim Otis, and tailback, John Brockington. We won the game 35–14.

Afterward, I didn't know what to expect. Sure, we'd won, but my defensive backfield had given up more than 400 passing yards, not the kind of day that earns a backfield coach a lot of accolades. Once the players showered and headed out of the locker room, Coach Hayes walked up behind me, put his hand on my shoulder, and said the two words I'd longed to hear since that first snowy day I'd arrived on campus: "Good game."

I was on top of the world. My first game on the Ohio State sidelines had been a success. I felt like I might finally have turned the corner and come into my own as a defensive coach. That feeling lasted about a day and a half. Then Coach Hayes fired me for some minor infraction—I think one of our safeties had laughed after we stuffed the offense in practice, and when I didn't jump down the athlete's throat, Coach jumped down mine, firing me on the spot. This was the first of no fewer than five or six firings I would receive during the year. Coach Hayes had warned me that this might happen. He'd said I should take him seriously only if he put it in writing, which he never did, although there were times when I longed for a memo instead of his verbal reprimands.

I soon found myself not only respecting him but loving him as well. Once, after another of his famous four-letter soliloquies, he waved his hand in my direction and said, "I don't know why I hired you." That fired me up, and I couldn't let it stand. So I said, "Because I'm the only decent backfield coach who'll put up with you." For a second I thought he was going to take my head off. But after staring holes through me for four or five seconds, he finally said, "You're probably right," and walked away. That was the only time I ever talked back to Coach Hayes. He gave me a pass the first time. I figured that the second time I might not be so lucky.

In our second game, we beat a very talented Oregon team 21–6. That's when we started feeling momentum build. We were young, but we had talent, and we were putting up numbers that boggled the mind at the time. Our offense averaged 440 yards a game, a staggering sum for that era when twenty passing plays a game was considered an all-out air assault. We had also outscored our first two opponents 56–20 and shut down the ground games of two very talented football teams. Our confidence built with each play. But the big test would come the next week, when we would host the number one team in the country: Purdue.

From the moment I arrived at Ohio State, Coach Hayes had left no ambiguity about my primary job. "You've got to figure out a way to shut down Purdue," he'd said. He felt the SMU and Oregon games, nonconference opponents, were exhibition games. The season started with Purdue, and we had to win. Anything less than a win was a personal disappointment.

So I spent the spring, summer, and early weeks of the fall studying the Purdue offense. What I discovered wasn't very encouraging. Purdue had a couple of All-Americans, quarterback Mike Phipps and running back Leroy Keyes, who appeared unstoppable. They were the complete package with running, passing, and blocking that ranked between good and outstanding. No position seemed weak. I knew that the young men on our team would have to have the game of their lives to win.

One night the staff was at the Grandview Inn listening to a performer named Bill Maxted. I was having a great time, and Hugh Hindman said,

"You won't feel so good when we play Purdue." I didn't flinch and said we would shut them out. Hugh quickly wrote it on a napkin, and we bet one hundred dollars and each signed it. I didn't mean it, but I wasn't about to back down. Plus, I had great faith in Bill Mallory, our defensive line coach, and Lou McCullough, our linebackers coach and defensive coordinator.

A few minutes before kickoff, I walked through the locker room and put my hand on each of our defensive players. They were as calm, focused, and ready to play as any group I'd ever coached. For the first time, I began to share the optimism Coach Hayes had expressed all year. Not only was it possible to upset the number one team in the nation, but I left the locker room thinking that we should beat them, and it didn't need to be close.

The first half was a defensive battle. Purdue's quick and shifting defense disrupted our offensive rhythm and kept us from scoring a single point. But our defense did the same to them. In their first three possessions, we hit Phipps and Keyes like they hadn't been hit all year, and you could see they were getting frustrated. We also shook their team's confidence. Each time we held them, our side felt the upset coming, and their side grew more and more impatient. The fact that we were playing at home was an asset. Every time we forced them to punt, the crowd started to believe.

When the gun sounded at halftime, we left the field exactly as we'd entered it: without a single point on either side of the board.

Even though the score was tied at 0, our players felt as if they were up by two touchdowns. Writers and commentators had talked about Purdue as if they were some unstoppable force of nature. After thirty minutes on the field with them, our athletes realized that they were just another good football team, one that could be beaten. All we had to do was continue holding them in the second half and put a few points on the board ourselves.

In the first series of the second half, Purdue's receiver ran an out-cut pattern on second down and Phipps threw a perfect pass. Fortunately for us, we had put in a special coverage and Jack Tatum jumped the out, reading the pass perfectly. The only person between Jack and the end zone was a cheerleader. But the ball hit him in the hands, and he dropped it.

That brought up third down, the biggest play of the game. Everybody on the Purdue sideline knew what a bullet they had just dodged. If Jack had intercepted that second-down pass and scored, the stadium would have erupted, and the momentum would have been tough to overcome. If, however, they could move the chains a few times in this series, they could silence the crowd and shift the momentum in their favor.

Phipps took the snap from center, and I immediately saw what was going to happen. The receiver on the opposite side of the ball from the previous play ran a curl pattern, and Phipps threw another beauty...right into the hands of our defensive back Ted Provost. Phipps was the only man who could have stopped Ted before he got to the end zone. That wasn't a contest. Ted would have run through anybody to score. He went in virtually untouched for the first touchdown of the game.

Purdue never recovered. Later in the quarter, we intercepted another pass and ran it back to Purdue's thirteen-yard line, and Bill Long scored from there to make the score 13–0. That's where it ended. The young, underrated Buckeyes walked off the field winners, defeating the number-one-ranked team in the nation in a dominating performance.

I was beside myself with joy. Not only had our defense shut down the best team in the country, we had done so at home, and in front of a nationwide audience. Because I'd grown up in the state, the win was thrilling for me, especially considering I had friends and family (including my uncle Lou) in the stands. I wanted to share the win with everyone I knew. I wanted to go out on the town, shake hands, relive the game with all the people from my hometown, and celebrate a win like none other I had ever experienced.

There was only one problem: Coach Hayes was already looking ahead to next week. In the locker room after the victory, he said: "I want all the assistants in the staff room at seven P.M."

"Tonight?" somebody asked.

"No, next Saturday. Of course, tonight!"

We all looked at one another, waiting for him to say, "Just kidding, guys, go out and have a good time," but we knew that such a statement wasn't coming. Coach Hayes appreciated the win over Purdue as much as we did, but he wasn't about to rest on one big win. We had Northwestern coming up the following Saturday, and Coach Hayes didn't want anything to distract us from the task at hand. His goal was to win every game. If that meant forgoing a late-night celebration after the biggest win of the year, that's exactly what we would all do. There would be plenty of time to party after the season ended. At that moment, we had to sacrifice for the greatness that was to come.

There was a lot of grumbling in the staff room that night, but later in the year, every assistant realized that Coach Hayes's demanding standards helped put us over the top. Great achievements require great sacrifice, and Coach Hayes never let his coaches or his team get too high or too low, and he never let us forget that each win was just one more step in a season-long process on our way to the prize we all cherished: a national championship.

Our season snowballed after the Purdue win. We trounced Northwestern the following Saturday by a score of 45–21, putting up 565 yards in total offense. Then we beat a very good Illinois team when Jim Otis ran for 129 yards. After that, the wins piled up. We beat Michigan State, Wisconsin, and Iowa, and entered the final game of the season as the number-two-ranked team in the nation.

Our final regular-season contest was a home game against Michigan, the one game every Ohio State fan lives for. There are some great rivalries in college football—Alabama-Auburn, USC-UCLA, Georgia–Georgia Tech, Army-Navy—but nothing matches the white-hot passion of the Ohio State–Michigan game. Part of the intensity of this rivalry stems from the quality of the teams. Year in and year out, Michigan and Ohio State are usually battling for the Big Ten championship. In the pre-BCS days, that meant a berth in the Rose Bowl. Another element is the sheer dislike many Ohioans have for Michigan and many Michiganders have for Ohio. In the late seventies, when the American automobile industry fell on hard times and towns like Flint, Michigan, became virtual ghost towns, a prominent bumper sticker read: "Hey, it could be worse.... We could be in Ohio."

These were two states and two schools that simply didn't like each other.

In our case, we needed to beat Michigan to go to the Rose Bowl to play the USC Trojans and their Heisman Trophy winner, O. J. Simpson. As if the interstate rivalry weren't big enough, Michigan was the only team standing between us and a berth in the national championship game. Nothing was going to stop us. However, if we lost, Michigan would go to the Rose Bowl, and we would stay at home during the bowl season. This game was "winner take all."

We led 21–14 at halftime, but to hear Coach Hayes rant in the locker room you would have thought we were losing by three touchdowns. He didn't want to beat Michigan, he wanted to demolish and embarrass them, which is exactly what we did. Our defense held them scoreless in the second half, while our offense poured on four more touchdowns.

When we scored the final time with under a minute remaining, Coach Hayes signaled that we were going for a two-point conversion. Everyone was surprised, especially our quarterback, who was casually trotting off the field after the touchdown. Coach Hayes frantically signaled the play, and our offense went into the end zone for the two-point conversion to make the final score 50–14.

After the game, reporters couldn't wait to ask Coach Hayes about the two-point conversion. "What were you thinking, Coach? Why'd you go for two?" one of them shouted.

Coach never hesitated. "Because they wouldn't let me go for three," he said.

Coach Hayes fired me for a fifth time in Pasadena approximately a week before the Rose Bowl. My previous four dismissals had come on or around campus, where such firings didn't attract much attention. But when you're playing on New Year's Day for the national championship, everything is magnified out of proportion. In this instance, Coach Hayes had put me in charge of the room assignments, which meant I not only had to make sure everybody knew where he was staying, I also had to guide the wives in and out of the hotel. It was one of those logistical jobs nobody liked, but it had to be done, and I was the guy Coach Hayes had assigned to do it.

I got the players and coaches into their rooms at the Hollywood Sheraton without any problems, and I had planned to greet the wives in the lobby when they arrived. But that evening, I was sitting in a traffic jam on Sunset Strip, where I remained for the better part of three hours. I'd never been to Los Angeles before, so I'd had no idea about the legendary traffic. I couldn't go forward. I couldn't go backward. I couldn't get out.

I couldn't do anything. So I finally abandoned my courtesy car, found the nearest pay phone, and called Tiger Ellison. I was frantic. I had to make bed check at 11 P.M., and it was obvious I wasn't going to make it.

"Tiger, it's Lou."

"Hey, Lou, where are you?"

"I'm at a pay phone on Sunset Strip."

"What in the world are you doing down there?"

"I'm stuck in traffic. I just left the car. I can't get out of here, and I need you to make bed check."

He laughed and said, "I'll take care of here. You take care out there."

I fought traffic, but didn't worry. I knew Tiger had taken care of things. He got the wives in the right rooms and made bed check at the prescribed time. Unfortunately for me, Coach Hayes wandered the halls while Tiger was making his rounds.

"Tiger, what are you doing?" he asked.

"I'm making bed check."

"Why? Where's Lou?"

"He's on Sunset Strip," Tiger said, failing to say, "He's stuck in traffic." Coach Hayes didn't know if I was stuck in my car, or carousing at the Whisky A Go-Go. All he knew was that instead of being where I should have been, I was out on Sunset Strip.

The next morning I got a heads-up on my way to breakfast. "Hey, Lou," George Chaump said to me as I walked toward the elevator. "You better watch out. Coach Hayes is looking for you, and he doesn't look happy."

Bill Mallory stopped me in the lobby and said, "You need to find Coach Hayes before he finds you, and you best avoid him."

When I finally saw Tiger, I said, "Hey, Tiger, thanks for taking care of bed check last night. Did you say anything about it to Coach Hayes?"

"Yeah," he said. "He saw me and asked where you were. I told him you were on Sunset Strip."

I never got to ask Tiger if he'd informed Coach Hayes that I'd been stuck in the world's longest traffic jam. Coach Hayes saw me and charged at me like an angry bull. He reprimanded me with every nasty word in the dictionary and many that weren't. For three minutes he stunned the entire hotel lobby into silence. Players, coaches, wives, reporters, even a few women who were sipping coffee before their morning game of bridge heard every foul syllable. Coach ended the rant by firing me. Then he stormed off to his room before I got a chance to say "Good morning," much less explain what had happened.

The restaurant remained silent for a good fifteen seconds after Coach Hayes's dramatic exit. Then I sat down and had a cup of coffee. As for breakfast, I found that I had suddenly lost my appetite.

Coach Hayes never was much for apologies. I don't think I ever heard him utter the words "I'm sorry," unless it was in the context of a rant, like, "I'm sorry I wasted this university's time and money on someone like you." But he had different ways of showing contrition. In the case of his breakfast tirade, after he learned why I had been late, he issued a very unique apology at the Big Ten banquet. With twenty-five hundred people in attendance, including legendary comedian Bob Hope, there wasn't a bigger event in town. During coffee and dessert, Coach Hayes said a few words about the game and how much the season had meant to him. Then he introduced his coaching staff. When he got around to introducing me, the accolades he showered upon me were so over the top it was embarrassing. He made it sound as if I had single-handedly gotten the team to the Rose Bowl, and that I would be the single biggest factor if we were to win that national championship.

I couldn't imagine what the crowd must have been thinking. The praise went on and on. Then I looked out into the audience and I saw my uncle Lou and my uncle Leo, who were there as my guests. As Coach finished his remarks, Uncle Lou was the proudest man in America. That's when I realized that Coach Hayes's apology was the best I could ever have received.

In one of the greatest games in Rose Bowl history, our Ohio State team charged back from a 10–0 deficit to win the game 27–16. At first it looked as though we were going to be in big trouble. Coach Hayes had warned me that O. J. Simpson had better not score a touchdown. In the second quarter, USC had the ball first and ten on their own twenty. O.J. took a handoff and went eighty yards for a touchdown. Coach Hayes hollered, "Why did O.J. go eighty yards?" I said, "Coach, that's all he needed."

We held Simpson to ninety yards on twenty-seven carries the rest of the day, while our sophomores came through on offense. It was one of the best games I've ever had the privilege to coach, and one of the greatest teams in the storied history of Ohio State University. We won the national championship by unanimous vote in both the coaches' and the writers' polls.

The title shined a spotlight on our young team, and onto many of our talented assistant coaches. Fortunately, I was one of those who garnered a lot of attention. In the summer immediately following our undefeated season, I got a call from Davis Y. Paschall, the president of the College of William and Mary, where I had spent three wonderful years as an assistant and where Beth and I still had many good friends. Marv Levy, the coach who had beaten me out for the top job, had just resigned to go to the Washington Redskins. President Paschall didn't want to assemble a search committee. The head-coaching job was mine if I wanted it. There is no doubt that the trainer, Mont Linkenauger, and the William and Mary team physician, George Oliver, were influential in his decision.

I accepted. Then I had to tell Coach Hayes. I called him at home and told him that I had to come over and see him. On the short drive between our house and his, I practiced what I was going to say, and tried to imagine what his reaction might be. When I got into his living room, my mouth dried up and my throat constricted and I almost blew my lines.

"Coach," I finally choked out, "I've been offered the head-coaching job at William and Mary. I'm going to take it."

The first words out of his mouth were unprintable. He stomped around his living room ranting and raving. Then he took off his glasses and threw them into his fireplace, where they broke. This set off another torrent of obscenities, although at that point I was biting my lip to keep from chuckling. Breaking his glasses in the fireplace was funny. I think finding humor in the situation loosened me up and allowed me to open up and share my feelings with Coach Hayes.

After his eruption lost its initial steam, I said, "Coach, I know this isn't what you wanted to hear, but I'm thirty-two years old, and my goal has been to become a head coach. This is that opportunity. I know that the people who made this possible are the ones I'm going to hurt the most, but this is what I've been working for my entire life. I know you're upset, but I really hope you'll support me in this decision."

The muscles in his face relaxed, and I think he actually sighed. "I understand," he said. "And I do support you. But I want you to do two things for me before you go."

"Absolutely, Coach, whatever you need," I said.

"Okay, I want you to spend time with whomever I hire to replace you so that he knows what we're doing in the secondary." All our players were returning, and he didn't want to change our coverages.

"Done." I would have done that without his asking, assuming he still wanted me around.

"And, second, I'm writing a book called **Hot Line to Victory**. I want you to write the chapter on pass defense."

"Sure, Coach," I said, although this request was a little tricky. I'd never written anything for publication at the time. Even though I knew the subject matter, I wasn't sure what Coach Hayes wanted to say or how he wanted to say it; but I was willing to give it a shot.

Within the month, Coach Hayes hired Dick Walker from the Naval Academy to replace me.

I stayed long enough to realize that Dick had his own thoughts about pass defense and wanted to put his own imprint on the defense, and I was more than happy to oblige. Every coach needs to have the respect and undivided attention of his players, and my presence after Dick Walker's hire was creating a distraction. So I departed as quickly as I could.

I also wrote, rewrote, edited, and finally finished the chapter Coach Hayes had requested for his book. He was in his office when I presented him with my chapter. "Good," he said, taking the file from me. He sat at his desk and started reading while I stood there like an anxious child awaiting affirmation from a teacher. He read, occasionally nodding, thumbing through the pages with great care. When he finally finished, he looked up and said, "Yeah, that's good."

His next move was to his back pocket—he took out a checkbook, filled out a check, and handed it to me.

My hands went up. "No, I'm not taking that," I said.

"You are taking it," he said.

"No, Coach, I can't. After all you've done for me, this was the least I could do for you."

"You're taking this check or you're not leaving this office," he said.

"No, I really can't."

So he folded the check and stuffed it into my shirt, ripping the stitches of the breast pocket. I didn't have many shirts at the time, and I was sure the check would go a long way toward replacing the one he'd just torn, but I couldn't accept payment from someone I admired as much as Coach Hayes. This was my final thank-you to a man who had taught me more in a year than I had learned in the previous decade.

I took out the check and, without looking at it, tore it to shreds.

"I can tear them up faster than you can write them," I said. "How long do you want to do this?"

With that, he finally smiled. Then he thanked me for all my hard work, shook my hand, and wished me well at William and Mary.

I think about Coach Hayes often these days, as I did throughout most of my coaching career. He was, as advertised, volatile, controversial, hard, tough, and as inspiring a person as I've ever been around. As time passed, after I left Ohio State and even after Coach Hayes left coaching, I realized what a great teacher and marvelous influence he was to me and countless others. I also realized that not all the people who positively affect our lives behave like saints. Sometimes it's the good-hearted man behind the foul mouth and rank veneer who teaches us the most, and whose influence continues to be felt long after he has gone. Coach Woody Hayes was that man for me, as he was for every player and coach who ever worked for him.

My only regret with Coach Hayes was never asking him what kind of number he'd written on the check I tore up. I've always wondered how much he thought that chapter was worth. Was it thirty dollars? Was it three thousand dollars? Unfortunately, I'll never know.

7

LEADING IS EASY WHEN PEOPLE WANT TO BE LED

A portrait as head football coach at William and Mary, 1969. It was my first job and I didn't real-ize that authority comes with the job: respect was what I needed to earn, and you earn respect only by proving yourself as a leader. **(Photograph by Thomas L. Williams / Courtesy of the College of William and Mary)**

I left for Williamsburg, but my wife remained in Ohio until she gave birth to our fourth and last child, Liz. After she was born on June 23, 1969, our entire family moved back to Williamsburg in August. While I wasn't awed by the responsibility of being a head coach, I did make some serious mistakes, as only I could do. First, I tried to establish my authority by intimidation with the players and with Marv Levy's staff, which I kept. What I didn't realize was that authority comes with the job: respect was what I needed to earn, and you earn respect only by proving yourself as a leader. I was young as a head coach, so I jumped in and changed almost everything. I was impatient with both the athletes and the coaches. I was trying to be Woody Hayes and not Lou Holtz. I didn't realize there was only one Coach Hayes. I worked them like Spartan soldiers, the same intense workouts I'd seen Coach Hayes put his players through. I implemented the Ohio State offense and defense, even though we didn't have the Ohio State talent pool on either side of the ball. My first year as a head football coach was anything but a success.

I also failed to anticipate the pressures that would come with the job. As an assistant coach, you have the luxury of focusing on your particular specialty and not worrying too much about anything else. If you are a backfield coach, you worry about your backs. If you're an offensive-line coach, you keep tabs on your linemen. Issues like who lines the football field, who returns phone calls from boosters, who coordinates the equipment transport, and who sorts the laundry are left to someone else. But as a head coach, not only was I responsible for every player in every position, I also had to handle the hundreds of issues not related to athletes that crossed my desk on a weekly basis. It was a lot different from my first stint at William and Mary. Then, football had dominated my life during the season, but I'd still had time to be a husband and father in the morning, while being on the practice field in the early afternoon, and I'd enjoyed a social life during the off-season. Beth and I had belonged to a bridge club when we first lived in Williamsburg. Now as a head coach, I didn't have time to kiss my wife and children good-bye. I went everywhere except to bed and talked to everyone except my wife.

By the time we lined up for our first game, the athletes were exhausted. There is a fine line between training and conditioning a team and working a group of athletes too hard. I didn't even see that line as I blew past it. We opened with Cincinnati and led for most of the game before losing in the fourth quarter. The only positive thing about that game was that Coach Hayes attended it and brought his quarterbacks. He made a very positive talk to our team after the game. The following week I got my first win as a head coach when we beat Temple. But the season was a disaster. We won three games and lost seven, a record that looked better on paper than it actually was. Were it not for some great individual performances by athletes, we might not have won a single game that year.

One particularly bitter loss came at the hands of West Virginia, coached by my good friend Bobby Bowden. In 1962, while I was an assistant at William and Mary, Beth and I went on a belated honeymoon to Florida, where we stayed with Bobby and his family. Bobby was an assistant coach at Florida State. We were friends, and remain so to this day. However, now he was the head coach of West Virginia University, one of our opponents, and that afternoon, Bobby kept in his two star running backs long after the game had been decided. The score was lopsided, but the West Virginia starters stayed in the game until the bitter end. Afterward I said, "Bobby, why did you do that? We're friends."

He looked me straight in the eye and said, "It's your job to keep the score down, not mine. If you don't like the score, either recruit harder or coach better. I've got to coach my team, and you've got to coach yours. You can coach only one team."

That stung, in part because I knew he was right. If I wanted to keep from being embarrassed, I needed to do a better job recruiting, a better job preparing, and a better job coaching. Blame for our season rested solely with me. I was the only one who could fix things the following year.

In the off-season, the winter of 1970, I knew I had to make some substantial changes. This wasn't as easy a decision as it sounds. I had taken the head-coaching job with some specific ideas and some firm beliefs about how to run a football team. The fact that those ideas hadn't worked surprised me. I'd taken all the good things I'd learned from Woody Hayes, Forest Evashevski, Rick Forzano, and Paul Dietzel and incorporated them into what I thought would be a winning plan. When we didn't win, I could have responded in one of several ways: I could have blamed the athletes for failing to buy into my style of football; I could have shaken up the staff—after all, it couldn't have been my fault; or I could have looked in the mirror and decided I needed to change the way I had approached this team.

Changing our approach was, of course, the logical answer. Unfortunately, self-examination can be tough. I can't count the numbers of people I've seen in business, football, and life in general who fail to see their own failings until it's too late.

I wasn't going to be one of those people. I don't believe in fixing what isn't broken. But if something isn't working, you need either to fix it or to abandon it. I wasn't about to leave William and Mary, so our only alternative was to identify and fix what was broken.

I called a staff meeting in the early weeks of the year. "We need to identify and list our assets and our liabilities," I told my assistants. "Okay, what are our assets?"

The room fell quiet for a full thirty seconds.

Finally, one of the assistants said, "We have a great center."

We did, indeed, have an outstanding center. That was about it. When I asked the staff about liabilities, everybody chimed in. We didn't have a quarterback who was a proven winner; we had only one returning receiver, and he had caught four passes but had also dropped eleven in the previous season; with the exception of the center, we were awfully weak in the offensive line; and we didn't have a running back who had enjoyed success on the college level. Our defense was better, but we lacked size, and no one had what today you would call "playmaker speed."

"Okay," I said after we had listed all the positives and negatives. "If we can't move the ball forward, let's at least not move it backward."

With that, we scrapped the Ohio State offense and implemented a precision option: the veer. We were one of the first teams to use the veer offense, and this turned out to be a great asset. Houston invented the veer, and William and Mary may have been the third team in the country to employ it. Eventually many teams would use the veer, and by the late seventies it became probably the most popular offense. Many high school teams still use it with great success. Mishawaka Penn High School won 60-plus regular-season games with it, and it was used by De La Salle in California, which just had its 150-plus-game winning streak stopped.

In simple terms, the veer is a triple-option offense that relies on execution and teamwork. I felt if we could learn to run it well, teams would have to execute on defense to stop us. After closely examining our competition, it became clear to me that most teams had better athletes, so we could not win based on our athleticism. In addition to playing a strong Southern Conference schedule, we were also playing North Carolina, Wake Forest, West Virginia, VPI (now known as Virginia Tech), Tulane, and Miami, all larger schools with strong football programs. If we were to stand a chance against any of those teams, we had to execute our offense better and more efficiently than our opponents could defend it.

We had recruited a couple of fine athletes named Phil Moser and Todd Bushnell who brought a lot of spark and speed to the offense. In his first year at William and Mary, Moser gained 1,300 yards, and Bushnell gained 780. The previous school rushing record had been 720, and it had stood for decades. Phil and Todd were able to run the ball because we worked on executing the veer again and again and again in practice until most of the young men could perform their assignments in their sleep. By the first of September, I felt that we had turned a corner. The team gained confidence with each repetition. They felt they could run the ball on anybody. And they no longer felt like I was asking them to do something that they couldn't do.

We didn't have a winning season, as North Carolina, Miami, West Virginia, and Wake Forest beat us, but our losses were because we couldn't stop them. We went into every game thinking we could score 30 points, and we usually did, even when we lost. We did, however, win the Southern Conference championship. That earned our team an invitation to the Tangerine Bowl, where we took on Toledo, the eleventh-ranked team in the nation. It was the third time the College of William and Mary had been to a postseason bowl game, and is still the school's only bowl. The athletes were thrilled, and I was overjoyed. Even though we lost to Toledo (after leading at halftime), I felt good about our future.

I had gained more confidence as a head coach as well. With two seasons behind me, I felt more at ease in the job, and felt as though the players and assistant coaches were more confident in the direction of the program. We weren't the only ones who noticed our improvement. In the off-season after winning our conference championship, I got a letter from the search committee at North Carolina State University. Their coach, Earl Edwards, had retired, and while they had an interim coach, they were searching for a permanent head football coach for N.C. State. I was one of many coaches they were considering. It was flattering to be sought out for a job after only two years of head-coaching experience, but I didn't think too much about it. Beth and I were very happy in Williamsburg and had no plans to leave.

Then Dr. Paschall, the president of William and Mary, and the man who had brought me to the school, retired. It had been Dr. Paschall's vision to elevate William and Mary athletics to the level of those schools in the Atlantic Coast Conference in the hopes of someday moving William and Mary into the ACC. I thought those were admirable and attainable goals. But when Dr. Paschall retired, so did his vision. The new president wanted to move athletics in a different direction: to Division I-AA.

I thought this was a mistake, but I didn't get caught up in the campus politics of the decision. Playing in the ACC meant playing in front of fifty thousand to seventy thousand people every week, on national television, recruiting the best athletes in the country who wanted to compete at the highest level, and reaping the financial rewards for the school that top-flight conference football brought. Division I-AA was a step back in terms of building the program. There was nothing wrong with that; it just was a different philosophy.

My job was to coach the football team. We had a solid recruiting year and a great spring practice. When the season rolled around, we played very well, beating Tulane in our third game and East Carolina the fourth week of the season. The fifth week, I got a call from athletic director Willis Casey, head of the N.C. State search committee. "We would like to meet with you to discuss the possibility of your coming to N.C. State," he said.

"Thank you, I'm flattered," I told him. "But I've made a commitment to William and Mary, and I can't talk to you until the end of the season. I'll be happy to meet with you then."

"That's too late," he said.

I understood what he meant. Recruits would make early commitments in December. They needed a coach in place before the recruiting season.

"I'm sorry," I said. "I have an obligation here. I hope you understand that I would say the same thing to another school if I were coaching at N.C. State."

"We understand," the director said. "But I'm afraid we can't wait that long. If that's your position, you're no longer a candidate."

I said, "That's disappointing, but I understand."

I figured that was the end of it. N.C. State would hire a coach before the end of the season, and I would continue coaching at William and Mary for the foreseeable future.

What I didn't realize was how closely the decision makers at N.C. State were scrutinizing me. After our football team had beaten a very good East Carolina team, East Carolina beat N.C. State by a big margin. This must have caught the attention of the N.C. State family.

Later in the season, we traveled to Chapel Hill to play the University of North Carolina. Our athletes played one of the best games in William and Mary football history. It was a great game. For fifty-nine minutes, we never trailed. First we led 7–0. Then it was 7–7. We went up 14–7, and they tied it up at 14. We led 21–14. Then it was 21 all. We jumped ahead 28–21; then it was 28–28; then we went ahead 35–28, which was where it stood with two minutes remaining in the game.

North Carolina took possession with two minutes to go, and we stopped them on two consecutive downs deep in their own territory. They had third down and ten, which meant we were two plays away from a major upset.

Their quarterback, Paul Miller, a left-hander, dropped back on third down and under heavy pressure threw a deep pass that bounced on the ground twice at our forty-five-yard line. The ball hit the turf right in front of me, so I assumed we were one play away from winning the football game. The sideline official ruled the pass incomplete, the right call in my opinion. But the backfield official, who had no visual angle whatsoever, called it a completion. There was a huddle of officials at midfield. When the conference broke, they ruled it a completed pass.

I got two fifteen-yard penalties for voicing my opinion very vocally. I did not use profanity, but I wasn't very polite either. The penalties were probably justified. The first one was because I ran on the field and the second was for unsportsmanlike conduct. This put the ball on our fifteen-yard line. UNC had gone from their twenty to our fifteen on an incomplete pass. With ten seconds left in the game, Paul Miller threw a pass into the end zone, and North Carolina was only one point behind. They went for two, as I had expected, and threw a delay pass. One of our linebackers deflected the ball, but the receiver, Louis Jolly, came back and made a great athletic grab on his knees to complete the conversion. North Carolina won the game 36–35. They would go on to win ten games that season, losing only to Notre Dame in a low-scoring game.

While we were playing North Carolina, N.C. State was losing badly twenty miles up I-40. I was told that the fans at N.C. State kept tabs on our game through the public address system at the stadium, and they heard the thrilling finish in their cars in the parking lot. Because our game was so high scoring, it lasted about forty minutes longer than N.C. State's game.

I hadn't been home from the North Carolina game thirty minutes when the phone rang. It was another member of the N.C. State selection committee. I was tired, and still a little upset after our loss when I got to the phone. The conversation was polite but curt.

"As I've told you, I can't talk about another job until this season is over," I said.

"We understand," the committeeman said. "All we want is for you to meet our athletic director, and let him tell you what the job is all about. This won't be a formal interview; it won't even be an official conversation. Meet with our AD, and if you like what you hear, we'll wait until your season is over to talk."

That seemed reasonable enough. "Okay," I said. "We're playing Wake Forest next week, so why don't we meet next Thursday in Danville, Virginia. That's about halfway for both of us."

Five days later, I drove to Danville, where I waited inside a gas station–convenience store for the N.C. State athletic director, whom I had never met. After spending several minutes standing in the parking lot, I saw a man looking at me for a few long seconds and finally said, "Are you Lou Holtz?"

"Yes, I am."

He extended his hand. "I'm Willis Casey, the athletic director at N.C. State."

We talked for the better part of two hours, and I liked Willis Casey instantly. He reminded me a lot of Coach Hayes in his direct no-nonsense style. There would never be a question about where you stood if you worked for him. I knew immediately that this man and I could work together. I also knew that N.C. State would provide greater opportunities for my family and me. It was a large state school with a lot of fine athletes and a lot of potential.

If Dr. Paschall had remained at William and Mary, I would have remained there as well. I might have retired there. That's how much we loved Williamsburg and the friends we made there. But with the athletic program at William and Mary downsizing, the opportunity at N.C. State seemed too good to pass up. It was a hard decision—another one that required a lot of soul-searching and honest self-evaluation. But after a lot of prayer and discussions at home, Beth and I agreed that this was the right move for us to make. I told Mr. Casey that I looked forward to speaking with him after the season. I was definitely interested in the job.

Unfortunately, as we were finishing out the season, the William and Mary Quarterback Club bought us a brand-new station wagon. They tried to give it to me at our last Quarterback Club meeting. I thanked them, but I just couldn't accept it. They said it was for what I had done for William and Mary. I felt it was a gift for what I would do in the future, so I couldn't accept it. At halftime of our last game, the public address announcer called Beth out of the stands and down to the fifty-yard line, where the president of the Quarterback Club presented her with a brand-new station wagon.

That night, when I learned what had happened, I said, "We can't keep it. We have to give it back."

Beth said, "We do not have to give it back. We have four small children. We need this car." She and the president of the Quarterback Club won the argument.

So we loaded up the children and drove to Raleigh in a one-week-old station wagon given to us by supporters of the school we had just left. To this day I'm still embarrassed about that.

When writing to his wife of the type of men he longed to command in the Continental Army, Colonel Henry Knox said: "We want great men who, when fortune frowns, will not be discouraged."

I found just such men in the football program at North Carolina State University. The N.C. State team had gone 3–8 for three consecutive years, and when I arrived on campus, I found a group of hungry, talented, committed, undiscouraged athletes who were sick and tired of losing and who were willing to run through walls to turn things around. All they needed was a little discipline, direction, and leadership, which I set about implementing. N.C. State was going to win regardless of who was going to coach them.

My first job was to convince the players, coaches, boosters, and fans that this was not a losing football team; it was simply a football team that had lost a lot of games. The difference between those two was the attitude and abilities of the players. A team that wins games, but has players who are discontented because their personal statistics aren't what they'd hoped, or point fingers at others for failures on the field: that is a losing team. But a team filled with players who believe in one another, and who believe they can win, who are willing to work hard and do the things necessary to become successful: that is a winning team regardless of their record. I had a winning team at N.C. State. We just hadn't won any games yet.

A good example of that was our young center, a fine young man from Pennsylvania named Bill Cowher. One day Bill fell asleep during study hall, a clear violation of our rules. When I called him in to talk about it, I said, "Okay, Bill, how long were you asleep?"

He answered honestly: "About twenty minutes."

"Fine," I said. "For the next twenty days, you are to run two miles at six o'clock in the morning."

Bill accepted his punishment without complaint, and every morning, without a coach there to make sure he did it, Bill Cowher showed up at the practice field and ran two miles around the track. But he had a dilemma. The semester ended, and he still had a week of running left. When he went home to Pennsylvania, it was windy, snowing, and dark at six in the morning. As he tells it, "I got up and went to the track, and there was snow everywhere. I'm thinking to myself, 'Coach Holtz isn't going to know if I run or not.'" This was true. I figured he might fudge a little in the final days. "I started to go back home, but then I thought, 'You know, he might find out,' so I ran my two miles every day."

Bill Cowher has gone on to become one of the most respected and successful coaches in the history of the NFL, winning his first Super Bowl after the 2005 season. He was also typical of the athletes we had at N.C. State. I've never coached a group of players who were hungrier to win. They were a joy to be around. They also had talent. In the off-season I'd recruited freshmen twins named Dave and Don Buckey out of Akron, Ohio. Dave was a quarterback and Don was a receiver. It was the first year freshmen were eligible for varsity play, and Don and Dave made the cover of **Sports Illustrated** under the headline "Freshmen Make an Impact." They certainly did. We were greatly rewarded for having them on our side of the ball.

Living in North Carolina was equally rewarding. I wasn't sure we could equal the life we'd had in Williamsburg, but I was pleasantly surprised to find out I was wrong. We moved into a home at the McGregor Downs Country Club in Cary, North Carolina, about ten miles from campus. Today, Cary is an enclave for computer programmers, biotech researchers, and pharmaceutical scientists, but in the early seventies, it was a small town with great amenities and great neighbors. The day we moved, I assembled a trampoline in the yard, and by sundown, every child in the neighborhood had come over to play. Our children made friends immediately, and loved the place from day one.

The football team responded to my coaching better than I'd expected as well. From the first day of practice, I used the ploy Coach Hayes had used at Ohio State the year we'd won the national championship: I not only encouraged that team to win, I let everyone know that I expected to win, and would be disappointed if we didn't. By raising the expectations, it was easier to raise the focus and intensity of our practice sessions. It also got everyone—players, coaches, trainers, administrators, students, boosters, and fans—excited about football. By dismissing what the polls and the experts were saying (just as Coach Hayes had done with his young 1968 team) and setting standards that exceeded anything N.C. State had experienced before, we entered the season with a group of disciplined, trained, and motivated athletes.

Our first game against Maryland ended in a tie, even though every pregame analyst had picked Maryland to win decisively. The following week we played Syracuse, where we were huge underdogs. We won that game handily, putting 42 points on the board.

After that win, people flocked to N.C. State games. In the previous three years, the stadium had never been full. In the four years I was there, we averaged fifty thousand spectators a game, which was quite an accomplishment, since the stadium sat only forty-two thousand. Fans brought blankets and lined the end zone hillside to see us play. That kind of attendance lifted the players' spirits, and helped our recruiting efforts. When a visiting prospect stood on the sidelines and saw a stadium jammed with enthusiastic fans, he was more likely to leave with a positive impression.

The victories certainly helped build momentum and enthusiasm on campus by the time we played in-state rival North Carolina in Chapel Hill. We fought hard, and by late in the fourth quarter we were tied at 28. I felt as though North Carolina was playing for the tie. After they held us on three downs, our punter dropped back. They didn't try to block the punt, but our punter dropped the snap, and by the time he picked up the ball, one of the defensive backs had charged from the outside and blocked the kick. They recovered on our one-yard line and went in to score the go-ahead touchdown. With one minute remaining, they led 35–28.

Our athletes never gave up. We drove the ball the length of the field in forty seconds. With ten seconds remaining on the clock, one of our receivers, Pat Kenny, caught a touchdown pass to make it 35–34. We never considered going for the tie. Our men lined up for a two-point conversion. We ran a delay pass that was unsuccessful. As we were running off the field after such a close loss, the North Carolina fans started yelling "Agriculture U and Moo U."

This upset me. Our players had played their hearts out. When I sat down for my postgame press conference, I said, "I just want to tell all those North Carolina fans who were yelling 'Agriculture U and Moo U' that agriculture is a hell of a lot better than no culture." This endeared me to the Wolfpack fans but made me unwelcome in Chapel Hill.

We didn't lose often that first year. With a 7–3–1 record going into our last game, I got a call from the president of the Peach Bowl. He said if we won our last game against Clemson, we would get a postseason bid to play in Atlanta. The game against Clemson was never close. We ended up winning 42–7.

I was especially thrilled to play in the Peach Bowl that year, not only for our athletes and staff who had done a spectacular job, but also because our opponent was West Virginia, still coached by my old friend Bobby Bowden. We entered the game as 13-point underdogs, in part because Bruce Shaw, the senior quarterback who had shared time with Dave Buckey all season, broke his arm in practice before Christmas and wouldn't be able to play. We had to rely solely on the freshman.

Late in the game, Dave Buckey completed a pass to his twin brother for a touchdown to make the score 48–13. I was delighted by the late score. After all, I could coach only one team. If Bobby didn't like the score, he needed either to recruit better or to coach better, because it was his job to keep the score down, not mine. As we shook hands at midfield, I said, "Good job," to my friend, and I made a couple of comments about some of the good backs I thought he had on his team.

Bobby said, "What can I say? You've got a very, very good football team."

We finished the 1972 season ranked seventeenth in the country, a good turnaround for a team that had won a total of nine games in the previous three years. Finishing in the top twenty in the country certainly helped us recruit for the 1973 season, but I also had to continue to motivate the team and keep them from having a letdown. That turned out to be one of the easiest parts of the job. As Vince Lombardi always said, "Nothing breeds future successes like present successes." Winning felt good, and our athletes didn't want to lose that feeling.

Our second year, we finished the regular season with an 8–3 record, and all of our losses could have gone our way. We came within a yard of beating Penn State on their home field when Don Buckey dropped a pass because he was trying to stretch into the end zone instead of catching the ball and going out of bounds on the one. But overall the season was everything we could have wanted. We beat Kansas 31–18 in the Liberty Bowl and finished the year ranked sixteenth in both the AP and coaches' polls.

Then we got on a roll. The strong freshmen and sophomores we had in 1972 were juniors and seniors by 1974. We played a strong schedule and won nine games, including victories over Penn State (a first in N.C. State history) and a 35–7 rout over nationally ranked Arizona State. Our only losses came against Georgia and Nebraska when both teams were ranked in the top five in the country. We won the Atlantic Coast Conference, and had one of the ten best records in the country. Yet we didn't have a bowl bid. This was before all bowls contracted with conferences, so winning the ACC didn't automatically get us anywhere. In fact, when we beat Penn State in our tenth game of the year, it was their team that was invited to the Cotton Bowl.

Finally, when we beat Arizona State, I got a call from Bill Yeoman, the legendary coach at the University of Houston. "Lou, we can't get anybody to come down and play us in the Bluebonnet Bowl," he said. "If you're still uncommitted, we'd love to have you down here and play us." I knew why nobody would play them. First, they were great, and second, it was on their home field.

Not only were we uncommitted, we were uninvited. I said, "Great. I hope we can be a worthy opponent."

The Bluebonnet Bowl turned out to be one of the best bowl games of the season. Both teams played great, and the game finished in a 31–31 tie. Two days later, the polls came out, and N.C.

State finished as the ninth-ranked team in the country.

The next spring, our neighborhood in Cary renamed the street we lived on after me. It was quite an honor, and a bit embarrassing. We didn't want to be treated differently just because I had coached a couple of winning football teams. By the same token, we felt blessed to be where we were. N.C. State was a wonderful school, and the people in Raleigh couldn't have been kinder to us. Beth was happy; our children were happy; the university was happy; and I was happy.

However, I ignored my own advice. Nothing is as good as it seems and nothing is as bad as it seems, but somewhere in between there reality falls. I labored under the misconception that I would never fall on hard times again. With this misconception, I was about to make a decision that would be unfair to my family, Leon Hess, Al Ward, the New York Jets, New York City, and the NFL.

8

A HALFHEARTED COMMITMENT IS WORSE THAN NO COMMITMENT AT ALL

With Joe Namath, 1976. Taking the Jets head-coaching job was the most regrettable mistake of my career. **(Courtesy of the New York Jets)**

We all make mistakes in life. Some are small—forgetting to take the garbage to the street on trash day—and some are not so small—investing your life savings in Global Crossing. The only things these mistakes have in common are the regret we feel initially when our error becomes apparent, and the extraordinary excuses some people use to rationalize their mistakes or shift blame to others.

You can tell a lot about a person's character, not by the mistakes he has made, but by how he has handled those mistakes. The person who takes responsibility for his errors and does what he can to fix the problems he's created is someone you should respect. The person who has never made a mistake in his own mind, who obfuscates and attempts to deflect blame, is someone you should approach cautiously. I've fouled up plenty in my life. In most of those circumstances, I've done my best to own up to my mistakes and take whatever steps I could to correct them. I've also worked to repair any injuries those errors might have caused. Mistakes are an inevitable part of life, but accepting responsibility and taking corrective action are not. This can be hard because our egos get in the way. You have to be a confident person to admit you fouled up.

One mistake that continues to bother me to this day was when I took the job with, and then abruptly left, the New York Jets. For three decades, my short-lived tenure in the NFL has been a source of embarrassment for me, not because the Jets didn't do very well under my leadership (they did not), but because making the jump to the NFL and then leaving the league were both decisions that were avoidable, because both grew out of a so-so commitment on my part.

Every athlete who has ever played for me has heard me preach against the pitfalls of entering anything halfway. In my mind, a halfhearted commitment is worse than no commitment at all. If you decide to take a class, you should give the professor and yourself the full benefit of your undivided attention. If you don't, you're wasting your time and taking up a valuable seat in the classroom. If you're on a team, you owe your coaches and teammates your total commitment. If you don't—if you're unhappy because the coach doesn't start you, or because you aren't getting as many touches as you think you should—you are hurting yourself and the entire organization. You and the team would be better off if you played somewhere else. If you take a job thinking you can coast along until you find another job, you are, in essence, stealing resources from your employer, no less than if you had broken in and robbed the place.

Commitment is the most critical component in any relationship. A marriage based on the premise "Well, let's give this a shot, and if it doesn't work out, or if we 'grow apart,' we can always get divorced," is doomed before the vows are complete. If you accept admission to a college and say to yourself, "Well, this wasn't my first choice, but I'll see how things pan out," you aren't going to perform very well. And if you say, "This job is a good stepping-stone, but I'm not thrilled about what I'll be doing," you might as well quit today.

In sports, it's become axiomatic: Commitment beats talent every time. At N.C. State we won a number of football games when we weren't the most talented or athletic team on the field. We won because from the athletic director's office to the redshirt freshmen on the sidelines, every person involved in that program committed himself to making the team a success. Willis Casey led the way in that regard. He was one of the most impressive athletic directors in the country, a man whose commitment was unwavering and unquestionable: a tough, creative, no-nonsense, get-it-done kind of guy whom I respected greatly.

One example of Casey's genius came when our NCAA championship basketball team led by David Thompson was to play John Wooden's

UCLA team at a neutral site in St. Louis. Mr. Casey called UCLA's athletic director to negotiate the finances of the game and said, "John, this is going to be one of the most watched nationally televised games of the year. Why don't you keep all the television revenues, and let us have all the gate receipts?"

UCLA agreed. What they didn't know was that the ACC required each school to share television revenues with the conference. Gate receipts were the sole property of the school. Conference officials found out about the deal late, and were furious. But Willis had done what was best for his school and his people. He took care of me as well as anyone I've ever worked for, but he was tough. After we accepted the Peach Bowl invitation in my first year, I went to Willis's office and asked about a bowl bonus.

"A what?" he asked.

"A bowl bonus," I said. "It's customary for the coaching staff to get a bowl bonus, usually a month's salary."

"Why?"

"Well," I said, "we played well enough to get a bowl invitation, we filled up the stadium, we're nationally ranked, alumni contributions are at an all-time high, and most schools give the coaches a month's salary for doing this."

He stared me in the eyes and said, "All of that is why I hired you. That's your job. I fired the guy before you because he didn't do those things. Don't come in here asking for a bonus for doing your job. I'm going to let you coach here again because you did those things."

The coaching staff did receive bowl bonuses every year I was at N.C. State, but I never asked for one again. I was hired to win and graduate our athletes, and failure to do so was bad luck.

In my fourth year at N.C. State, we lost a couple of games early. Many athletes in key positions had graduated, so the team we fielded was young and relatively inexperienced. But that didn't dampen our commitment. After a disappointing loss to Michigan State (where our athletes played on Astroturf for the first time) I decided to start two freshmen running backs: Ted Brown, who would go on to a successful career with the Minnesota Vikings, and Ricky Adams.

The following week we played Indiana University coached by Lee Corso, who is now my colleague at ESPN. Ted Brown, in his first college start, rushed for more than two hundred yards, and N.C. State beat Indiana by a score of 27–0. We finished the regular season with a record of 7–3–1, and got another invitation to the Peach Bowl. That's when Al Ward of the New York Jets called.

Since their upset Super Bowl victory over the Baltimore Colts seven years before, the Jets had failed to make a return trip to the championship game, and after the retirement of their legendary coach Weeb Eubank, the team had struggled. Their owner, oil magnate Leon Hess, was looking for a new coach to lead the team back to greatness. I was their first choice.

This was ego-inflating stuff for a young head coach. Going to the NFL meant reaching the pinnacle of the coaching pyramid. There was no higher league. Unlike college, where a great team might have three or four games televised a season, the NFL teams were on television every Sunday. Those teams that won received national acclaim, and championship coaches became celebrities. NFL team owners usually reserved those select coaching spots for older, more experienced veterans, men with a little gray hair around their temples and a lot of wins under their belts. I was a few days away from celebrating my thirty-ninth birthday. It was an honor even to be considered for the job.

The problem was, I didn't really want to leave N.C. State. My family was settled; our teams had been to four consecutive bowl games; our recruiting efforts were paying great dividends; I had the support of the university administration; and I was happy. Some of my fondest memories of college coaching came from that time.

One particularly good memory was made in 1974, when I accepted an offer to speak at the Birmingham, Alabama, Touchdown Club. We had just beaten Maryland on national television, and we had an open date the following week, so I flew to Birmingham to speak on Monday night. When I got there, the president of the club asked if I would like to go to an Alabama practice before I spoke. I didn't know Coach Paul "Bear" Bryant at the time, so the thought of meeting him and watching him work excited me.

My contacts at the Touchdown Club set up a meeting, and I drove to Tuscaloosa, where I sat patiently outside Coach Bryant's office for a good twenty minutes. When the Bear finally came out, he greeted me as if we were old friends, saying, "Coach, let's go to practice."

I stood on the field, as I did at our practices, while Coach Bryant climbed into his famous watchtower. After a couple of minutes, I heard the booming baritone voice from the top of the tower: "Coach, come up here."

It wasn't a request. I climbed those stairs as fast as I could. When I got up there, we stood for a few more minutes in dead silence before he said, "How did you beat Maryland and my boy Jerry Claiborne?"

I knew he wasn't talking about our play calling, so I told him what I'd done to motivate our athletes for the game. "They had such a great offense and defense that I knew we needed to do something special," I said. "So for television, I had the announcers introduce our special teams before the game. We played a good game, but our special teams had an outstanding game. That was the difference."

He nodded and grunted. I assumed that meant he approved. Then he pointed to the field as his offensive squad ran a down-the-line option. "We're having trouble with that," he said. "What do you do?"

I explained how we felt the secret to this play was to crack the linebacker and seal the inside. Without another word, Coach Bryant climbed down out of his tower and implemented my suggestions on the field. When I watched him at work, he reminded me a great deal of Woody Hayes. He demanded the absolute best from those who worked for him and played for him, and if he didn't get it, he let them know. That week, Alabama beat Tennessee badly. The following Monday, Coach Bryant called me and said, "Lou, I want to apologize to you. **Sports Illustrated** covered the game, and wrote, 'Only Coach Bryant would think of introducing his special teams instead of his offense and defense.' I didn't say that. The writer jumped to that conclusion on his own, and I'm really sorry."

I laughed and said, "That's nothing to worry about, Coach. I'm just glad it worked out for you as well as it did for us."

Before we hung up, he invited me down to his home. "I'm having a clinic for all the former Alabama players who are now coaches," he said. "I'd like for you to come speak."

The following summer I went down to Coach Bryant's clinic in Tuscaloosa, where I stayed in his house, ate his home-cooked biscuits, and enjoyed his hospitality. I met his wife, a wonderful woman who went way out of her way to make me feel at home, and Coach Bryant himself couldn't have been nicer. One night, he took several of us out to dinner at his country club. We had a private dining room, but the room didn't have a television, and Coach Bryant wanted to watch his former quarterback Ken Stabler, who played for the Oakland Raiders, in a televised preseason game. The club manager rectified this problem by taking the television out of the club's lounge and putting it in our private dining room, even though the lounge was full. That was the kind of weight Bear Bryant carried throughout his tenure at Alabama. It was an honor to know him.

Those were the kinds of memories I'd accumulated at N.C. State, and one of the primary reasons I was not eager to leave. I also loved the lifestyle there. During the winter and spring I would play pickup basketball with our players, and during the summer I would play golf with our neighbors and other members of the university staff. Our children were in great schools, and they had lots of friends. We were an established part of the community. The thought of uprooting everyone was unsettling. Coaching was still a full commitment, but I did discover you must have balance in your life.

After our season-ending banquet in January of 1976, I called Al Ward back and told him I wasn't interested in moving to New York or the NFL. It had nothing to do with the Jets organization. I was happy at N.C. State, and my family and I weren't ready to move anywhere.

"But you're our first choice," he said.

"I understand, and you don't know how much it means to me to be thought of that way. But I'm just not ready to make any sort of move."

Al appreciated what I was saying, but he didn't give up. "Why don't you just come up and meet with Mr. Hess," he said. "We'll fly you up, take you to dinner, and talk about it. Then you can turn us down with no hard feelings."

"I'm not sure anything will change," I said.

"Then you'll get a nice meal and a trip to the city out of the deal," he said.

I agreed, and on February 19, I flew from Raleigh-Durham to La Guardia airport, from where a limo driver transported me to a posh French restaurant in midtown Manhattan. Al Ward and Jets' president Phil Iselin met me there. A few minutes later, Leon Hess joined us, and the tone of the lunch changed immediately. To say Leon Hess had a commanding presence would not do justice to the power and character the man exuded. His grace, humility, honesty, empathy, and integrity impressed me from the first moment I met him. He cared about people. During my time with the Jets, Mr. Hess constantly reminded me of my obligations to my family and my faith. He was a very generous man who consistently donated to every worthwhile cause that was in need. Here was a man of Jewish faith who built Hess Oil by working with Arab Muslims. His ability to communicate is rarely duplicated.

Mr. Hess outlined the job for me and explained, very honestly, why I was their candidate. Before dessert and coffee, I knew I couldn't say no to this man. His charisma persuaded me to accept a job I really didn't want.

And that was the problem.

Had I been more mature, more self-confident, and less inclined to be swayed by the accolades of others, I probably would have thanked Mr. Hess for the fine dinner, told him it was an honor and a pleasure to meet him, and politely declined his job offer. Instead, I reluctantly became the head coach of the New York Jets.

I spent the night in Manhattan, which I would have enjoyed if I hadn't been so conflicted about the decision I'd just made. When I called home and told Beth what I'd done, the response was lukewarm at best. She supported me, as always, but in addition to thinking about uprooting the family and moving to New York, she feared that I had made this monumental decision in haste without considering all the long-term consequences. She was right, but I didn't see it at the time. I felt conflicted about leaving N.C. State, a school and program that I loved, filled with people who I admired and respected. But I also felt that I had finally reached the mountaintop. I was about to be named head coach of the New York Jets. What could be better than that?

On February 20, Leon Hess introduced me at a press conference as his team's new head coach, and I got my first taste of the New York press. The questions ranged from legitimate—"How will your lack of NFL experience affect your performance?"—to absurd—"Do you plan to have Joe Namath run the option?" I answered all their questions, and tried to inject a little humor into the proceedings. I understand the New York media are a little different because the competition is so keen. They are talented, and I believe they treated me fairly.

Even my family came around. They still weren't thrilled about leaving our house and friends—our daughters got pretty emotional when they learned that we were moving—but they warmed to the idea once one of the local television stations did a story on the four years I'd spent at N.C. State. When the anchor ended the story by saying, "Good luck to Coach Holtz. We all wish him well," the children decided that this might not be such a bad move after all, particularly when the background music was "Leaving on a Jet Plane."

The problems I had in New York had nothing to do with the Jets organization, the management, the players, or the press. My problems in the NFL were all self-inflicted. First, I had committed to this move without really committing. My body was in New York and my name was on the coaching roster of the New York Jets, but my mind and soul were still stuck in the college game. I could no longer run an option offense, but would have to install a very complex passing game.

I started my new job in February, a time when Beth didn't want to take the children out of school, so I moved up on my own. This gave me plenty of time to work, and even more time to lie awake at night questioning the decision I'd made. Home prices were a shock. We couldn't come close to finding a comparable home in New York in a neighborhood like the one we had in Cary. Westchester was pretty, but the home prices were so far out of our reach that we didn't bother looking. Beth finally settled on a place called Cold Spring Harbor, which was nice. Then I got my first taste of New York commuting. If I left the house at the right time, my drive to the office and practice field took forty-five minutes. If I left at the wrong time—and in New York anytime has the potential to be the wrong time—it could take me two hours or longer to get to work. In North

Carolina, I could leave the office by six o'clock, drive to Durham, speak to an alumni group, and be home by seven thirty.

Then there was the weather. August days were as hot or hotter than anything we dealt with in North Carolina, but when the February nor'easters blew through, I felt as if we had moved inside the Arctic Circle.

Assembling a coaching staff for the Jets was not a problem, and probably one of the best things I did in my brief tenure in the NFL. I knew that to be successful in the NFL, you needed professional experience. I didn't have any, so I had to hire a solid group of assistants who did. Fortunately, I had no trouble attracting talented coaches. The Jets had one of the premier organizations in football, and plenty of quality coaches wanted to be part of it. My first hire was to bring Walt Michaels back to the franchise as my defensive coordinator. He had been with the Jets when they won the Super Bowl, and had moved to Philadelphia to be the defensive coordinator for the Eagles. He was excited to get back to New York, and I was thrilled to have him. Then I hired Bob Crow, who had been the Jets tackles coach, and hired him as our defensive-line coach. My offensive-line coach came from the Saint Louis Cardinals, and my special-teams coach, one of the only coaches not in the NFL, came from the University of Maryland. The only off-the-wall assistant I hired was a guy who had played for me and been a backfield coach at Florida State University, and who was out of a job and working as a night watchman at the World Trade Center. He was Dan Henning, currently recognized as one of the most successful offensive minds of professional football. I think history has proven that I made some good hires.

As for the players and front office, I had all the support I needed to be successful, but the environment was definitely different. My first day on the job, I asked my secretary, Eloise, to get Joe Namath, our starting quarterback, on the phone.

"I can't," she said.

"Sure you can," I said. "Just pick up the phone, call him, and then transfer him to my office."

"No, I mean I can't call him. I don't have his number."

"Oh?"

"No, I have to call his agent."

Turns out the only person who knew Joe's number was his agent, Jimmy Walsh, one of the best sports agents in the business.

So I called Jimmy. "I need Joe's phone number," I said. "I need to set up a meeting with him."

"I can't give you Joe's number," he said.

"You're kidding, right?"

"No, I'm not. Why don't you give me your number, and I'll have Joe call you."

It's hard to express how much this surprised me. I was the head football coach, and the only way I could schedule a meeting with my starting quarterback was to call his agent and have him arrange for Joe to call me back! I wondered how Woody Hayes would have handled that situation.

I quickly let the procedural problems with reaching Joe slide once he called me. Not only was he prompt in getting back to me, I found him to be one of the most professional and dedicated athletes I have ever worked with. There was never a time when I asked him to do something that he didn't do it. He was a winner, a leader, and an all-around class act.

I remembered Joe from his high school days in western Pennsylvania. He played about twenty-five miles from my hometown, and everybody talked about him. I first met him when I was a graduate assistant at the University of Iowa. Joe visited campus as a recruit, and I was the guy responsible for getting him fed and making sure he was in the right place at the right time. Even then, charm and intensity oozed naturally from him. I couldn't tell at the time what kind of quarterback he would become, but I knew he was a special person, a natural leader who would be successful at anything he tried.

Even though his well-documented knee injuries had slowed him down, he was still one of the most talented quarterbacks I had ever seen. Contrary to what was written at the time, and what some have said since, Joe and I never had a problem. I never, as was widely written after the fact, designed running plays for the quarterback in the Jets offense. I knew what we had in terms of a quarterback, and I believe I knew what we needed to do to get the most out of the team's assets.

My initial frustrations with the NFL stemmed not from what was happening with our team, but from the system in general. When I signed on to coach the Jets, they had one of the best running backs in the game in John Riggins. He was a bull of a runner with the potential to do for the Jets what Larry Csonka had done for the Miami Dolphins in the early seventies. But before the snow melted in Manhattan, John Riggins declared free agency and signed with the Washington Redskins, where he went on to become a Super Bowl MVP, and the kind of bruising back I had envisioned, only with another team. I never got a chance to try to talk Riggins into staying. His free-agency deal with Washington closed between the time I was announced as head coach and my first day of work. Those kinds of things happened in professional football, and they were a shock to my system. I had never dealt with anything like that in the college game. Sure, we had athletes at William and Mary and N.C. State who had trouble in school, or who needed to be motivated to go to the weight room in the off-season, but I never had to worry about free agents moving to another team inside a week.

In many respects, it was easier dealing with pros than with college students. Discipline was less of an issue, because professional athletes are just that: professional. They are mature, and they approach the game as their livelihood. In college, if we recruited twenty-two athletes, eleven of them might not turn out to be as good as we thought they were when we signed them. Of the remaining eleven, four or five might not be the kind of motivated people we needed to win football games, and two or three others might have trouble in school. My job as a college coach had been to motivate, coerce, teach, cajole, and mold those young men into winners on the field, in the classroom, and in life. In the NFL, if we had a player who wasn't getting the job done, we cut him or traded him and found someone else to do his job. The entire professional league is a pass-through—athletes play only until someone else comes along who can do the job better.

As a result, there is a built-in motivation. If you don't do your job as well as or better than you did it last year, last month, or last game, you can be fired, and some eager young athlete will jump into your position. Every game could be your last. That is true of football at every level, but in the pros, the athletes play for a paycheck. It's their career, not a pastime, that is at stake.

This adds a lot of pressure to perform, and to follow coaching. The athletes know who makes personnel decisions, and it's not them. If you want to play in the NFL, you listen to your coach and do what he says. Otherwise, you're trying out at minicamp for a different team next year.

This also breeds an inherent lack of loyalty in the NFL. If a player doesn't work out, the coach doesn't have the time or resources to mold and teach him. You cut him and move on. Players have to look out for their own interests as well. If a free agent has a chance to make more money or win more games wearing a different uniform, no one in the professional game should begrudge that athlete's looking out for himself.

Had I been an assistant a few years in the NFL, I would have understood the culture a little better, and might have adapted a lot easier. All coaches who jump from college to the NFL go through a transition period, even today. Some are successful; some aren't. I was in the latter category.

Before we ever played a game, I was brutalized in the New York press for "wasting" a first-round draft pick on a quarterback out of Alabama named Richard Todd. Todd had been a wishbone quarterback at Alabama, which meant he had gained more yards with his legs than he had with his arm. The speculation in the sports community was that I wanted to bring a college-style running game to the pros, and that I wanted to replace the legendary Joe Namath with a rookie quarterback who could run the option. Of course, this was silly. Dan Henning and I went down to Alabama during camps and worked Todd extensively. He had a strong arm, a good head, and the kind of overall athleticism that the Jets needed. He also had great interpersonal skills, which were a must in New York. Obviously, our decision proved to be correct. Richard Todd became one of the most successful quarterbacks in Jets franchise history. But if you read the papers at the time, you would have thought we had thrown our first-round draft pick down a Bronx sewer.

During our workout of Richard Todd, Dan and I spent some time with Bear Bryant, and I asked him about Joe Namath. It hadn't taken me long to realize that Joe idolized Coach Bryant, talking about Bear as if the coach sat at the side of God. Coach Bryant chewed his lip, and his eyes got narrow. "Joe's a good man," he said, high praise from Bear. "Course, I had to discipline him quite a bit, but once I got his attention he was fine. He was a heck of a competitor."

That came through the first day I saw Joe on the practice field. When he was off the field, he was a calm, smiling, friendly, confident fellow who never met a stranger or an enemy. When the helmet went on, he became as fierce a competitor as I've ever seen. Joe as team leader was like having another coach on the field. The offense responded to him, and they performed at a high level because they didn't want to disappoint Joe.

I did not socialize with Joe, or any other player for that matter. As head coach my job was to lead the team. If I became too friendly with any of my players I ran the risk of blurring the lines of authority. Other coaches have been able to play golf and go out to dinner with their players, but I always felt that that kind of fraternization bred too much familiarity, which would lead to problems. After I left New York, however, I ran into Joe many times, and he could not have been nicer. My last year coaching at South Carolina I ran into him when we played Alabama, and asked him if he would mind coming into the locker room to say a few words to our football team. He acted as if it were a great honor to be asked. Our athletes loved hearing him. They were so fired up, they beat Alabama handily.

I wish we'd had such good fortune in New York. It was obvious early that we would struggle. The Jets' record the previous season was 3–11, and that was with John Riggins. Our first four games were on the road, and we lost every one of them. Cleveland, Denver, Miami, and San Francisco all beat us as we started out 0–4. It wasn't until week five, when we finally came home, that we won our first game, a squeaker against Buffalo, 17–14. We would beat Buffalo again in Buffalo. Not that the game was memorable, but when you win only three games in a fourteen-game season, you savor every good memory you can. Our only other win came at home against Tampa Bay, the franchise that held the NFL's longest losing streak.

We had talented football players—Burgess Owens at safety, tight end Rich Caster, and our offensive guard Randy Rasmussen, to name a few—but we just didn't have enough of them. The biggest problem, however, was me. I was used to winning. Losing didn't sit well with me, and I did a poor job of leading.

In early September, Phil Iselin, the team's president, died suddenly from cardiac arrest. This sent shock waves through the organization just as we were getting the season under way. Then rumors began floating that Namath would retire, or that his contract would be waived at the end of the season. This presented more distractions to a team that couldn't afford to lose focus for a second. Throw in the fact that the season was longer than I was used to, the scrutiny was greater than anything I'd ever experienced, and the injuries were overwhelming—at one point, we had twenty players out of forty-four suffering from some form of injury—and it was easy to see how I could ask myself, "How do we get better under these conditions?" The answer kept coming back, "We can't."

Instead of looking for solutions, I couldn't take my eyes off the problems. That came from a lack of maturity and experience. Had I spent several years in the NFL, I would have understood that parity in the league means you're going to lose some games, and when injuries hamper your team, you'll likely have a bad season. At the time I didn't have the patience to see that. Plus, I was getting hammered in the press, and I didn't have the friendships that I had been able to develop in Raleigh, or Williamsburg, or Columbus for that matter. New York is a tough town under the best of circumstances; when you're under the microscope of coaching one of the city's NFL franchises, and you're being questioned because of your college credentials, it's easy to get worn down.

My problems did not stem from a lack of organizational support. Leon Hess gave me everything I wanted, and assured me that I had his full backing. But I kept hearing rumors (unfounded) that the team was for sale, and that a new owner planned to make many changes, including me. I should have taken those rumors for what they were worth, and continued to do my job. But by early December, I was exhausted and discouraged.

On Pearl Harbor Day, December 7, 1976, I got a call at home from Frank Broyles, the head coach at the University of Arkansas. Frank told me that he was retiring from coaching to take on the role of athletic director full-time. He was one of the few men who had been successful wearing both the head coach's and athletic director's hats. By the winter of 1976, he was ready to move solely into administration. He wanted me to take over for him as head coach.

I had never been to Fayetteville, Arkansas, and wasn't sure I could find it on the atlas when I said yes to Frank's offer.

I called Al Ward and told him that I would be leaving to take the job at Arkansas. Al didn't over-react. He was always a calm person who rarely raised his voice and never spoke without consid-ering his words carefully. He asked if I was sure about this decision, and he asked if there was anything that the organization had done to pre-cipitate my leaving.

I assured him that I was, indeed, sure, although I really wasn't. In hindsight, I didn't know what I wanted. Maybe I wanted somebody to talk me out of leaving, to alleviate my unfounded concerns and tell me everything was going to be hunky-dory. I told Al that I would honor my commit-ment through the end of the season, but that I would be leaving as soon as we played our last game.

He said, "No, if you're going to leave, we'd prefer you do now so we can start over immedi-ately." That was the right call on his part.

Leon Hess was out of the country when Frank Broyles called me. Had I been able to sit down with Mr. Hess, I might have made a different deci-sion. I'm sure Mr. Hess would have given me the assurances I needed to stay with the Jets. He had always been fair and honest, and I have no reason to believe that he would not have been in this situation. But because he could not be reached, I made an impetuous decision to resign from a job I hadn't fully committed to in the first place. It was a series of events that I regret to this day.

Thankfully, I had plenty of opportunities to apologize to Mr. Hess, and many of the players on that team. The year we won the national championship at Notre Dame I was asked to speak at the Hall of Fame induction dinner in New York in early December. Before I got up to speak, I felt a tap on my shoulder. When I turned, I saw a smiling Leon Hess with his hand extended. We shook hands and hugged, and I told Mr. Hess how sorry I was for the way I had handled the whole situation. "I let you down," I said. "There's nothing I can do about that now but apologize and hope you understand."

He waved and smiled as if it were nothing. "Everything in the past is past," he said. "It's over. Of course, I accept your apology."

On December 9, 1976, I officially resigned as the head coach of the New York Jets. Two days later, Joe Namath played his last game in a Jets uniform. I wish I could have done more to make Joe's final season in New York more memorable. But more than that, I wish to this day that I had either fully committed to the Jets organization, or not committed at all. Not doing either has bothered me for thirty years. And it will continue to bother me for as long as I live.

9

WHAT BEHAVIOR ARE YOU WILLING TO ACCEPT?

To Lou Holtz
with admiration
and thanks for
your fine work
(and sharp wit even
at my expense!)
Bill Clinton
10/9/79

Bill Clinton represented me as a young Arkansas attorney general in a case that could have destroyed my career. He signed this photo for me: "To Lou Holtz, With admiration and thanks for your fine work (and sharp wit, even at my expense!), Bill Clinton 10/9/79."

The one word most often used to describe my coaching style through the years has been "disciplinarian." Some people look at this as a derogatory comment, but I think being called a "disciplinarian" is a compliment. I don't know how anyone can be a successful parent, teacher, coach, manager, entrepreneur, husband, wife, or friend without understanding the role discipline plays in life, and without in some form or another being a good disciplinarian. Far from shying away from it, I've worked hard to be the firmest and fairest disciplinarian possible, whether it has been as a parent, a coach, or the manager of a staff. Discipline is not what you do to someone, but what you do for them.

Every construct in life requires discipline. Marriages require both spouses to suppress their selfish urges for the good of the relationship. That is a form of discipline, and the consequences of not following those rules are a troubled marriage. If you don't have enough self-discipline to pay your monthly bills, you will soon suffer the consequences while sitting in the dark. If, as a parent, you don't discipline your children, they grow up without any boundaries, which damages them well into adulthood. If you have no discipline in the workplace, then an "anything goes" attitude will soon prevail, and your company will be in trouble. In government, we have laws that impose consequences upon certain actions society deems unacceptable. And in my profession, achievement, performance, and teamwork are rewarded, while a lack of those qualities requires corrective action: discipline. If enforcing standards has made me a disciplinarian, then I gladly accept the title and plead guilty as charged.

A parable I always use to make the point about the importance of discipline involves two young men, each of whom owned a new puppy. The first young man showered his puppy with love and affection, and allowed the dog to do whatever it wanted. No restrictions, only unconditional love and freedom. The other young man loved his puppy as well, but he also put a choke collar on the animal. Anytime the dog behaved improperly, the young man would tug on the choke collar. It didn't take long for that dog to realize that there were limitations on his freedom.

A year later, the second young man was able to take the choke collar off of his dog, and the dog roamed the neighborhood. The owner didn't worry, because he knew that the dog would obey his commands, that he wouldn't bite anyone or destroy property, and he wouldn't abuse the free-

doms the owner had given him. The dog understood that actions had consequences. The first
young man could not give his dog those same
freedoms. If let loose, the first dog would have
terrorized the neighborhood, destroyed property,
and possibly harmed someone. For those reasons,
the dog had to remain confined indoors.

The freedom the first young man thought he
was giving his dog by not disciplining him turned
out to be exactly the opposite. The lack of discipline became a lack of freedom. The dog that had
been properly disciplined and shown the boundaries of acceptable behavior was allowed to run
free, because the owner loved the dog enough to
discipline it.

When I finish telling this story, I always ask the
athletes who have been forced to listen, "Now, the
question I have for you is, do you want a choke
collar for a year so that you can enjoy freedom for
the rest of your life? Or do you want to be coddled
and never be free?" It is a rhetorical question, but
the point gets across. My job as a coach was to
prepare the young men on our teams for a life of
success and happiness. That life had to start with
discipline.

Unfortunately some people confuse discipline with harassment, when the two could not be
more diametrically opposite. Discipline is administered out of love and caring. If the consequence
for a particular action will teach a valuable lesson

and make the recipient a better person, then you have properly used discipline. If none of those things are true, if no one learns anything from your actions, and the person on the receiving end is not made better because of what you've done, then you're simply harassing that person, not disciplining him.

Of course, no discipline is fun. As the apostle Paul wrote in Hebrews 12:11: "No discipline seems pleasant at the time, but painful. Later on, however, it produces a harvest of righteousness and peace for those who have been trained by it."

I've had people say many times, "Man, it must have been tough being one of your children." Fortunately, none of them were my children. Sure I was a tough disciplinarian at home. The most important thing I think you can teach a child is respect for authority: respect for parents, elders, teachers, coaches, and certainly law enforcement. This should be reinforced in the school. Many problems young people face today are a direct result of their lack of respect for authority. I believe it's important for children to learn to say "Yes, sir" and "No, sir," shake hands firmly, and look people in the eye. If you respect yourself, it is easy to show respect to others.

Every child in our family grew up with responsibilities. It may have been nothing more than putting a spoon on the table for dinner. This way everybody contributed to the welfare of the family. I swatted the boys when they needed it. I had a pledge paddle, and they would get one swat or two depending on the severity of their actions. I never spanked the girls. All I had to do was look at the girls sternly.

We had plenty of discipline and responsibility in our household, but all our children will say that they had fun growing up. And I advise parents now to be sure to have fun with your children. When Liz was going to her junior prom, I put on my tuxedo, greeted her date at the door, and said I was going with her. Liz was mortified, but her date thought it was quite funny.

We didn't have a lot of rules, but we did have a lot of customs. One of them was answering the phone. The youngest teenager who was home answered the first phone call of the evening. Whoever was the recipient of the call had to answer the next call by the second ring. They were also expected to answer properly: "Holtz residence, this is Liz. How may I help you?"

We are a strong religious family, and this goes back to my wife's spiritual beliefs as well as mine. We always tried to go to Sunday mass as a family whenever possible, believing fully that a family that prays together stays together. After mass we would go out for breakfast. Many times the bill was much higher than what I had budgeted, so I would say, "The person who comes the closest to guessing the amount of the check receives a dollar in cash." At first they didn't have a clue. But the dollar incentive made them pay attention, and eventually they qualified for our family version of **The Price Is Right**. Twenty-five years later, when we go out to dinner, they still guess the check. The reward is still one dollar.

Throughout my career, I tried to be fair but firm to everyone I met, and I tried to be just as creative in teaching football as I was in teaching my children the value of a meal in a restaurant. If a football player failed to meet my expectations on the field, in the classroom, or in his general comportment, I always gave him a chance to make things right. But if he failed, then he could be assured that the consequences for his behavior would be meted out swiftly. Life is a matter of choices. It is imperative that the person in charge enforce the decisions people make.

One player, who shall remain nameless, tested that theory when I gave him one semester to improve his classroom attendance and pull up his grades. "If you don't do those things, I will suspend you," I told him. He promised me that he would, and I promised him that I would keep my word if he didn't. At the end of the semester, he had failed to keep his promise, but I did not fail to keep mine. Even though he pleaded for a second chance—and my compassion for this person tugged at me to give him a break—I knew that if my word was going to mean anything, and if the rules we had established for our team were to have any weight at all, I had to follow through with my promise. I suspended the player, and, hopefully, made him a better man. Whenever I suspended a person, I always gave him a plan on how to rejoin the team. I never shut the door completely, but he would have to adjust his behavior and make better choices to be reinstated.

Discipline is all about what you deem acceptable and what you do not. You can yell at the top of your lungs, swear that you're going to do this or that if certain boundaries are violated, but until you are put to the test, until you actually have to follow through with enforcing a rule, keeping your word, and making sure that the consequences for unacceptable behavior are met, you never know how people are going to respond to you. I came to realize this in a very public way during my first season as head coach at the University of Arkansas.

When I arrived in Fayetteville, I felt as if I'd come back home, even though I'd never been to the university or the town before. It reminded us a lot of East Liverpool. I bought a home on a hill and installed the trampoline, and the children set out making new friends just as they had in North Carolina. We had plenty of acreage and a lot of houses around us. Beth didn't like the kitchen, so she set out on a remodeling project that she loved. She loved it so much, in fact, that it went on for months. I finally had to intervene. After three months of our house looking like a hard-hat area, I came home one afternoon and told the decorators and builders, "I love what you guys have done, but you're leaving a week from Monday. I hope you're finished, because that's when you're out of here." They finished the project one day before I evicted them.

I hired some of the staff members who had worked with me in the past—men like Larry Bechtel, who had been with me at William and Mary, and John Konstantinos, who was one of my best friends and a former teammate and fraternity brother at Kent State. I also hired Monty Kiffin, who was the defensive coordinator at Nebraska. By the time I was done, I felt that we had one of the finest coaching staffs in college football.

We also had a heck of a good football team. Arkansas had gone 5–5 the year before I arrived, but Frank Broyles had brought up some outstanding athletes. Ben Cowens and Jerry Eckwood were excellent running backs. And we were able to fill in some gaps with a great recruiting year. Our first game was against New Mexico State in Little Rock, and I had one of my strangest experiences as a coach. On the first play from scrimmage, our quarterback, Ron Calcagne from Youngstown, Ohio, threw a pass to a wideout running a curl pattern, and the ball was intercepted. The New Mexico State defender ran back for a touchdown, but our fans cheered because they had never seen an Arkansas team throw a pass on first down, much less on the first play of the game. They couldn't have cared less that we were down 7–0. The fact that we had thrown a pass was worthy of applause. We went on to win that game 58–7, the start of a very good year.

We were rolling along until we played the University of Texas in Fayetteville, Arkansas. They were the number one team in the country at the time, primarily because of a big tailback named Earl Campbell. Earl was the first back I can remember in college football who combined breakaway speed, slashing quickness, and size. He was bigger than most of our linebackers, and faster than any man on our team. If he ever made it into the secondary, he was virtually unstoppable.

I was scared to death of Earl Campbell. Texas had other weapons, including a very effective quarterback, but their offense centered on Campbell. To beat them, you had to stop the tailback by having at least one linebacker focused solely on Campbell.

Our defense played great that day. We led by six points in a low-scoring game with three minutes to go. Texas had the football on their own twenty-five on third down when their quarterback, Randy Meecham, threw a flat pass to Campbell. Earl stumbled and made a first down by inches. Later in the drive, on third and long again, Earl caught a screen pass, and we finally pushed him out of bounds at the one-yard line. They scored two plays later. Texas beat us by one point that afternoon. It would turn out to be our only loss of the season.

After the loss, our team got much better. Our athletes improved with each practice, and their confidence grew after each win. We were ranked fifth in the country going into our final two games. That's when I got a call from the president of the Orange Bowl committee. He told me that if we beat SMU in our upcoming game, we would get a chance to play Oklahoma in the Orange Bowl.

At the time, Oklahoma was the second-ranked team in the country behind Texas. Oklahoma was also a neighboring state. But proximity hadn't built much of a football rivalry. The only time Arkansas had ever played Oklahoma had been in the 1920s, and Oklahoma won by a score of 100–0. Fans of the Razorbacks had always lived in the shadow of their neighbors, always ranked below the Sooner teams, even though Frank Broyles had some outstanding Arkansas football teams. So even though the teams hadn't met on the field in more than half a century, there was definitely some bitterness between Norman and Fayetteville.

Our players knew the importance of the game and reacted accordingly, and we beat SMU convincingly in front of a national television audience.

The outcome of the game was no longer in doubt as we entered the fourth quarter. So out of boredom, the fans showered the field with oranges.

In the postgame press conference, the first question I was asked was, "Coach, what do you think about fans throwing oranges on the field?"

I said, "Thank God we didn't get invited to the Gator Bowl."

That sound bite played nationally for the rest of the weekend and throughout most of the bowl season. For many, it was their first introduction to my dry sense of humor. I only wish the rest of the year was that funny.

My biggest fear was that our team would have a letdown after beating SMU. We were in the Orange Bowl and would take on the second-ranked team in the country, a team the entire state of Arkansas wanted to beat more than anything. As one elderly fan told me, "I'd pull for Russia if they were playing Oklahoma." That was the prevailing sentiment throughout the state. Virtually the entire state of Arkansas was pulling for us because they loved the Razorbacks, and the other 25 percent pulled for us because they disliked Oklahoma. The Razorback fans are the most loyal and vocal I have ever seen. They are knowledgeable football fans, and they raise their sons and daughters to be Razorbacks. The first words their children are taught are "Woo—PIG—Sooie," the Razorback rally cry.

I knew we still had another regular-season game to play, and we could ruin our season if we didn't beat a lower-ranked Texas Tech team in Lubbock. Adding to my concern, a former player, one whom I did not know, was killed in a car crash the same weekend we beat SMU. His funeral was scheduled for Tuesday, and the entire team planned to attend. We didn't practice on Sunday, and I spent most of Monday calming the team down after the big win. On Wednesday, we left for Lubbock to play the Red Raiders of Texas Tech on Thanksgiving Day in a game that would be televised, which meant we would play a very good team having had zero practice.

The game was too close for comfort, in part because Texas Tech played a tremendous defensive football game. We finally won 17–14. Afterward, I was so impressed by how well the Red Raiders had played on defense that I asked someone, "Who's their defensive coordinator?"

The answer was, "A young guy named Bill Parcells."

We avoided an upset at Texas Tech, but we weren't going to take anything for granted the rest of the year. We prepared our team for the Orange Bowl the same way I'd seen Woody Hayes get Ohio State ready for the Rose Bowl. We practiced every weekday between the Monday after Thanksgiving and December 20, with the exception of final exams. Then, I intended to let the players go home for Christmas. We would fly to Miami late on the twenty-fifth. This would allow our players to spend Christmas Eve and Christmas morning with their families.

During the three weeks we practiced, our team studied film on Oklahoma, and we began planting the seeds of what I thought could be a tremendous success. "They're a very good football team," I told our players, "but they're also predictable. If we line up in a particular formation, we can predict what their response will be. If they have a particular down and yardage, you can predict what play they're going to run. If we can predict what they're going to do, we can beat them."

I truly believed not only that we could beat Oklahoma, but that we had the potential to dominate the game. We added some wrinkles into our offense based on what we'd seen them do throughout the year, and Monty Kiffin, now defensive coordinator for the Tampa Bay Buccaneers, and Pete Carroll, presently the head football coach at Southern Cal, had some strong thoughts on how to defend Oklahoma's wishbone attack. At the time we had the best defense in the country. As good as Oklahoma was, I felt sure we could stop them. I was feeling so good about our bowl preparations that I asked Frank Broyles, "If we win this game by thirty points, do you think we've got a chance at the national championship?" Frank laughed and looked at me as if I had a fever, but I believed we could do it.

Then things got very complicated.

On the night of December 20, after we had wrapped up practice, I was in the football office reviewing film. We were to gather the team together early the next morning to review film of our most recent scrimmage. Then we would send them home for Christmas. It was eight thirty, and I was only halfway through the film. At that rate, I'd be in the office until ten, and probably wouldn't get to sleep until midnight.

I jumped when the phone rang. Not many people knew where I was, so I wasn't expecting a phone call at that time of the evening. My heart rate jumped several beats a minute when the caller identified himself as a sergeant with the campus police.

My first thought was my family. As a parent, anytime a police officer tracks you down at night, your mind races home to your children. Thankfully, my family was fine. But otherwise, the news couldn't have been more devastating. At the exact moment the police sergeant began to fill me in on the reason for his call, another phone rang in the office. It was the Reverend H. D. McCarty. He was the pastor of the local Baptist church, a devoted Christian, and a caring person. On Sunday our sons would go to a Catholic mass with our family and then go to the Baptist service with their friends because Mr. McCarty was such a positive leader. He had called to tell me the same news I was getting from the police.

"Three of the players are in police custody," Mr. McCarty said.

"What did they do?" I asked.

When he explained why, my heart sank. They were involved in an incident in the players' dorm with a young woman. I sat silently for a couple of seconds as my mind tried to process what my ears had just heard.

"The police are holding the men," he continued. "I have the girl with me."

I hung up the phone and stared at the practice film, grainy black-and-white images on a cream screen, the soft clicking of the reel-to-reel projector breaking the silence in the room. All of a sudden, the world had gotten very small. I couldn't believe what I had heard. These players were fine young men. I had never had a problem with them.

The players weren't in cells. They hadn't been charged, fingerprinted, or photographed. The investigation was still ongoing, but they were in a heap of trouble. I sat down across from them in an office in the police station and gave them one opportunity to tell me exactly what had happened. They understood that any variances from the truth at this stage wouldn't be tolerated. The police needed to know the truth, and so did I.

It took a half hour before I got the full story. I was floored.

To call this a terrible situation did not do it justice. The girl wanted action taken. But the police and the university wanted no part of it. The athletes had not been charged, and if local law enforcement had anything to do with it, they would not be. The university took the position that if there were no charges, there was no crime, so the school was able to wash its hands of the matter as well.

If the same series of events had taken place in 1997 instead of 1977, the situation would have been out of my hands. Given the information that everyone stipulated was true, the athletes would have been arrested and charged. But in those days it was up to the police and prosecutors to determine someone's intent and state of mind and to weigh the circumstances surrounding the event.

Still, the police weren't aggressive about pressing charges. The players were the offensive stars of our football team. Among them, they had scored 78 percent of our touchdowns that season. When I met with McCarty, he told me the girl would not press charges if I and the university would take disciplinary actions. If the girl didn't press charges, the police had a perfect excuse to walk away. To press charges, they said, they needed a cooperative victim. The university, however, could take whatever action it deemed fit, but no administrator wanted to get involved. They were all perfectly content to leave any and all action to me.

Turning a situation like this over to a football coach seemed outrageous to me at the time, and is even more unbelievable when I think back on it today. For the principal figures in a state university to turn a blind eye was, in my mind, unthinkable. This incident occurred in a university dorm on the Arkansas campus and consequently fell under their jurisdiction. Yet, the fate of the athletes and our team was left up to me.

Administrators were conveniently "unavailable" when I tried to talk to someone about this situation. I don't know if the president, the dean, or any members of the board of trustees knew all the details at the time, because I never got a chance to talk to any of them. What I do know is that I might as well have been alone on a deserted island when it came time to handle the situation. I don't know how much the politics of the times played into this, but I do know that nobody at the University of Arkansas outside the football program stepped up and did the right thing. In fact, I have yet to hear from anyone.

I called an emergency staff meeting at 11 P.M. where I discussed what had happened. One or two people put forth the argument that if the police had found no cause to make any arrests, then there was no reason for the incident to become public. No harm, no foul. I didn't see things that way. The moment I took my first head-coaching job, I instituted something I called my "Do right" rules. They were very simple. I expected all my players and coaches to do right and avoid wrong. The rules I instituted were based on the premise that college athletes knew right from wrong, and were old enough to make proper choices. Being late for practice or a team meeting was a wrong choice. Disobeying coaches or professors was a wrong choice. Comporting themselves as anything other than gentlemen was a wrong choice. If ever there was a situation that violated the "Do right" rules, this was it. As I evaluated the situation, it became obvious that I could not let them play in the bowl game. I felt that if I overlooked this, it would mean anything goes.

I told our staff that they weren't going to play in the game, and I still believed we were going to win. "Those young men will not be going to Miami," I said. "Look, I know they haven't been charged, and probably won't be charged, but if you excuse this kind of behavior, what won't you excuse? If what they did is acceptable, what is unacceptable?" I don't believe in making important decisions late at night. I told the staff that we would see if we felt the same way in the morning.

With that, the meeting adjourned. I got home a little after one in the morning. Beth was asleep. I knew the fallout from the events of the night would be huge, so I wanted to talk everything through with her and hear her opinions. I nudged her a few times. When she didn't respond, I went to bed and stared at the ceiling the rest of the night.

The following morning, I left the house before Beth got up. I met with the staff early and said, "I feel the same today as I did last night." The decision was now in cement. I then met with the three players and told them that the police were not filing charges, but that they would not be playing in the Orange Bowl. At the time, they understood my decision, apologized for their actions, and wished us well in Miami.

An hour later, I issued a press release where I said, in part, that three of our best athletes had violated the "Do right" rule and would not be playing in the Orange Bowl. No details were mentioned, and I would have nothing else to say in the matter.

Then I went through the daily agenda as if nothing had happened. We met with the team and went over the scrimmage film. We gave everyone a list of things we expected during their four-day break. At the end of the meeting, I informed the team about the suspensions. When one of the players asked what rules his three teammates had broken, I said, "They violated the 'Do right' rule, and that's all you need to know. They know what they did, most of the team knows what they did, and I know what they did. That's all that matters."

I then entertained questions. There were a few about the suspensions, but most of them were about winning. I could tell that the team had compassion for the suspended players, but the players accepted our decision. I was very emphatic that the decision had been made and was irrevocable. I wished the players a Merry Christmas and dismissed them. I only wished I had shown them the film the preceding day and sent them home for Christmas the previous evening. If I had, the problem wouldn't have come up, because they would have been home. I hadn't gone that route, because I hadn't wanted them driving home late at night. The last thing I wanted was one of them getting into an auto accident. I figured if they were on campus, they wouldn't get into any trouble. I was dead wrong.

That night, Beth and I traveled to Little Rock for a dinner with some friends. I avoided the subject of the suspensions in front of our dinner guests, but then the restaurant manager came by our table and said, "Coach, you need to be prepared when you leave. Every television truck in Arkansas is set up in the parking lot."

Beth said, "Why are television trucks out front?"

"If you hadn't slept so soundly last night, you'd know why," I said.

To this day, I have no idea how the press got wind of where I would be that night. When I told

Beth and our friends what was happening, the room became very somber. A few minutes later, Beth and I walked out and faced the spotlights. Most of the reporters wanted to know what rules had been violated. I replied that the press release said it all. The accusations made against the athletes were serious, but since the police had taken no action, it would have been grossly unfair to have them aired in the press. Actions or inactions of law enforcement and the university could be debated over time; having the charges broadcast all over the country would have been a terrible disservice to everyone involved.

The press didn't like it when I refused to answer their questions, so they jumped to their own conclusions. Stories ran speculating that I had suspended the best players on our team over some minor infractions. Columnists accused me of being unfair to the Orange Bowl because some players missed a curfew. I was portrayed as a power-mad disciplinarian who would rather lose football games than act reasonably.

The speculation wasn't limited to the local press, either. National media outlets picked up the story, each couching the events in such a way as to make it look as if I had been frivolous in handing out the suspensions. This was hurtful. As a football coach, my job was not to suspend players, but to do my best to keep them eligible and playing so that we could grow and enjoy success in the classroom, on the field, and in life. Keeping players out of a game was the most self-defeating thing I could do. If I handed down suspensions casually and carelessly, the players would not follow my leadership, and I would have been out of a job. Even though I wouldn't go into any detail about the suspensions, I felt the media should respect that my intentions were honest and in the best interest of the University of Arkansas. In fairness, some members of the media did so, but at the time it seemed as if the entire country was against me.

The state of Arkansas went into an uproar when the news broke. When Beth and I arrived home from Little Rock, we were shocked. We always had a listed phone number in the event a person or a coach needed to call me at home, and our children had already received numerous obscene phone calls. The calls continued until we left for Miami.

Still, there was silence from the university administration. Whether it was written, verbal, or simply understood, school administrators and university boards adopted a hands-off policy. Not once did I receive a phone call from anyone associated with the University of Arkansas either supporting me or questioning what had happened. No one in a position of authority stood up for me. No one came out and said that I had made the right decision and had done the right thing by not revealing the details of the suspension. In fairness to the university, no one criticized my decision publicly or privately. Coach Broyles supported me privately and probably felt he didn't need to defend me publicly. I had great respect for Coach Broyles then and I still do. He is an exceptional leader and person.

The one positive thing about this tragic situation was the support I received from the football staff and my family. Beth took great offense that so many people took such a see-no-evil approach to the charges. But she couldn't have been more supportive of me during the ordeal. I only wish our children had not been exposed to such viciousness. In retrospect, they also learned a lot about human nature and the price for doing what is right.

The problems grew worse when accusations became racial. One day after the news broke about the suspensions, I received notice of a petition filed by a lawyer named John Walker on behalf of the suspended players. The petition claimed that I had wrongly suspended these players because they were African American, in violation of their civil rights. Lawyer John Walker was seeking an injunction that would allow the players to play. He also notified me of his intent to file a civil-rights lawsuit on behalf of the three players against me and the university. Mr. Walker then called me and said that twelve of our best African American athletes had told him that, in solidarity with the suspended teammates, they would not play in the Orange Bowl unless the suspensions were lifted.

This disturbed me. Race relations in the South in 1977 were not what they could have been, and certainly the sting of discrimination could still be felt through Arkansas as well as the rest of the country. After all, we were not a full decade removed from Martin Luther King Jr.'s assassination, an event that had shaped the worldview of many of the young men who now played football at the University of Arkansas. Those same young men had been children when John Carlos and Tommie Smith had raised their gloved fists on the medal stand during the Mexico City Olympic Games, an event that set off a firestorm of controversy that continued for many years. Southwest Conference football had been integrated only for eight years when I took over as head coach at the University of Arkansas, even though it had been almost a quarter century since the **Brown v. Board of Education** decision, and thirteen years since passage of the Civil Rights Act. And in many places, minorities were subjected to awful slurs and mistreatment. It was particularly painful to me because it seemed like only yesterday when I read of Governor Orval Faubus refusing to admit African American students to Little Rock Central High School.

Our football team was not one of those places. In 1977, 30 to 40 percent of the athletes on our team were African American. They were treated with the same dignity and respect as anyone else; they abided by the same rules and codes of conduct; they were expected to do the same things as their white, Asian, and Latino counterparts in the classroom and on the field; and they received the same praise and were subject to the same discipline as any other athletes on our team. We were as color-blind as any institution in the country because I, like the Reverend Martin Luther King Jr., expected people to be judged, not by the color of their skin, but by the content of their character. To suggest otherwise was an affront to our fine football program, and an insult to every player and coach on our team.

John Walker was a high-profile and very respected lawyer in the state of Arkansas. What concerned me was the fact that he seldom lost a case. Most of these were settled out of court. It was my impression that he had contacted the athletes and said, "I can help you play in the game." This got the players' attention. All they wanted to do was play against Oklahoma. I honestly felt that Mr. Walker thought we would capitulate because this episode could end my coaching career. I informed my wife of this. We agreed that if this was the result, so be it. I must tell you I have never prayed so hard in my life, and God gave me a peace about the entire situation.

I then issued my second press release. As I best remember, I said, "Twenty-six of our African American players have told Mr. Walker they will not play in the game unless I reinstate the three suspended players. I have always told our players that they must think for themselves and stand up for the things they believe. I respect their decision not to play, but the fact remains, the suspensions will not be lifted, we will play Oklahoma in the Orange Bowl with them or without them, and we will play a great game."

The first question I received was that I said twenty-six, but Mr. Walker's number was twelve. I replied, "Maybe some of them have changed their minds." I wanted it to appear that the boycott was breaking and not growing.

In fact, I had pulled the number twenty-six out of thin air. I knew how many African American players we had, and I figured that a large percentage of them wanted to support their suspended teammates, particularly if this was the consensus. I also knew they loved football and wanted to play in the Orange Bowl.

By the time I got home that night, I already had half a dozen messages from players. When I called back, each player said, "I'm with you, Coach. No matter what anybody else says, I'm ready to play."

By nightfall, I knew that the threat of a mass boycott by our African American players had ended before it ever materialized. I will always be especially grateful to George Stewart and his family. George was a high-profile player from Little Rock with great parents. George not only blasted any idea of a boycott, but he and his parents were vocal supporters at a time when supporting me wasn't the most popular position an African American athlete could take. George went on to become our team captain and an All-American.

Even with the support of players like George, I still needed to hire a lawyer to defend my position in court. I said, "Why do I need a lawyer, because I made a difficult decision? No, I'm not hiring a lawyer."

Finally, I got a call I didn't expect, and one that I will never forget. It came from the Arkansas attorney general. He said, "Coach Holtz, my job is to represent the state of Arkansas. You're a state employee. I'll represent you."

The attorney general agreed to put his holiday plans aside and do whatever it took to vigorously represent my interests and the interests of the university in court. His name was Bill Clinton, and I couldn't have been happier to have him represent me.

On December 24, I received a phone call from Dr. Ray Miller, an African American who was on the University of Arkansas's board of trustees. He said he had a few of our athletes in his home who were confused about whether to play or not. I flew to Little Rock immediately. When I got there, we prayed together and then I told them I understood their confusion. What I didn't tell them (or anyone else other than future president Clinton) was that if I hadn't suspended the players, the young lady would have pressed charges. Consequences from that action would have been far greater for them than missing a football game.

I did tell them that I was fully aware we wouldn't have had such a successful season without their three teammates. These were great players, but I had no choice. I answered all my players' questions and then I hugged each one of them. It was well after midnight when I got home. I had missed Christmas Eve with my family. I felt sorry for myself. Then I thought about the players and people who didn't have families. Even though the trial loomed, as well as a bowl game against a great Oklahoma opponent, I went to bed thankful for my family, my friends, and the blessings I had.

We were in Miami when the judge finally heard the case. I had a football game to prepare for, and I had an attorney who was more than capable of representing my interests. Sitting in a courtroom would have been a waste of my time.

Attorney General Clinton kept me apprised by telephone of all the developments. It seemed like every time my phone rang it was him saying, "Lou, it's Bill Clinton. I'm afraid the motion didn't go our way."

After a while, I said, "Bill, are you holding out on the good news, or is everything going against us?"

"So far, everything's going against us," he said. "But don't worry. We're still in the fight."

It wasn't until midmorning that I got some good news. One of the three athletes had been evasive on the stand, insinuating that some minor infraction had led to the suspensions. That was the opening Bill Clinton needed.

On cross-examination, the attorney general exposed the woman's accusation, and the fact that another player had called police to the scene. It was my understanding that John Walker then asked for and was granted a recess, and the petition was withdrawn before the lunch break.

When I got another call from Bill Clinton, I thought the worst. My heart jumped when I heard the attorney general say, "Lou, I've got some great news."

I will forever be indebted to President Clinton for the caring way in which he handled my case. He could have gone home for Christmas and said, "Oh, well, I hope things work out," but he didn't. He put aside his holiday plans and did what he thought was right, and did so in a professional manner. No matter what your political beliefs are, I will always be thankful for the effort he put in and the things he did on my behalf.

My Christmas nightmare of 1977 was almost over. Unfortunately, the Arkansas team practiced like the 24-point underdog they were. The players appeared distracted and disheartened. Things got so bad that I canceled practice one day and took the team to an alligator farm, and let them swim in the hotel pool all afternoon. It pleased them but didn't improve their performance. Practices were slow and the execution was sloppy. There is always going to be rust on a team when you have a month between games, but these practice sessions had more to do with attitude than lack of repetitions. I knew we were good enough to compete with Oklahoma, but our team didn't know it.

Finally on the twenty-ninth, three days before the game, I called a team meeting. As the players came in, they didn't talk to one another; they wouldn't look at me or laugh at my jokes. I said, "Okay, I know all the reasons we can't win this football game. If I want a few more, all I've got to do is pick up the newspapers. I've read about all the great players from Oklahoma who will be playing, and all the great players from Arkansas that won't be playing. I've read how their offense is unstoppable, and how we won't be able to gain any yardage on their defense. I've read all of that, and more. But what I haven't heard or read is anything positive about the people in this room. So I want to hear from you why we have a chance to win this game."

It didn't take long for one of our defensive players to say, "Coach, we have the number one defense in the country"—which we did—"so we aren't going to get beat nearly as bad as everyone thinks." Well, it wasn't what I wanted to hear, but it was a step in the proper direction.

Another player said, "We have a great offensive line, and they can block Oklahoma."

"There you go," I said, pointing to the player as if he'd just stated the obvious.

Then they all started to get excited. Another said, "Our quarterback is a great leader and a great competitor." Others chimed in with the fact that we had fantastic special teams. Our punter and placekicker were among the best in the country. When the players left the room, they were a different team. Why? Because they focused on what we had and not on what we had lost. They were no longer thinking about the fact that we would be playing without the leading rusher in the Southwest Conference, the starting fullback, and the starting flanker.

The next day, I attended the Orange Bowl luncheon, where I couldn't have been in a better mood. I felt good about our team and the game plan, and the legal problems were behind us. The fact that we were 24-point underdogs didn't bother me. I still believed we were going to win the game. At the luncheon, I entertained the crowd with a few jokes and a couple of magic tricks. (One of my 108 personal goals was to learn to juggle and do magic.)

After I performed the "Anderson Tear Newspaper Trick" I said, "How many of you would like to see me do this on **The Tonight Show** with Johnny Carson on February twelfth?" A cheer went up in the room. "That's great!" I said. "I've checked my calendar, and I'm free that day, so if you'll be kind enough to call Johnny Carson and tell him you'd like to see me on his show, I would appreciate it."

After lunch, a man walked up and said, "Coach, my name is Merl Slauser, and I'm president of NBC. I want to tell you, you're going to be on **The Tonight Show**. And you're no twelve forty-five guest, either." That's when the show ran from 11:30 P.M. to 1:00 A.M. "You're eleven forty-five material."

I thanked him and said, "You know, we might get beat badly."

"I don't care," he said. "You can count on it."

On January eighth, Merl Slauser was fired as president of NBC, which hired Fred Silverman. I always figured Merl lost his job because the network found out he had invited me to be on **The Tonight Show**.

On New Year's Day of 1978, we entered the Orange Bowl as one of the biggest underdogs of the year. Texas had been beaten by Notre Dame in the Cotton Bowl before our game began, which meant that Oklahoma could sew up a national championship with a victory over us.

When we left the locker room before the game, I felt we could win. Our team was ready. I tried to lighten the mood by saying to them on the way out, "Oklahoma is big, mean, strong, and aggressive, and our last eleven out of the locker room will have to start." They all laughed, and we charged onto the field for the biggest game in University of Arkansas history.

NBC had worried about the television audience for a game that was supposed to be a rout, so the network had gone out of its way to play up the controversy surrounding the suspensions in order to drive more viewers to what it thought would be a pretty lopsided game. It turned out to be the most watched game of the 1977 season.

The first play from scrimmage, Oklahoma attempted to run the ball up the middle, and our defense swarmed. We had ten out of eleven players in on the tackle for no gain. So impressive was that play that the university commissioned a painting of all ten players gang-tackling the Oklahoma runner. It was one of the bestselling memorabilia items in the school's history.

On offense, Roland Sales, our third-string back, rushed for 206 yards, an Orange Bowl record, while our fourth-string tailback, Barnabus White, rushed for 60 yards in the fourth quarter. We won the game 31–6 and finished the year ranked third in the nation. It wasn't the 30-point victory I had predicted to Frank Broyles in early December, but it was still a dominant performance by a group of unforgettable athletes.

I've often wondered what might have happened if Arkansas had lost that Orange Bowl game, or what might have happened if Bill Clinton hadn't volunteered to represent me in court, or what would have become of my career if the ruling in those proceedings had gone another way. Things would certainly have been different. I became a national figure after that, which bothered me a little. I hadn't done anything special. I had followed the rules I set up for myself and for our team, and we won a football game. Those were not extraordinary feats, and to be praised for doing the right thing made me feel uneasy. But even if we had lost that game, even if I hadn't gone on to win a national championship at Notre Dame, appear on **The Tonight Show** three times, visit the White House six times, and become one of the most sought-after public speakers in the country, I know that I could have lived with myself. The decision I made to discipline those Arkansas athletes was rooted in a very simple philosophy: Do what's right, and avoid what's wrong. If I hadn't followed that rule, winning football games and appearing on television shows would have meant nothing. And if those things had never happened in my life, but I had done the right thing, I know that I could have lived at peace for the rest of my days.

Am I a disciplinarian? Absolutely, and I do not apologize for it. There were other times when I had to suspend players for violating team rules, being late, or doing poorly in the classroom. I never liked it, and often thought about overlooking the violations and giving the players a break. But that wouldn't have been fair to them. Discipline is a teaching tool. I've tried to teach athletes how to succeed in life. Hopefully, I've succeeded. But even if I haven't, I've done what I thought was right. And that's all that can be asked of a life. Have I made mistakes? Certainly. Am I liked by all the athletes I have coached? Of course not. Nobody likes to be told what to do, especially today's youth. But it has been my experience that those who want to succeed in life will eventually call or write to say, "Thank you." Those who don't understand the importance that discipline plays in a successful life will continue to blame me and others for their failures.

10

BAD THINGS SOMETIMES HAPPEN FOR A GOOD REASON

In December 1983, I was named the new head coach of the University of Minnesota. Not only was it too cold there, but the football program was in chaos. I had my work cut out for me. **(AP Photo/ Larry Salzman)**

On July 22, 1982, I was in Milwaukee, Wisconsin, where I had been invited to speak to the sales force of Northwestern Mutual. After a long flight, I checked into the new Hyatt Regency, picked up my room key, and rushed up to my room, needing to shower, unpack, and collect myself before heading out to give my speech. When I reached my room on the eleventh floor, suitcase in hand, I inserted the key in the door, and promptly broke it off in the keyhole. This provoked me to pitch a little fit in the hallway. Then I got the hotel security and maintenance staff involved. Thirty minutes later, nobody could get the door open, and I had reached the boiling point. I was supposed to be standing at a podium giving a speech in an hour, and I still hadn't showered, shaved, or brushed my teeth. I kept asking myself how such bad luck could befall me. Why was it that Murphy's Law of things going wrong seemed always to apply when I was running late? In frustration, I kicked the door.

Someone from the twelfth floor of the atrium yelled down, "Lou Holtz, if you do that again, I'm calling the police."

I looked up and saw Bob Hope leaning over the railing, laughing at me.

"What are you doing?" Bob asked. He and I had become good friends since our first meeting at the Rose Bowl Banquet when I was an assistant coach at Ohio State. I had played in his celebrity pro-am golf tournament in Palm Springs several times, and done my comedy and magic routine at his pretournament dinner. But I didn't expect to see him in Milwaukee.

"Bob, my key's broken off in the door," I said. "I'm supposed to speak in an hour, and I can't get in to take a shower."

"Come on up," he said. "You can use my shower."

I went up to Bob's suite, where he graciously allowed me to prepare for my speech. Before I left, he said, "Listen, there's no need to get another room. I've got two bedrooms and this huge living area. It's just me up here. Stay with me. After your speech, we'll have dinner before my show."

I did just that. Afterward, as he was preparing to leave for his show for the same group, I said, "Bob, can you do me one favor?" As if letting me stay in his suite weren't favor enough.

"Sure," he said.

"Today's my anniversary. Would you call Beth and wish her a happy anniversary?"

I dialed our home number and gave the phone to Bob. I heard him say, "Beth, this is Bob Hope calling, and I just wanted to wish you a happy anniversary." He went on to talk about how special anniversaries were and how he and his wife, Dolores, cherished theirs. He then said, "Let me speak to Lou.... What do you mean he's not there?...You mean, he's not home on your anniversary?" I was standing next to him thinking what natural talent he possessed. He had great writers, but he was unique and caring.

That was one of the best anniversary presents from a friend Beth ever got, one we still talk and laugh about to this day. I also had a day with Bob Hope, a treat I would have missed had it not been for the misfortune of breaking my key off in my hotel room door.

That is one small example of a life axiom I have found to be true: Sometimes bad things happen for a good reason. My mother was someone who constantly reinforced the notion of "God's will" ruling our lives, and that everything that happened, good and bad, was part of an overarching strategy. I heard her words, and believed them, but I also thought the Good Lord looked after those who looked after themselves. There were times when I figured I could shape my life based on **my** will, and God could come along for the ride. I couldn't have been more wrong. As the saying goes, if you want to make God laugh, tell him your plans for the future.

Time and again I've seen terrible things happen to people who have done nothing to deserve their fate. In those times, I've asked myself, "Why has this bad thing happened to these good people? What sort of plan could the Almighty have that would include this kind of suffering?" Days, months, sometimes years later, those same people told me how their tragedy became a blessing in disguise. I can't tell you the number of times people have said things like, "I didn't know if I was going to make it when my father passed away, but it brought me closer to my mother than I've ever been. I guess it was a blessing in disguise." Or, "When I lost my job, I thought our world was going to collapse. But if I hadn't gotten fired, I never would have had the impetus to start my own business. Losing that job was the best thing that ever happened to me."

Stories of this type would fill volumes, and many good books have been written on this subject. Still, most people have to learn this for themselves: the tragedies in our lives seem unfair at the moment they happen, and the tendency is to feel despair. But sometimes, tragedies come our way for a good reason. Maybe we need a shock to show us what is really important; maybe we need a little shove to rekindle a shattered family relationship; or maybe we need to be nudged out the door to make that important career move we've been putting off.

It isn't easy when bad things happen, and it's never fun. As Mom always said, "God never promised it would be easy." He only promised love and blessings based on His plan, not ours. And God's ability to take a long-term approach far exceeds anything we humans can comprehend.

I thought I had seen the plan for my life after the 1978 Orange Bowl game. I had done what I thought was the right thing before that game, and, because of the national exposure I received, people wanted me to speak at their banquets, or say a few words at their sales seminars. I completed several of the items on the list I'd written back when I was unemployed in South Carolina, including several appearances on **The Tonight Show**, where I combined comedy and a few magic tricks, something no football coach had ever done before on a talk show. I dined at the White House, one of four visits there, traveled around the world, and made lots of friends like Bob Hope, Dinah Shore, Arnold Palmer, Glen Campbell, Zig Ziglar, and Colin Powell, wonderful down-to-earth people whom I would never have had the opportunity to know if we hadn't enjoyed success at the University of Arkansas.

I figured my career was set. I loved my job; my family loved where we lived; the children couldn't have been happier in school and with the friends they had made; and we were winning. In 1978 our team went 9–2 and tied UCLA 10–10 in the Fiesta Bowl.

Following the Fiesta Bowl, I took my family and my mother to Hawaii, where I was to coach in the Hula Bowl. Coach Hayes had just been fired for losing his temper on the sidelines during the Gator Bowl and striking a Clemson player in the helmet after the player intercepted a pass, ran out of bounds in front of the Ohio State bench, and said something to the coaches and players. The trip was sad for me because I couldn't get my mind off of Coach Hayes. He was one of the greatest coaches in history, and one of the greatest men I had ever known, but I knew that, in his lifetime at least, all the great things he had done would be overshadowed by this one incident. It was a terrible way for an exceptional man to go out, and my sympathy for him and his family put a damper on my trip.

Plus, speculation was rampant that I would be offered the head-coaching job at Ohio State. Sure enough, the following day I received a phone call at my hotel in Hawaii from Hugh Hindman, the athletic director at Ohio State.

"Lou," he said, "we would like you to apply for the head-coaching position here. We want to interview you."

"Hugh, how many coaches are being interviewed?"

He said, "About six, but you're on the short list."

I said, "Hugh, we coached together, won a national championship together at Ohio State with you as the line coach. You know me as both a person and a coach. I've got a track record and a winning percentage, and if that's not enough, you can check with people I coached at William and Mary, N.C. State, or Arkansas. There is nothing you or anyone else can learn from an interview. Now, I love Ohio State. I'm from Ohio. But I love Arkansas and the people here, too. Hog fans think Arkansas is as good a job as Ohio State, and for me to 'apply' for any job would be an insult to them. If you offer me the job at Ohio State, the odds are pretty good I'm going to accept. But I am happy, and it would be unfair for me to apply anywhere, even Ohio State."

He said, "Well, if you change your mind, call me."

"Don't stay home waiting for my call," I said.

When I hung up, Beth asked, "Are we going back home to Ohio?"

I said, "We are at home, honey: in Arkansas."

In 1979 we lost a lot of athletes to graduation, but still went 10–1 in the regular season and played Alabama in the Sugar Bowl for the national championship. Alabama won that game 24–9, and afterward Coach Bryant told me that it was the best game Alabama had played in five years. I said, "Gee, I'm glad I got to see it."

We had a slightly tougher year in 1980, when we won only seven games. Recruiting was never easy in the Southwest Conference. Good athletes wanted to come to Arkansas, and good parents wanted their sons to be part of our program, but we missed some players, especially to one conference school that would later have its entire football program ripped out from under it by the NCAA. Famous Fort Worth writer Dan Jenkins wrote a couple of bestselling comedy-novels based on the shenanigans that went on in our conference during that time. Living it wasn't quite as funny. I remember recruiting one athlete who had verbally committed to Arkansas, but two days before signing day, he informed me that he was going to Dallas. When I asked him why, he said: "I just think I'll be happier there." This came as quite a surprise, since he had never visited their campus. But that was how things went back then. Still, we signed our fair share of top-notch athletes, and we beat Tulane in the All-American Bowl that year.

Our next two years, we played exceptionally well, finishing the season 8–3 in 1981 before losing to North Carolina in the Gator Bowl, and in 1982 we won nine games, lost once, and had one tie. When we beat the Florida Gators in the Bluebonnet Bowl, we finished the year ranked ninth in the nation, the fourth time in six years we had finished as one of the top ten teams in college football.

Things couldn't have been better from my perspective. The University of Arkansas put my picture on recruiting posters aimed at boosting enrollment. I wasn't sure how my face on a poster would lure anyone anywhere, but enrollment went up after the campaign began. I decided I could be very happy in Arkansas for the rest of my career. Our daughter Luanne had graduated from high school in Fayetteville, gone to the University of Arkansas, and married an Arkansas graduate named Terry Altenbaumer. Our oldest son, Skip, also finished high school in Arkansas and was attending Notre Dame. I had visions of Beth and me spending our empty-nest years in our house on the hill in Fayetteville, and then throwing a nice Razorback party for all our friends when I retired.

In the winter of 1983, all those plans were destroyed. Our team had gone only 6–5 that season, but it might have been one of our better coaching jobs. We had a slew of injuries and were forced to play a freshman quarterback. We had graduated most of our team from 1982, but our schedule hadn't gotten any easier. I had also lost a number of assistant coaches to head-coaching jobs, moves I wholeheartedly encouraged.

We were invited to a bowl game for the seventh straight year, but we declined to accept it, and it was the first time since I was at William and Mary that a team I coached hadn't won at least seven games.

It wasn't a time to panic. The Arkansas team I'd inherited had gone 5–5 the year before I arrived. That coach, Frank Broyles, had the athletic center named after him. A 6–5 record wasn't acceptable, but most of our team was returning, and I was determined to make the 1984 season the best year ever.

I had just returned from church on a Sunday morning when Frank called my house and asked me to come by his office. I didn't think twice about it. Sure, it was unusual for Frank to call on a Sunday, but I was more curious than concerned. I had no idea what the meeting was about or why it was important that we meet at his office on a Sunday afternoon. When I got there, Frank wasted no time.

"Lou," he said. "I want you to resign."

To call what I felt shock would be an understatement. Had I heard him right? Was this an April Fools' joke in January? Frank's expression told me that he was deadly serious. It took a second for me to collect myself. Then I asked the only question that came to my mind: "Why?"

"I just think it's best for the program," he said, and that was the only answer I ever got. Despite having the best win-loss record in the history of the University of Arkansas, I was, technically, fired that Sunday without any notice or explanation.

I always had a fine relationship with Frank. Even though he had been a successful head football coach before moving into the athletic director's office, he never interfered with the program while I was the head coach. There were times when I initiated football conversations where he would offer some tidbit of advice, but it was always when I brought the subject up. He never tried to step back or second-guess what I did on the football field. He is a great man. The Razorbacks had been wildly successful during my tenure, and we had no problems with the NCAA in a conference where many considered playing by the rules a joke.

I bet Frank and I never had a dozen cross words between us during my tenure. Sure, I was disappointed when he wasn't more out front during the Orange Bowl scandal, but that was long forgotten. We won that game, and the school was better off for how things worked out. I guess I had rubbed a few people the wrong way in the years I'd been in Fayetteville. You're never more popular at a school than the first day you show up. The second day you're there, you might do something that's different from how it's always been done, and the third day, you might not recruit a kid that a donor thought you should have signed. Before the first year is over, you're going to have to turn down a speech or two. Those things pile up. It happens at every school, but the coach usually has some sense, some warning, when he's fallen out of favor. To this day, I have no idea what precipitated my firing from the University of Arkansas.

In hindsight, the only thing I might have done to prompt such an out-of-the-blue reaction was shoot a campaign commercial for North Carolina senatorial candidate Jesse Helms. Jesse had been an enormous help to me when I was at N.C. State. He got us coverage on local Raleigh television, and opened doors for me in the state that I would never have walked through otherwise. When he ran for the U.S. Senate in 1980, Jesse asked me to do an ad for him. I did, but when I got home, I felt uncomfortable. The politics of football is tough enough; injecting myself into a Senate race didn't seem to make a lot of sense. So I called Jesse and told him how uncomfortable I felt. He understood, and the ad never aired.

If a political ad for a North Carolina Senate race that never aired had anything to do with my dismissal at Arkansas, no one ever told me. Even today, the reason for my firing is one of the great unsolved mysteries of my life.

At the time, the news hit me like a brick. It was even a harder hammer blow when I saw the effect the news had on my family. None of us could believe it. Liz, our second daughter, who was a sophomore in high school, cried, and our son Kevin got mad at how unfair the system was. I couldn't blame either of them for those emotions. I felt the same way. I had been loyal and hardworking. I ran a clean program and had received seven consecutive bowl bids, attendance at our games was at an all-time high, and most of our athletes had graduated. If those things weren't enough, I didn't know what else to do. Being fired left me bitter, disappointed, angry, depressed, and questioning the goodness of mankind. It was a bad day all around.

I got home at one o'clock on Sunday afternoon, shared the sad news with my family, and then turned on the television to another shock: at three o'clock the networks broke the story that I had resigned as head coach at the University of Arkansas. I hadn't even called my other two children, my mother, or any of our friends before the story was broadcast to the world. The players were home for Christmas break, so I hadn't had a chance to speak to any of them, either. This really upset me. My whole world crashed down in only one afternoon.

The phone started ringing the second the news broke. Talking was the last thing I wanted to do. What was I supposed to say? "Yeah, I thought about it at mass this morning and decided to resign for no apparent reason." Or should I tell the truth: "I was fired without being given any reason." I wasn't comfortable with either comment, and I had long ago learned not to make any rash comments in the heat of emotion. I needed to calm down, get away, and contemplate my future in a rational way. That was tough given the way my afternoon had gone so far.

One of the only phone calls I took came from a man named Harvey Mackay. I'd met Harvey at a meeting where we had both been speakers. Once you meet Harvey you never forget him. When he was twenty-six years old, he started the Mackay Envelope Company, which he quickly grew into a multimillion-dollar business. But Harvey wasn't satisfied being a successful entrepreneur: he wanted to share his success secrets with everyone. So he wrote two **New York Times** number one bestsellers: **Swim With the Sharks Without Being Eaten Alive** and **Beware the Naked Man Who Offers You His Shirt**. Those books have now been translated into thirty-five languages and sold in eighty countries. According to the **Times,** they are among the top fifteen bestselling inspirational business books of all time. But he didn't stop with two bestsellers. Harvey went on to write four more books and a nationally syndicated weekly column on business. He also served as a director of Robert Redford's Sundance Institute, ran ten marathons, and was the number-one-ranked senior tennis player in Minnesota.

Harvey had a tremendously commanding presence. He was the kind of guy who could convince the Saudis to buy sand. We became as close as brothers. I respected him and loved him like a sibling, and he has been quoted as saying, "Never take any golf advice from Lou. However, if my son or daughters were to ask me to name one person to go to outside of their old man for any other kind of advice, I'd name Lou Holtz."

It took every ounce of salesmanship Harvey could muster to convince me to do what he proposed. He had just seen news of my resignation, and wanted me to come to the University of Minnesota.

The only thing I knew about the state of Minnesota was that every time I looked at the back page of **USA Today,** the temperature there was in the single digits or teens, sometimes above zero, and sometimes below. I wasn't happy when the temperature in Arkansas dipped below fifty. Minnesota might as well have been the North Pole. In addition, I knew that the University of Minnesota football program was in chaos. They had lost seventeen of eighteen games by an average score of 47–13. The school was without a head coach not because it was taking its time and being choosy, but because the five people it had offered the job to had all turned it down.

Harvey was helping the school's athletic director, Paul Giel, who was recovering from heart bypass surgery. "I would love for you to come up and talk to us," Harvey said.

Had it been anyone other than Harvey Mackay, I would probably have politely declined while thinking to myself, "What, are you nuts?" However, I remembered that in 1960 Minnesota had won the national championship. I was a graduate assistant at Iowa at the time, and Minnesota had handed us our only loss of the season. Plus, I knew that Harvey wouldn't accept no for an answer.

I wasn't excited by the idea of flying to Minnesota, but I had to get out of Arkansas. The last thing I needed was a crowd of reporters hanging out in my yard wanting interviews. I told Harvey I'd see him soon, and called the airlines to book four tickets from Tulsa to Minneapolis for the following day. Perhaps auspiciously, I was first informed the flight was sold out, but before I could hang up, the flight had a cancellation of four seats.

I still felt terrible. I had accumulated a 60–21–2 record, and had been let go. It was a low moment in my head-coaching career, one that had me questioning the choices I'd made. Minnesota was a fine school, and Harvey Mackay was a fantastic fellow, but that didn't soften the sting of my situation. To add a final element of insult to my injury, snow fell hard between Fayetteville and Tulsa. With the car slipping and sliding on the highway, I decided to turn around, go home, and forget about the trip.

"No," Beth said. "We're more than halfway to the airport, and the snow is easing up. Plus, there's nothing waiting for us back home."

She was right. Our days in Arkansas were over. We might as well spend a couple of days in Minnesota.

Harvey met us at the airport and gave us the presidential tour. We went to the hospital and met with Paul Giel, one of the all-time great players in Minnesota history. Harvey never showed me the campus or the facilities, but I did meet many of the most powerful CEOs in the state, and they assured me I would have all the support I needed to build a winning program. I didn't realize it until later, but Harvey never let me set foot outside. Everywhere we visited had a covered garage and enclosed walkways between buildings. It was December, and I had no idea how cold it was. Harvey knew that if I took one step outdoors, I would no longer be a candidate.

Paul Giel offered me the job from his hospital bed. I wasn't ready to say yes, but I didn't want to say no. I didn't have a job, and I didn't want to go home and start searching for one. So I asked for a little time to discuss it with Beth and the children.

This wasn't an excuse. Family decisions required the entire family. A decision as big as

moving to Minnesota required input from everyone. Harvey took us to our hotel, where he had
booked a three-bedroom suite. We sat in the living area and talked about what we had seen. Not
much came out of our initial discussions. I think
Liz and Kevin were still shell-shocked from the
events of the previous twenty-four hours. I can't
say I blame them. We had gone from a stable situation on Saturday, when I had spent the weekend
interviewing John Gutekunst to come to Arkansas as my new defensive coordinator, to sitting in
a Minneapolis hotel suite wondering if this would
be our new home.

"I think we all need to go into separate rooms
and pray about this," I finally said. "This is a big
decision. We need to reflect on it. We're not going
to talk for at least thirty minutes. During that
time, I want everyone to ask God what He thinks.
After that, we'll meet again in this room."

Everyone agreed, and each of us went into a
separate room and prayed. The suite was silent as
a rectory. We took our time, praying, reflecting,
and trying to come to grips with where we were
and where the Good Lord wanted to take us.
When we came out thirty minutes later, the suite
took on a different atmosphere. Everyone was at
peace with the decision to move to Minnesota.

It was during that prayer session with my wife
and two of our children that I felt moved to come
to Minnesota. But I was moved in another direc-

tion as well. Something in that afternoon meditation led me to insist on a clause in my contract, an unprecedented request, one I thought might be a deal breaker, but one I knew I had to have before I could accept the job. It was a simple paragraph in a lengthy legal document that became known informally as the "Notre Dame Clause."

I had no reason to believe that Notre Dame would ever try to hire me except that Gene Corrigan, the former athletic director at the University of Virginia, was now the athletic director at Notre Dame, and he had tried to hire me three different times. I felt that if we were successful at the University of Minnesota, and if Notre Dame was looking for a coach, I would be a strong candidate.

The clause was short and direct: If Minnesota accepted a bowl bid during my tenure, and I was contacted and offered the job as head coach at the University of Notre Dame, I was free to terminate my contract with Minnesota. The logic behind the wording of the clause was that if we made it to a bowl game, my staff and I would have turned the program around. The university would then have little difficulty hiring a very capable coach to replace me. When you've lost seventeen of eighteen games by an average margin of thirty points, you're going to have trouble hiring a coach, as Minnesota had had with the five coaches who had turned them down. But a bowl team was a winning team, which meant recruiting would be easier, the talent level above average, and the attitude positive. Replacing the head coach in that situation would not be as tough.

As for the second provision, I would never initiate contact with Notre Dame even if the job became vacant. Notre Dame had to contact me. I could not pursue it. Notre Dame had a coach in place, a fine man named Gerry Faust, and there was no indication he would not be successful. However, if the situation at Notre Dame changed and the school contacted me, I didn't want any hard feelings if I made the move.

Notre Dame was the Catholic college of America, and I, like many practicing Catholics, felt as though it was the one institution where I could coach and still express my faith without the ACLU calling the president of the school and lodging a complaint. I was taught by the sisters of Notre Dame, and every day at recess, noon, and dismissal, we marched out to the Notre Dame victory march. Every time the job opened up at Notre Dame (which wasn't very often), I wished somebody from the university would call me. I'd be on the road, and call Beth and ask, "Did they call today? Did anybody call?" I didn't know it at the time, but Moose Krause, the former athletic director, and a man known around campus as "Mr. Notre Dame," had lobbied on my behalf in 1980 when Dan Devine retired. Moose had heard and read about the suspensions before the 1978 Orange Bowl, and he liked the attitude I brought to the Arkansas program. In the end, the university hired Gerry Faust, one of the most successful high school coaches in the country, and a fine individual. At the time I was happy for Gerry, but I must admit, I was a little envious. I considered the head-coaching position at Notre Dame to be the best job in the world because of what it stood for in terms of values and ethics.

The administration of Minnesota wasn't thrilled when I broached the subject of the Notre Dame Clause. They felt that I was taking the job at Minnesota with my sights already set on another job. I explained that this wasn't the case at all. In order for the clause to become effective, Minnesota had to go to a bowl game. If I wasn't focused on Minnesota football, the clause was moot because we couldn't win. Second, the Irish had a coach, and Minnesota did not. If they would accept my one unusual condition, the Golden Gophers would have a coach as well.

At the time, the prospects of Minnesota going to a bowl seemed so remote that the risk of the clause seemed worth it to the administration. Plus, they didn't have anybody else. If I turned them down, they would be zero-for-six in their hiring efforts. After some deliberation and soul-searching of their own, Minnesota agreed to the

Notre Dame Clause, and we came to terms. For the 1984 season, I would be the new head football coach at the University of Minnesota.

Had it not been for the bad things that happened to my family and me on that Sunday afternoon in Arkansas, I would never have gotten the call from Harvey Mackay; never gone to Minnesota; never had that afternoon prayer session with my family; and never been led to include the Notre Dame Clause in my contract with the University of Minnesota. I would never have had the opportunity to accomplish the things we did in Minnesota, and probably would not have been in a position to spend a successful eleven seasons at the University of Notre Dame.

If I had been given the gift of seeing the future, I might have hugged Frank Broyles the day he asked for my resignation. The fact that I considered it a low point of my head-coaching career proves the point: You never know when bad things are intended to lead you in good directions.

Of course, I arrived in Minnesota with no more knowledge of the future than I'd had when I left Arkansas. All I knew at the time was that we had a lot of work ahead of us. We had more than twenty athletes who had played the previous season who were ineligible because of academics. We had forty-seven players on scholarship and had every problem known to man. Academics ranged from being a low priority to being a joke among the players. Their work habits more closely resembled those of a prison chain gang than of a disciplined football team. There was racial strife, a lack of trust among the players, and little respect for coaches. The athletes expected to lose, because that was what they had always done.

They were defeated, cynical, and completely undisciplined. The fact that I was the head coach had little effect on their attitude toward authority. After giving them a reasonable adjustment period to realize we were committed to building a winner, I laid down the law. If they weren't there to graduate and win, they should quit. Their choice was to either change their attitude and behavior or change their mailing addresses.

Most of the players responded positively to the changes. Minnesotans are a hardworking people by nature. They also love football. The fact that the state university football program had fallen so low disheartened many good people in the state, so when I came in and insisted that the program become more disciplined and hardworking, I had lots of support in the community and on the team. Players like Peter Nigerian, an excellent linebacker whose father was one of the most successful transplant surgeons in the country, encouraged others to believe. But we needed more.

I met with Harvey Mackay and a local sports editor named Sid Hartman every night. We would

toss around ideas on how to generate more interest and enthusiasm for the program. Our first
accomplishment was agreeing to play all our home
games in the Metrodome. This decision was controversial, but we were able to persuade people
that it was the only logical course of action. The
university stadium needed extensive repairs and
modifications, and a cost-benefit analysis showed
that it was cheaper to lease the dome than to fully
renovate the stadium. I also made personal pleas
to the community. "We need the help and support of anyone who has ever picked up a snow
shovel."

That one comment sparked an outpouring of
enthusiastic support from within the state. People
in Minnesota were eager to get involved and contribute to the success of our program. All they
needed was an invitation to help, which I extended
to them. If we were to build a winning program,
it was critical that we entice the high school athletes to remain in-state. Over the previous several
years good athletes from Minnesota had signed to
play for Iowa, Nebraska, Wisconsin, and others.
I appeared on statewide television and implored
all our high school prospects to attend the University of Minnesota. I also asked their families
to encourage their sons to do so. "The heart and
soul of our team must come from Minnesota," I
said. I then looked into the camera and said, "But

you do realize the arms and legs must come from elsewhere. It is hard to run in snowshoes."

For the next two years, we signed every prospect in the state except one.

To give people a reason to come out and support the program, I split the spring team into two squads, and named those squads "Minneapolis" and "St. Paul." The university had averaged twenty-eight thousands fans in attendance at home games the year before. For the spring game between Minneapolis and St. Paul, we had more than forty thousand attendees.

Fan support was crucial, but fans didn't play the games. For that we needed good athletes, solid coaches, and a new attitude at every level of the program. I brought in many of the coaches who had been with me at Arkansas. Frank Broyles didn't fire my assistants when he fired me, but new coaches have a tendency to release more assistants than they keep. I had no problem convincing Pete Cordelli, Jim Strong, and George Stewart to follow me to Minnesota.

George was a great story. He had been an All-American for us at Arkansas, and had been drafted by the Kansas City Chiefs. He went to the NFL a few credits shy of graduation, which didn't make his mother happy. When George injured his knee, left football, and began selling cars, his mother phoned me and said, "You promised me that George would graduate. He hasn't, and now he's selling cars."

I said, "You're right." So I called George and said, "George, I promised your mother you were going to get your degree, and that's exactly what you're going to do. I want you to come up here, go back to school, and work for me as a student coach."

My call caught George by surprise. He said, "Coach, I appreciate the offer, but I'm very happy selling cars and making a lot of money."

I informed him that he wouldn't be happy if I called his mother and told her he had turned me down. "You're coming back to finish your degree," I said. "If you want to sell cars after that, fine."

This was not a request, and George knew it. George loved his mother, and I did too. She was a great woman who had raised a first-class son. Not only did George come back to Arkansas and get his degree, but he was a natural as a coach. I put him on staff after he finished school and hired him the minute I got to Minnesota.

On the first day of spring practice, I set the tone by going berserk when the offensive unit meandered into their huddle. Some players had their hands on their knees, while others cocked their hips and put their hands on their sides as if they were waiting in the popcorn line at the theater. When the huddle broke, the players clapped sporadically. It sounded like a group of misfiring cap guns.

"Hold it!" I yelled, charging out into the middle of things. "That's not the way we do it."

They had no idea what I was talking about, so the coaching staff and I explained how they were to stand in the huddle, how far apart they were to keep their feet, where they were to be looking, and where they were to hold their hands. When the huddle broke, they were to clap authoritatively and in unison. After the play, they were to run back to the huddle. There would be no loping or wandering around the field in a slow stroll. If you had somewhere to be, you were to get there in a hurry. If you didn't have somewhere to be, you needed to get off the field. I informed them that we might not be able to block and tackle, but we would be the best-looking team in the country until the ball was snapped.

In 1981, when I was at Arkansas, we played Texas, the number one team in the country. At halftime we were ahead 42–3, and we won the game decisively. The next day, I was watching film of the game when Roy Kidd, the very successful coach of Eastern Kentucky, called. He said, "Coach, tell me about your huddle and how you coach it."

I explained why and how we taught our huddle. He thanked me and prepared to hang up.

"Aren't you interested in our offense and defense?" I asked.

He said, "No, I saw your game on television. The thing that impressed me most was your huddle."

In Minnesota, that huddle took a lot of work. The second play of that first spring practice the huddle still looked like hooligans gathered on a street corner. When practice was over, I kept the offense out, and for thirty minutes we practiced it further. After that our huddles improved.

A lot of people questioned my obsession with something they considered minor. Certainly the team had more serious deficiencies. But execution is about paying attention to details. If a team looks sloppy in the huddle, it will look sloppy during the play. If players are unruly on the sidelines, they will be undisciplined on the field. We set standards in that spring practice that many of those athletes had never seen before. Those who responded positively made up the nucleus of our 1984 team.

Once we found our core upperclassmen, we filled out the team with quality recruits such as Ricky Fogge, a quarterback out of North Carolina, and Gary Couch, a running back out of Iowa. We also convinced the university and the boosters to build an indoor practice facility and upgrade the quality of the weight-training room. Once everyone saw the commitment from the university, fans, coaches, and players, enthusiasm snowballed.

We didn't have any superstars at Minnesota, but we won four games in 1984 with athletes who believed in hard work, discipline, attitude, and execution, proving again that anything is possible when you have enough support. We lost to Nebraska 31–6 in Lincoln. Our fans were encouraged because the previous year they had beaten Minnesota 84–13 at our place. We upset nationally ranked Wisconsin in Madison on national television. This game gave us possession of "Paul Bunyan's Axe," which goes to the winner. We played Michigan tough, but they won and kept the "Little Brown Jug." In our last game of the year, we defeated a nationally ranked University of Iowa football team and claimed the pig trophy "Floyd of Rosedale." No one doubted that we were moving in the right direction. We had won two of the three rivalry games we played annually and had the ax and the pig in our trophy case.

In the off-season, Dr. Kenneth Keller, interim president of the university, asked for a meeting. He wanted the Notre Dame Clause expunged from my contract. After our first year, going to a bowl game no longer seemed such a far-fetched notion. Plus, Gerry Faust, for all his great qualities, was struggling at Notre Dame. His contract was up at the end of the 1985 season, and while no one in South Bend would say so officially, it looked as though he would need to have a good season. I felt he would; obviously, the administration at the University of Minnesota didn't share my sentiments. The perfect storm of provisions in my Notre Dame Clause appeared to be lining up. Dr. Keller said, "We have a proposal to get rid of the Notre Dame Clause. We are willing to give you a lifetime contract, and make you athletic director if you'll take that clause out."

This was an appealing offer. I had been at Minnesota only one year. Moving again wasn't high on my priority list. Plus, I loved the people of Minnesota and was thrilled by the progress we were making. The entire state got behind us, which was proof of my theory that if enough people care, anything is possible. I wanted to be fair to my friends and the people who supported me, so I told Dr. Keller that I would take the Notre Dame Clause out of my contract if he made me associate athletic director. Paul Giel was the athletic director, and I felt that this offer might push Paul out of a job. That was the last thing I wanted. But if I could be associate athletic director, taking some of the burden off of Paul but leaving him in the role of athletic director, free to attend to all the public relations aspects of the job, then I would agree to remove the Notre Dame Clause. My only stipulation was that the deal had to be agreed to by Paul. I had great respect for him, and with his heart condition, I felt I might be doing him a favor by taking on some of the responsibilities.

These negotiations occurred during July 1985. It was my understanding that Paul agreed, but something went wrong. Dr. Keller said, "I can't put this together at this time."

I said, "No problem. You approached me. I didn't approach you."

In 1985, our second year, we won a good number of games, beating Purdue badly. We had them down 42–7 at halftime and cruised to a lopsided win. This came one week after Purdue had beaten Notre Dame in the Hoosier Dome. We beat Wisconsin again to retain the ax, and barely lost to Oklahoma, where we were down by five points with a first-and-ten on their twelve-yard line with two minutes to play but couldn't find a way to score. Oklahoma won by five, went on to finish the year undefeated, and won the national championship. The following week, Oklahoma called and canceled our 1986 game with them.

That's when Dr. Keller called to set up a meeting. He wanted to revisit the Notre Dame Clause a second time. Rumors swirled that Gerry Faust might not be retained, and television commentators were openly talking about my Notre Dame Clause at Minnesota. By 1985, ESPN had grown from a curious little cable channel in Connecticut that showed Australian Rules Football and motorcross racing to a big-time sports/news out-let. The anchors of **SportsCenter,** the network's most watched show, speculated that I would be contacted by Notre Dame the minute the season ended.

I never got to talk to Dr. Keller. He had some-one else in his office at eleven o'clock when I arrived on time for my appointment. At eleven forty-five I told his secretary that I had to leave. Our game with Ohio State was to be televised nationally, and I had a twelve o'clock meeting with Keith Jackson, the ABC commentator for the game. I left and was halfway back to my office when an out-of-breath Dr. Keller caught up to me and said, "What do we have to do to get rid of that Notre Dame Clause?"

At that point, I put my hand on his shoulder and said, "There are some things that are meant to be, and some things that aren't meant to be. Let's just let nature take its course."

I wasn't being coy. I truly believed that this situation had happened for a reason, just as my epiphany to include the Notre Dame Clause in the first place had been for a reason, and my being forced out at Arkansas had been for a reason. I had done everything I could to turn Minnesota into a winning football program. If things worked out and I stayed at Minnesota for ten or fifteen years, I would be very happy. If Minnesota accepted a bowl bid and I got a call to talk to the University of Notre Dame, I would also be happy. I had done all I could do in my capacity as a coach. Everything else was up to a higher power.

We lost a close game to Ohio State on a blown call and then lost our final game of the year against a very good Iowa football team to finish with a record of 6–5. Despite the latter loss, two representatives from the Independence Bowl in Shreveport, Louisiana, approached me in the locker room and offered us a berth in their game on December 31 against an as-yet-unnamed ACC opponent.

Paul Giel was in the locker room when this happened. I said, "What do you think."

"We have to take it," he said.

"Paul, you know that if we accept this bid, the Notre Dame Clause goes into effect."

He was quiet for a couple of seconds. Then he said, "I know, but this is too important to the program. Tell them we would be honored to play in the Independence Bowl."

We accepted the offer, and told our team that they would be playing in a bowl game. The locker room erupted in cheers. It was a great way to off-set the negative feelings that came with losing the final game of the regular season.

Two days later, I flew to Shreveport for the press conference at the Independence Bowl. Clemson would be our opponent. Ironically, this was the same team Coach Hayes had played in the Gator Bowl when he lost his poise, hit the athlete (sparking a bench-clearing brawl), and was fired from Ohio State. I couldn't have been more excited about our opponent, our opportunity, and our venue. My daughter Luanne and her husband lived in Shreveport, so this would be a great holiday for the Holtz family. Plus, our recruiting efforts were already under way at Minnesota, and it looked as if we would have a great incoming freshman class. Throw in the fact that we had sold out every home game for the 1986 season with season tickets, and it was easy to conclude that Minnesota football was on the way up.

Then, a week after I got home from Shreveport, the phone rang at 11 A.M. When I answered, I heard a voice I recognized.

"Lou Holtz, this is Father Joyce from Notre Dame." He was vice president of Notre Dame in charge of athletics, and he had called me on the recommendation of Gene Corrigan, the athletic director at Notre Dame. Father Edmund Joyce and Father Theodore Hesburgh, the president of the university, had been ordained together, were the closest of friends, and had ruled Notre Dame for thirty-five years; now they are legends.

Father Joyce said, "We would like to talk with you about becoming the next head football coach at the University of Notre Dame."

Examining the convergence of events that made this moment possible led me to only one logical conclusion: It's critical to have goals in life, and to work as hard as you can to achieve those goals, but in the end, the Lord works in mysterious ways.

Hard times will come. They always do. But when it happens, remember that deep faith, hard work, and an unwavering commitment to your goals will turn today's tragedy into tomorrow's triumphs.

11

GETTING RID OF EXCUSES

On the field at Notre Dame. Notre Dame was not a place you attended to learn to do something; it was a place you attended to learn to be somebody.

If I didn't already understand the strict standards at the University of Notre Dame, I got a quick lesson in my first conversation with Father Joyce. After he offered me the job as head coach, he said: "Before you accept, there are a few things you need to consider. We have certain rules that might not apply at other universities, but that are nonnegotiable here at Notre Dame. First, we will not redshirt an athlete, and we will not accept a transfer from another school or junior college. The head football coach has nothing to do with admissions. In order for a student-athlete to be accepted at Notre Dame, he will have to have good college boards and solid grades with at least sixteen core curriculum credits. Our athletes live in the dorms on campus, and come under the sole jurisdiction of the dorm rector. Also, you will never be able to talk to a professor about a student's academics. That is the job of the academic counseling office. Do you understand?"

"I do," I said. This came as no surprise: I knew that the standards at Notre Dame were high and the rules were rigid; still, to hear them laid out in such cut-and-dried detail made me realize what an exacting and different place the university really was.

"That's not all," Father Joyce said. "We will always play a difficult schedule, the most difficult we can find. And we expect to win. Your players will miss or be late for practice if it conflicts with classes or labs. And finally, the head football coach will never make more than the president of the university."

I gulped at that last one. The president of Notre Dame, Father Hesburgh, was a priest who had taken a vow of poverty.

"If you can accept those terms, we would love to have you join us at the University of Notre Dame," he said.

I could certainly accept the terms. In fact, I looked forward to working in an environment where the rules were that clear and nonnegotiable. Father Joyce was right: the things he had outlined did not apply at many other universities, but very few universities could compare with Notre Dame. The rules he had just outlined were based on Christian teachings, Church doctrine, and standards of conduct that made Notre Dame one of the most highly respected institutions in the world. Notre Dame was not a place you attended to learn to do something; it was a place you attended to learn to be somebody. The rules reflected that. I couldn't wait to get there. In addition, he did not mention a single thing that would keep us from winning. He didn't say we must play with only eight players while the opponent could use eleven.

But I had to talk things over with my family. As much as I had always wanted to be the head football coach at Notre Dame, I still had a daughter in high school and a son who had enrolled at the University of Minnesota at our insistence. Kevin had been a diabetic since age fifteen, and had to take insulin injections four times a day. We wanted him at Minnesota so we could be close in case he needed our help. We had to make sure he was mature enough to handle his own medical needs. Plus, accepting the job at Notre Dame meant moving a second time in just over two years. I had to make sure the family agreed to all of this before I accepted. I knew Skip would be excited, because he was a junior at Notre Dame.

Father Joyce understood completely. Notre Dame had one more game against Miami, and even though they were not going to renew Gerry Faust's contract, they were in no rush to make any announcements. I took the call from Father Joyce on Monday morning, and promised to call him back on Tuesday.

I could never have expected the kind of reaction I got at home. Liz was thrilled. Not only did she insist that I take the job, she said she couldn't wait to finish her senior year of high school in South Bend. Beth was equally ecstatic. She knew this had been my lifelong dream, and she was overjoyed that it had finally come true. Kevin assured his mother and me that he would be fine, and that he could indeed handle his own health-care needs. With the decision made, I went back to the bedroom to make some notes about things I needed to do and people I needed to call.

A few minutes later, the phone rang. It was Dr. Mike Magee, the athletic director from the University of Southern California. He told me that there might be a vacancy at USC, and if that did occur, he would like for me to be Southern Cal's new head coach. Before I could answer, Dr. Magee went into a long speech on the advantages of Southern Cal over Notre Dame, telling me why I would be better off in California than South Bend. This struck me as funny, since I was the head coach at Minnesota, and nobody outside my family knew that I had even spoken to anyone at Notre Dame.

"Dr. Magee, why would you think Notre Dame would consider me?" I asked.

"You're the logical choice," he said.

I gave no hint that I had already decided to accept the job. "Thank you, Dr. Magee," I said, "but I'm under contract with the University of Minnesota. There is only one school I'm free to talk to, and that school will remain nameless."

In the morning, I told Paul Giel that I would accept the job at Notre Dame. He was disappointed but not surprised. That was not the general reaction throughout Minnesota when the news became public. Everyone in the state who read a newspaper or cared about football did not know the requirements of my Notre Dame Clause and they felt I had left Minnesota for selfish reasons. It angered most Minnesotans that I was leaving for South Bend.

Paul and I agreed that I should not coach the team in the Independence Bowl. This is fairly standard when a coaching change is made before a bowl game. High school seniors begin signing commitment letters the first week of January, which is why you see so many college coaching changes prior to the New Year's Day bowl games. Schools want to have their head coach in place prior to "commitment date." Minnesota was no different. My defensive coordinator, John Gutekunst, would take over as head coach. I had great respect for John and knew that he would do an outstanding job, and in fact the University of Minnesota would win a 20–13 victory over Clemson on New Year's Eve.

I knew it was best for me to leave the scene with as little fanfare as possible. The only problem was that Father Joyce had asked that we keep the news confidential, since Gerry Faust had one more game to coach in Miami. The press confer-

ence announcing the change would come the following Monday. We needed to keep the secret for
six days.

That plan lasted less than eight hours. Before
the close of business on Tuesday, Father Joyce
called me back. "Too many people are speculating
about who the new coach will be." The announce-
ment that Coach Faust's contract would not be
renewed occurred one hour before Father Joyce
called me and offered me the job. He added, "We
need to move the press conference up."

I understood Father Joyce's predicament. He
wanted to respect the tenure and authority of his
head coach, but he couldn't lie to members of
the media who were questioning him concerning
Gerry Faust's replacement. In addition, alums
were starting to argue over who they thought the
new coach should be.

"When would you like for me to be there?" I
asked.

"Tomorrow," he said.

Beth, Liz, Kevin, and I flew to South Bend on
Wednesday, one day after I had formally accepted
Father Joyce's offer, for my first press conference
as the incoming head coach at Notre Dame. Skip
joined us up there.

The press had a lot of questions. I tried to
be thorough and honest in my answers, and
lighten the room with a little humor. At one
point I said, "What I want to do is function as the

head coach in a quiet, nonconfrontational manner." That sparked a good deal of laughter. I also said, "My mother is extremely happy these days. She believes that once you go to Notre Dame, you're in heaven." When asked if I saw myself as the model coach for this university, I said, "Just look at me: I'm five foot ten, a hundred fifty-two pounds. I wear glasses, speak with a lisp, and have a physique that makes it appear I've been afflicted with scurvy most of my life. I ranked low in my graduating class of two seventy-eight coming out of high school. And here I am, a head football coach at Notre Dame."

I became deadly serious when the subject turned to the man I was replacing. "I only hope I can display the same type of character and integrity that Gerry Faust has in the last five years," I said. "I don't think I can recall an individual who has handled himself better in all situations or been a more positive influence in bringing optimism to people who are down and depressed. I don't think we in this room or Gerry himself realize how many lives he has touched."

When I first met Gerry Faust, I thought he had to be a phony. My instinct told me that nobody could be that nice, upbeat, and considerate all the time. He had to be putting us on. The more I got to know him, the more it became clear that Gerry was, indeed, one of the most positive, kind, considerate, and energetic people you will ever meet.

He simply was put in a tough situation. He had come from one of the most successful high school programs in the country directly into the pressure cooker of major-college football at Notre Dame. I felt terrible that Gerry's career at Notre Dame was ending the way it was, and I wanted everyone to know what a true gentleman I felt I was replacing.

Then I turned my attention to the future. "I'm not a prognosticator," I said. "I wanted to buy one of the first Edsels that came on the market, and you see how well that worked out. So I can't really tell what the future holds."

I had no more insight into the future than anyone else, but I had a pretty good idea what was going to happen during the upcoming Notre Dame–Miami game. Gerry Faust had been through a tough week. I knew it would be hard to get those athletes to overcome the distractions and focus on the game. I hoped I was wrong. I hoped the team would respond positively and give Gerry a victory as a going-away present. But Miami was a powerhouse. The score ended up being 58–7.

I watched the game in Palm Springs, at the home of Mr. Don Knutson, a loyal Minnesota alumni who was disappointed that I was leaving his school, but happy for Beth and me. I was also joined by a reporter from **Sports Illustrated** who had asked to sit with me to chronicle my reaction to the team I was inheriting. What I felt was disappointment for Gerry Faust. It's hard to get a team motivated when the players know you're not going to be there the next day. I learned that myself when I announced my retirement a week before the final game of the 1996 season at Notre Dame, and again in 2002 when I retired from South Carolina in the penultimate week of the season. In both those instances, our teams didn't perform well in the final game of the season. It's a fact of life: teams lose focus when they know their coach is leaving. Some of the underclassmen are debating whether or not they want to stay at the school after "their" coach leaves, while others get caught up in the speculation about who's going to replace their outgoing coach. Many of the assistant coaches wonder if they're going to have jobs after the season, so their focus isn't totally on the game at hand. It's a natural, time-tested reaction. Players might want to "win one for the outgoing coach," but it's hard to get their minds completely committed to the task with so many distractions in the works. I should have expected my Notre Dame and South Carolina teams to lose after I announced my retirement from those schools. I'd seen the same thing happen that afternoon with Gerry. But I guess it was one of those lessons you have to learn through experience.

That afternoon, as I watched the Hurricanes roll over the Irish, my disappointment grew to anger, and my anger to resolve. I didn't feel that this Notre Dame football team played with the kind of urgency the situation warranted. It became obvious that my first job at Notre Dame was to recruit the players we already had.

Monday morning, I arrived in South Bend and got to work. The team sat in the meeting room, kicked back. I could tell they were either feeling sorry for themselves after their big loss, or taking a lackadaisical attitude toward my arrival. Both were unacceptable.

"Sit up, gentlemen!" My tone wasn't quite a shout, but I got their attention.

Junior quarterback Steve Beuerlein looked stunned. He turned around and made eye contact with wide receiver Tim Brown. Both young men had "what's this all about?" expressions on their faces.

One of the players who didn't respond was center Chuck Lanza, a great young man who would go on to be an All-American and our team captain. He had his feet propped up, and was examining his fingernails. I stepped toward Chuck and said, "Young man, how long have you been playing football?"

He looked up and said, "I don't know...ten, eleven years."

"Well, if you ever want to play another down, you will put your feet on the floor, sit up straight, and pay attention."

Then I addressed the entire team. "That goes for every man in this room. I want you to sit up straight, put your feet on the floor, keep your heads up, your eyes forward, and get ready to talk about winning football games. As a team, we have two purposes for having meetings: one is to gather information, and the second is to disseminate information. While I'm not a particularly good speaker, I do expect your full, undivided attention for the duration of any meeting we might have."

I could tell that it had been a while since these players had been talked to like this, if they ever had. But I had to make a statement early. The only player in the room who knew me at all was a junior fourth-string flanker named Skip Holtz, whose mother happened to be my wife. The rest of those athletes knew of me—some might even have seen me telling jokes and doing magic tricks on television—but they had no relationship with me, and no idea what to expect. It was important that I set the tone of my relationship with the team from the outset. I cared about each of them deeply, but I was not going to be their friend. I wasn't going to hang out and joke with them; I was going to be their coach. I would love them and treat them fairly, but I would also keep a professional distance. I would be there for them when they needed me, but as an authority figure, not as a pal. This team needed to know that there was a plan, **my** plan, and they could either get on board, or get off. Either way, the plan was going ahead with or without them.

After he'd hired me, Father Hesburgh had said, "Lou, I can name you the head coach, but I can't name you the leader. Titles come from above. Leaders are selected by those under you. They will follow you if you have a vision and a plan."

"I know you did not select me to be your football coach," I said to the players. "In fact, if you had any say in the matter, I would be the last person you would select as your coach. That's not important. What is important is that I selected you. I came here because of you. I want all of you to know that I did not come here to try to change Notre Dame, and Notre Dame did not bring me here to try to change me. This institution will not compromise, and neither will I.

"The standard has been set for us at Notre Dame by Knute Rockne, Moose Krause, Ara Parseghian, Frank Leahy, Dan Devine, and all the other fine coaches and athletes who preceded you and me here. That standard is: We are going to play the best, and be committed to being the best we can be. We are going to do it the right way, with honesty, integrity, class, and togetherness, not only within the letter of the law, but in the spirit of the law as well."

I had their attention, so I talked about the direction we would be heading in the upcoming year, and what was expected out of each and every one of them. We would set the bar high. And I let them know, in no uncertain terms, that we would accept no excuses. The time for making excuses was over. The time to become a team, and perform as a team, had begun.

"I ask each of you to follow three basic rules: Do what is right. Do your very best. Treat others like you'd like to be treated. Those rules answer the three basic questions I'm going to ask of each of you, and I expect you to ask me and the other coaches. The questions are: Can I trust you? Are you committed? And do you care about me? This is what I believe and what I practice.

"These three rules are all you need, whether you are a coach, a player, a parent, a child, an employer, or an employee. Everyone you meet asks three questions mentally: Can I trust you? Are you committed to excellence? Do you care about me? The three rules answer these three questions positively. If you can trust someone, know he is committed to excellence, and cares about you, hug him and never let him go, because he is a winner. It would behoove you to remember that these are the same three questions everyone asks about you. For this reason, it is imperative that you always follow these three rules also.

"We're not going to win football games because I'm here any more than someone can fix a flat tire by changing the person driving the car. If we're going to be successful, we have to get rid of excuses for why we can't win."

Then I handed out the questionnaires. No one was ready for the type of test I gave out. It included such questions as "What does Notre Dame mean to you?" and "What are your most important goals in life?" and "What do you hope others will say about you when you're gone?" and "Name the five most important relationships in your life, and explain why." These were not multiple-choice questions. I expected student-athletes at Notre Dame to be able to compose essay answers. I also expected them to put a lot of thought into what they wrote. This was their first opportunity to make an impression on their new coach. I hoped they would take full advantage.

What I didn't expect was essays that required a desktop dictionary to read. This group might not have mastered the play-action pass, but they had a good command of the English language. I read through each of those essays to get a sense of where these players were in their maturity as human beings, and how disciplined they were in their goal setting.

From the outset I emphasized to each athlete the importance of setting lofty goals and developing a detailed plan to reach those goals. For the Notre Dame football team, the goals were to return the program to its former glory, and be in the hunt for a national championship as soon as possible. To get there, we had to get better in a lot of areas, none more so than the team's conditioning.

In my first week as the head coach, I instituted a rigorous winter workout program that began every morning at six. Most of the drills were agility and conditioning related. We broke the players down into small groups and set up different stations. One minute we had them high-stepping over dummies; at another station they bear-crawled on a wrestling mat; at another they zigzagged back and forth through some ropes; at another they ran in place, dropped to the ground, and rolled on command. Every station was run at maximum speed, and each group ran between stations. Running back Mark Green, who went on to a successful NFL career, called it the toughest thing he'd ever done in football, including the pros. Within a week, the players had nicknamed the winter workout "the pukefest."

I agree it was tough. In fact, I told them from the beginning that it was the toughest winter program I had ever put a team through. (I might have exaggerated a little in that claim: I'd had some equally tough ones at other schools.) Throughout the winter, I emphasized that if they made it through this workout, they were a very special group. I wanted those athletes to start believing in themselves again. I also believed that if a person was forced to pay a very dear price to be part of an organization, he would be more apt to cherish and defend that organization.

Our winter program had to be difficult because of the work ethic I knew it was going to take to succeed. I wasn't trying to punish the athletes, but I did want them to know that success came at a price. The athletes got up in the dark, in the cold winter South Bend mornings, and walked, often in the snow, to the training facility for six o'clock workouts. We were done by seven thirty, and they were exhausted. Then they had to go to class.

I didn't expect all of the athletes to make it through the winter. Others would be weeded out in the spring. What I did expect was to enter the summer with a core group of committed athletes who would be ready to do whatever it took to play Notre Dame football.

Among those athletes I had to test early was our quarterback, Steve Beuerlein. In my first meeting with Steve I said, "You had a tough junior year."

He said, "Yes, sir, I went through some injuries. But I'm ready to go now."

I knew about the injuries he'd suffered. I also knew that he had a tendency to get tunnel vision during pass plays, falling in love with a single receiver, and throwing a lot more interceptions than the team could afford. "You also have a tendency to throw a lot of passes to the other team," I said. "Well, I can guarantee you one thing: you won't throw more than seven interceptions next year."

Steve's eyes got big. He said, "Wow, Coach, that's great. How are we going to do that? Do you have a special way of reading coverages?"

I shook my head. "No," I said. "Once you throw the sixth interception, you aren't going to play. We can't win if the quarterback doesn't protect the football."

Beuerlein would end up being drafted by the Chicago Bears, and would go on to have a successful career as an NFL quarterback. He rarely tells football stories these days when this story doesn't come up. Steve laughs about it now, but at the time, he felt a lot of pressure. That was exactly what I had hoped he would feel. I knew that if I didn't put a lot of pressure on these players to perform, they would be unprepared and unable to handle the pressures of a big game.

I also felt responsible for preparing them for the enormous pressures that awaited them once they left the University of Notre Dame. My job was to build men of character. A Notre Dame man does not lose that title when he leaves the university. Notre Dame men are ambassadors for the university for the rest of their lives. We had to prepare these players to carry on the legacy of

Notre Dame football long after they left the campus. To do that, we had to educate them through hard work, demanding standards, and tough discipline. It would have been easier to take an anything-goes approach, but that was not what I had been hired to do, and not what was expected at Notre Dame.

It is always critical to hire an excellent staff, but even more so at Notre Dame. With the challenges that lay ahead, including a difficult schedule, I needed assistant coaches that understood Notre Dame, who were great teachers, and who wanted to be there. Notre Dame, for all its successes in the past, was one of the poorer jobs financially for a coach. I needed committed winners, who could put financial considerations aside in order to achieve something special at a very special institution.

I was able to hire an excellent coaching staff. Vinny Cerrato, a twenty-six-year-old assistant whom I had hired at Minnesota, came in to handle recruiting. He was the best, a fact proven by his current job as director of player personnel for the Washington Redskins. I also hired Jim Strong, my offensive backfield coach from Arkansas. I had promised John Gutekunst that I wouldn't strip him of all his assistants. That wouldn't have been fair to him given how hard we had worked together to build the Minnesota program. George Stewart, who had been with me at Arkansas and

Minnesota, was an exception. I also shuffled some of the existing staff and kept several of Gerry's assistants.

With the coaches in place, we set out on an aggressive recruiting campaign. Unfortunately, the negativity that had seeped into some of our players had found a home at many of the high schools we visited as well. It seemed like every time I went into a young man's home that first year, he pulled out a stack of articles saying Notre Dame couldn't win anymore because the schedule was too tough, the academic standards were too rigid, not being in a conference kept the best athletes out, and on and on. These were the same tired excuses you read about Notre Dame every year they didn't win the national championship.

Despite the late start and the negativity, we had a good recruiting year. We took a gamble on some athletes that weren't highly recruited, such as Anthony Johnson, a fine athlete from South Bend who was only the third leading rusher on his high school team. He was known more for his soccer than his football skills, but he would play nine years in the NFL. We also signed an obscure offensive guard named Tim Grunhard from Chicago, who would go on to play many successful seasons in the NFL. The quarterback situation concerned me. I visited a young man from South Carolina named Tony Rice, a good athlete and a great competitor. We had great chemistry from our first meeting. He was smart, disciplined, and motivated to succeed. I made a commitment to Tony during one of our meetings. I wanted him to come to Notre Dame, and he wanted to attend. He was exactly the kind of athlete we were looking for, and the kind of student that would be a great asset to Notre Dame. I felt certain that he would have no problem gaining admission to the school.

That turned out to be a gargantuan mistake. Our admissions director informed me very quickly that Tony Rice would not be accepted as a student. This stunned me. Tony was a great young man and a fine student, the sort of person the University of Notre Dame prided itself on. Having his admission rejected was the last thing I had considered.

This was my first real crisis at Notre Dame. I didn't think we needed Tony Rice to win football games—even if he had been admitted and made eligible, he probably wouldn't have played many downs his freshman year. The issue was that I had made a commitment to Tony. I had told him he was in. Thinking everything was set at Notre Dame, Tony informed other schools that he had committed to Notre Dame. I should have told Tony that I suspected he wouldn't have any trouble getting into Notre Dame based on his grades, but that I didn't have any control over admissions. That was what I had meant, but it was not what

I had said. I made an innocent but inappropriate representation to Tony, and violated one of my own basic rules: Say what you mean and mean what you say.

The only recourse I had was to go to Father Joyce and ask for his help. I was incredibly anxious when I met with him. Admissions was not my domain. That had been made clear to me in my first phone call with Father Joyce. But I had made what I considered an awful but innocent error, one I hoped the father would help me resolve. "I've made a terrible mistake," I said, and I explained what had transpired in the recruiting process.

Father Joyce's face tensed as he listened. He didn't say anything for a couple of seconds. Then he leaned forward and said very quietly but sternly, "This is not acceptable."

He lectured me in a kind but stern voice about my role within the university system, and my responsibility to use care when speaking of what would and would not happen at Notre Dame. Then he said, "I will help you, and I will help this student, but there will be a number of restrictions."

Those restrictions included strict academic requirements for Tony in his first year. He received a scholarship, but he could not, in any way, have contact with anyone involved in the football program during his entire freshman year. We didn't

306 | LOU HOLTZ

redshirt at Notre Dame, and Father Joyce did not want to give the impression that athletes received preferential treatment when it came to getting into the university. Tony's restrictions meant that he could not meet with a coach, practice, lift weights, or set foot in the locker room or football office during his first year. He would come to Notre Dame as a student, not a football player. If he proved himself in the classroom, he could join the team as a sophomore, which meant he would miss both the season and spring practice.

Then Father Joyce ended our discussion with a proclamation I would never forget. "Coach, I just want you to know one thing," he said. "This will never, ever happen again."

Tony accepted Father Joyce's decision, which surprised Notre Dame and me. I expected him to say, "Gee, thanks, but I think I'll go to Southern Cal," or one of the other schools that wanted him. When he accepted Father Joyce's restrictive terms, I knew that Tony had chosen Notre Dame for the right reasons. He could have gone to other schools, played as a freshman, and had an easier road academically, but he wanted to be challenged, and he wanted to be remembered as a Notre Dame man. As we entered our first season, I hoped I could find other men, eligible men, with the same commitment I saw in Tony Rice.

Through the spring and summer, we did many things to build a cohesive team with people who believed in themselves and in what we were trying to do. We were forced to change some of our offensive and defensive schemes to utilize the talent we inherited without altering our philosophy. We installed a few option plays, even though Steve Beuerlein was not a running quarterback. This would force defenses to play basic, stay-at-home, defender-versus-blocker football.

It would also reduce the pressure they could put on our passer. Steve was a solid passer and a smart quarterback, but Notre Dame had members of the band who were faster. In one scrimmage, we called an option, and Steve kept the ball and ran for a 40-yard gain before being tackled. He was so slow that a fifty-year-old coach ran with him stride for stride. Before Steve got back to the huddle I was in his face yelling, "Pitch that ball! We did not put in this option play to have Steve Beuerlein run the football. We put it in for you to pitch it to someone who is faster than you. And that list includes every back and every manager on our team."

Steve was a quick learner and he improved with each practice. He had a lot of physical skills, but his greatest asset was his brain and his ability to remain calm under adverse conditions. This is an essential quality a quarterback must possess. I always believed that intelligence in football far outweighed speed or strength. When you're the smallest and one of the slowest players on your college team, as I was, you must play smart. What I learned as a coach was that it was better to have a slow player running in the right direction than a fast one running the wrong way. Steve might not set any world speed records, but he would always run in the right direction.

Steve's arm was impressive as well. If we could get him to eliminate the bad plays, I felt, we had a chance to be a good offensive team, which meant putting some points on the scoreboard against some quality defenses. One of the reasons I was so optimistic was the quality of receivers Steve had catching his passes.

When reporters swarmed me after practice during that first week—a media throng I was unprepared for when I came to Notre Dame—I found myself in the middle of an impromptu press conference, which turned out to be a daily occurrence. Notre Dame attracted more media than anywhere I had ever coached, including the New York Jets. Every year I was in South Bend, I turned down more media requests for me and my players than I was ever extended in my entire tenures at other universities. When Beth got a haircut or we celebrated one of our children's birthdays, it was news, something I had never experienced before, but an occurrence I adjusted to quickly. In my first ad hoc press conference, the first question was, "What do you think of the talent?"

"Tim Brown is something really special," I said. "He's one of the best I've seen."

A few days later Tim came to see me and said, "Coach Holtz, did you really say that?"

"I did, Tim, and I meant it."

I didn't realize that short conversation would have such a positive effect on Tim Brown's future. He hadn't been highly recruited. In fact, he had been the quarterback on a 2–8 high school team in Dallas who never made all-state in Texas. Gerry Faust noticed him on film while he was recruiting another player. Fortunately for Notre Dame, Coach Faust saw a lot of potential in Tim and offered him a scholarship. All he needed was a boost of confidence to become a superstar.

People constantly underestimate their abilities, and it is the responsibility of parents, coaches, and teachers to raise their self-image and expectations. When you find a talented athlete like a Tim Brown, the right kind of coaching—encouraging him to believe in himself, pushing him toward greatness, and expecting more from him than he expects from himself—can turn a talented player into an All-American, Heisman Trophy–winning, All-Pro superstar. Some players respond to the demands coaches make of them by elevating their performances beyond all expectations. Others rebel against that kind of authority, and their talent goes to waste. I felt certain that Tim Brown was one who would respond positively. Eighteen months after that first meeting, Tim and I were together at the New York Athletic Club as he received the Heisman Trophy. After that, he went on to have what was unquestionably a Hall of Fame NFL career.

In my first season, I was less interested in individual performances, and more interested in building a team. Teams win when everyone subjugates his own personal welfare for the benefit of the unit. A team is capable of accomplishing things that no individual can regardless of how multitalented he may be. The team player recognizes this fact, and does whatever it takes to make the team better.

One player who understood this better than most was Mark Green. We did not have a healthy tailback when I arrived in South Bend. Alan Pinkett, Notre Dame's all-time leading rusher, had completed his eligibility, and the two returning tailbacks had knee problems and could play only a limited role. I asked Mark Green to change from his wide-receiver position (we had plenty of good wide receivers, including Tim Brown) and become our tailback. Mark had never played running back, but he unselfishly made the switch. Not only did he have some outstanding games at Notre Dame in that position, he went on to play a couple of seasons in the NFL.

The first time I recall having a private meeting with Mark was a couple of weeks after I arrived at Notre Dame. I was asked to inform Mark that his only living parent had just passed away. He was understandably devastated. He could easily have fallen into a pit of self-pity. I'd seen a lot of people who never recovered from the loss of a loved one. Mark grieved, but he chose to honor his parent's memory by working harder than ever. The example he set inspired our team and showed me that Mark Green was a man of the highest character. One of the special things about the Notre Dame family is how they support an individual in a time of need. This includes the priests, students, teammates, and faculty.

After spring practice Beth moved to South Bend. She had stayed in Minnesota until we sold the house, so I spent the winter and early spring living in the Morris Inn with my daughter Liz, who started at Saint Joseph High School right after Christmas break. Those months Liz and I spent alone together brought us closer than we had ever been. Then Beth moved and shocked me.

"I've been praying about it, and I think Kevin should transfer to Notre Dame," she said.

"That's not up to me," I told her. "I don't make those decisions, and I don't think Kevin's grades are such that he'll be allowed to transfer."

"Can you ask Father Joyce?"

I did, and Father Joyce informed me that Dean Robert Waddick handled all transfers. Dean Waddick looked at Kevin's transcripts, met with him, and gave him a chance. Not only did Kevin excel as an undergraduate at Notre Dame, but he was accepted by and eventually graduated from the law school. Notre Dame seemed to be good for all of us. I just hoped the football team responded as well to me as my family and I were responding to Notre Dame.

By the time we played our first game, most of the eleven teams we had on our schedule were ranked in the top fifteen in the country. I joked to the media that there was a chance we could go 0–11 and be the twelfth-best team in the country.

The difficult schedule we faced was no joke. My biggest concern was how we were going to gain confidence in ourselves as a team. If you aren't confident in your future, you will always be making excuses and pointing your finger at others. My conclusion was that I would lead by example. I would be very negative about us publicly but breathe confidence into the team in all meetings and on the field. The reason I was negative about our team and so positive about our opponent was to take the pressure off of us. Our team was told by me on several occasions, "Don't believe what you read but believe what I tell you. I will never lie to you."

The pep rallies at Notre Dame were special. At my first pep rally, before the Michigan game, I told the two thousand fans in attendance: "The student body here has always been the twelfth man. Well, we have such a difficult schedule this year that twelve might not do it. We might need thirteen men."

I made those comments on Friday, and spent the rest of that night and most of Saturday morning wondering where we might find that twelfth and thirteenth man. Michigan, coached by Bo Schembechler, entered the season opener ranked second in the nation. We were going to be tested early.

In years past, the team would go to mass early, then return to their dorm rooms before the pregame meal. I didn't want the players getting together at mass, then separating. I felt the entire day should be team oriented, so I changed the itinerary. We went to the pregame meal, then took the players to the wrestling room, where they could meditate together. Then they put on their coats and ties and went to mass, administered by Father James Riehle, at Dillon Dorm. We came out of the mass together as a team and walked to the stadium.

A lot of people have asked me about my thoughts and impressions as I walked into Notre Dame Stadium for my first game as head coach. My main focus was on how we could beat Michigan, with their great quarterback, Jim Harbaugh. I know everyone talks about Notre Dame's tradition, and I was aware of it, but I also believe tradition never graduates. It is always under construction, and it is yours to create or destroy. It was our mandate to build onto Notre Dame's great tradition, and the best way to do this was to win.

The only things I remember were a sheet someone had draped from a dorm-room window that said "John 3:16/Lou 12–0" and a skirmish that erupted in the end zone. Because of the configuration of Notre Dame Stadium, both teams had to enter through the same tunnel. When both teams came out at the same time, pushing and shoving became inevitable. This time it escalated quickly, and we had our first lapse in discipline before we ever played a down.

We played a great game, putting up 455 yards and 23 points on the offensive side of the ball. Unfortunately, we gave up 24 points. Our defense did not play badly, but we had six critical mistakes: two fumbles, an interception in the end zone, a bobbled kickoff, a missed extra point, and, on the final play of the game, a missed 45-yard field goal that would have won the game. John Carney, who became one of the great NFL field-goal kickers, had made fifteen of his previous sixteen kicks from 40 to 49 yards before missing at the end of the game.

Afterward I said, "John's made some great ones in the past and he'll make some great ones in the future. One play and one player did not determine the outcome of this game. We didn't do the little things, and that was the difference in the game.

"What can I say but that it was a heck of a football game. But let's remember that there are no moral victories at Notre Dame."

As disappointing as the loss was, our performance gave reason for encouragement. Unfortunately, it also gave the alumni false hope that we were going to have a great year. The following week, we lost to Michigan State by a score of 20–15. We beat Purdue in week three, but lost to Alabama in Birmingham. In that one, we were driving for the go-ahead touchdown when we called a bootleg pass. Cornelius Bennett, Alabama's All-American linebacker who had a great career with the Atlanta Falcons, blitzed and separated Beuerlein from the ball. It was a vicious hit, one that stopped our drive, took away any momentum we had generated, and excited the crowd and the Alabama team. For all intents and purposes, the game was lost. Oddly enough, from that moment forward, whenever we called that bootleg pass play, Beuerlein audibled out of it.

Then we lost to Pittsburgh at home by a score of 10–9 when we missed another field goal and had a punt blocked, all in the final two minutes of the game. Then we had an open date. During this week, we went back to teaching fundamentals and toughness.

I was still concerned that our players were pointing fingers at one another for our problems. We had a lot more excuses than we had wins. Improvement in the fundamentals will take a team only so far. In order for a team to make the leap from solid performers to true winners, you have to eliminate excuses and finger-pointing and take every accomplishment and setback as if the entire team is responsible. During the open date, we made two major decisions, and one of them had a positive effect on our team, not only for the 1986 season but for years to come.

Our special teams were average at best. There was no pride, enthusiasm, or execution. So our coaches picked the players they thought had the best attitudes on the team and asked them to be on the special-team units. Many of them were walk-ons and third-teamers, but all of them wanted to play. Our first game after the open date was against Air Force, and on the first kickoff return, Tim Brown ran 100 yards for a touchdown. In life as on special teams, success starts with attitude.

The second change occurred in the kicking game. I was mystified why John Carney had missed so many field goals when he made everything in practice. In studying film, I saw nothing different in John Carney's execution, but I did notice the holder held the ball differently in critical situations, applying more pressure on the football for a game-winning attempt than, say, on an extra point with the game well in hand. This subtle difference, in my opinion, caused John to miss the kicks. We replaced the holder, and John Carney became Mr. Automatic once again. For the next twenty years in the NFL, he rarely missed.

As the season progressed, I could see that we had a chance to be pretty good before the end of the season. Daily, I could see us improve in every facet of the game. In a single week, we had become a solid team, and when we played Air Force, the fans couldn't believe this was the same team that was 1–4. We followed this up with convincing wins over a good SMU team and Navy. We were facing three excellent opponents to end the season: top-ranked Penn State; LSU, ranked number five; and our archrival, Southern Cal, also nationally ranked. During practice before the Penn State game, an episode happened on the practice field that made a lasting impression. As our offense prepared to run a play, an offensive lineman jumped offside. This was the last straw. I had seen us lose focus too often in practice to put up with any more mistakes. If we had only three games left in the season and were still having false starts in practice, we were a long way from being a winning football team. Practice does not make perfect. Perfect practice makes perfect.

I grabbed our quarterback, Steve Beuerlein, and said, "Get off the field."

Steve threw his hands up and said, "Why? I didn't jump offside."

I responded in a voice loud enough for every player to hear: "You're the quarterback. You are responsible for this offense. You are the leader. Now hit the showers."

Everyone stood silently as Steve went to the locker room. Then I reinforced the point, telling our team, "You aren't out here playing for you, and you aren't out here playing for me. You're out here playing for the man next to you. If you aren't trying to win for your teammates, the men who are sacrificing beside you, you have no business putting on that gold helmet on Saturday. It is not a right to play for Notre Dame, it is a privilege. Act like it."

Even though we lost two more heartbreakers to Penn State and LSU, I was proud of our progress. At Penn State, the team that would go on to win the national championship, we had two touchdowns called back, and Steve hit a receiver in the end zone for what would have been the go-ahead touchdown with less than a minute to play. But the receiver dropped the pass, and we lost by five, having outplayed Penn State for most of the day.

At LSU, we scored with four minutes to go to pull within two of the lead. Our two-point conversation failed, but the defense played great, and held them to third-and-nine on their own nine-yard line. Tommy Hodson, LSU's great quarterback, went back for a pass, which we had covered. He should have been sacked, which would have left us in field-goal range. Unfortunately, Hodson scrambled for the first down, and we lost another game by less than a touchdown. That loss ensured a second consecutive losing season for Notre Dame.

With each heartbreaking loss, we were able to show the team that it was caused by a player trying to make a great play. I was convinced they wanted to win, but they didn't have confidence in their teammates. Instead of trying to play their position, they tried to win the game by themselves. Then in our final game against the University of Southern California at the Los Angeles Memorial Coliseum, I witnessed a remarkable turnaround. We were losing the game 30–20 when Steve Beuerlein threw his seventh interception of the season.

As he came to the sideline, I said, "Steve, I promised you that if you threw one more interception you would not play anymore. Take a seat."

Our defense held and USC lined up for a punt. We called for a punt block, but instead of blocking the kick, one of the players on our punt-return team roughed the punter, giving them an automatic first down. To make matters worse, the player who roughed the kicker was named Skip Holtz. Asked about the play afterward, I said, "Now I know why some species of animals devour their young."

USC scored to go up 37–20. Then, as we lined up to accept the kickoff after the touchdown, I saw a change. The return team all said to one another, "We're going to run this back," and they believed it. Each man said to the one next to him, "You get your guy; I'll get my guy, and we'll run this back." It was not "Tim Brown is going to run it back." They said "we" in a way that the word hadn't been spoken all year.

As we lined up to receive the kickoff, Steve Beuerlein came up to me almost in tears. He said, "Coach, don't let me end my career like this. This is my hometown. I am a four-year starter. This is my last game. This is USC. I promise I won't throw another interception."

Tim Brown took the kickoff and ran it back 57 yards. I turned to Steve and said, "Convince me."

The team played as if they were possessed. Steve led us to a quick touchdown. This encouraged the defense. I heard them saying, "Three and out! Three and out!" They held USC on the next series.

Nine minutes later, we had scored eighteen points; the last three points came on a John Carney field goal on the last play of the game. We upset USC by a score of 38–37. At that moment, I felt the spirit of Notre Dame. We were down by seventeen points with nine minutes to go and came back to win. That was when I felt we came together as a team.

I was happy for our seniors. After the game I told them that when Notre Dame won the championship, they could say, "We laid the foundation."

For the next ten years, the Notre Dame Fighting Irish won 80 percent of their football games and went to nine consecutive New Year's Day bowl games. No team had ever done that before. And none has done it since.

It took ten games, one full year of frustrations, but we finally put away the excuses and pulled together as a team. Our athletes realized that excuses come only out of the losing locker room. Winners don't need to make excuses, and they don't have time because they are too busy finding solutions. Only when you adopt this philosophy is the winner inside you free to come out and realize his full potential.

12

SUCCESS IS A
MATTER OF FAITH

With Tim Brown and Steve Beuerlein, who would go on to great success in the NFL. It was our mandate to build on Notre Dame's great tradition, with superior athletes and a winning philosophy.

Before joining the Notre Dame family, I heard a lot about the spirit of Notre Dame, but I wasn't sure what that meant. The people were spiritual, and the leaders of the university were driven by the Holy Spirit, of that I had no doubt. But I wasn't convinced the campus itself held anything spiritual. Then, in my first year, I made an interesting observation. I realized that if you don't believe in the omnipresent spirit of Notre Dame, you never feel it. I made up my mind that I was going to believe in this spirit. The moment I started believing, I started feeling it. And the feeling never left. I am often asked to explain the mystique of Notre Dame. I reply, "If you were there, no explanation is necessary. If you weren't, no explanation is satisfactory."

I became a much better Catholic at Notre Dame, going to mass every day if possible, a practice my grandmother had kept her entire life, and striving to live a life that would be pleasing to Christ. Faith was the only thing that allowed me to cope with the responsibilities and expectations of my job. I believed I had been led to Notre Dame for a reason, and that as long as I did my best, things would work out. This was not based on anything factual: the Lord hadn't left me any voice-mail messages. I believed it as a matter of faith: the same kind of faith that had been leading people to Notre Dame for more than a century.

In 1880, only a few years after Father Edward Sorin and five brave French priests settled in northern Indiana and founded Notre Dame, the Golden Dome, the symbol of faith that dominates the campus, burned to the ground. Far from being dejected or questioning himself, Father Sorin said that the reason it had burned was because it was not big enough. He said, "We're going to make the dome so big that people will see Our Lady on the Dome from miles away. And when people want to know what makes Notre Dame great, they will have to look no further than the Lady on the Dome." This was before Notre Dame had ever played a football game.

Our Lady lives at Notre Dame. That belief is what makes Notre Dame a special place for me and millions like me. When I first came to Notre Dame, I thought it might be nice to dress up the solid gold headgear worn by the players by putting an "ND" on them. I was told very quickly that the gold helmets represented the Golden Dome, and they would remain unmarked. The helmets are just one of many symbols of faith at Notre Dame, symbols that are far more important than football.

Certainly, football was still important. Even though we saw great improvement, and the athletes showed tremendous character in coming together despite more close, heartbreaking losses than I'd ever seen in a year, it was still a losing season. Being competitive at Notre Dame meant winning, not coming close. And when the alumni talked about winning, they meant winning them all, and winning by large margins. I was never pressured to win, but it was an unwritten rule that if you were the head coach at Notre Dame, you competed for the national championship on a regular basis.

I never had a contract at Notre Dame. They never offered, and I never asked. When I took the job, Father Joyce and I agreed on a salary, and that we would give it four years. If I turned things around, he felt sure I could stay. If I didn't, we both agreed that I should go somewhere else. I trusted Father Joyce to be good to his word, just as I trusted Father Hesburgh and Gene Corrigan. Unfortunately, early in my second year, all three of those men left. Fathers Joyce and Hesburgh, two of the greatest men I've ever had the privilege of knowing, retired after thirty-five years of leading Notre Dame.

Gene Corrigan, the athletic director and my immediate boss, had shepherded me through my first year as head coach. He was firm, fair, open, friendly, and a devoted husband and father, and

I respect and love him and his family. I was honored when Gene called me into his office and told me that he had been offered the job as commissioner of the Atlantic Coast Conference, but that he was going to turn down the offer because he had hired me, and with Fathers Joyce and Hesburgh retiring, he didn't feel comfortable leaving me alone after just one year, particularly a losing one.

This was typical Gene: totally selfless. He was willing to forgo a great opportunity, one that might not come again in his career, to be there for me.

"Gene, I'm honored, but I think you should take the job," I said. "This is a great opportunity for you and your family. There's no way you should pass this up because of me."

"But I'm the one who hired you, and I feel responsible," he said.

"And I will forever be indebted to you," I said. "But I would have come to Notre Dame if you and Father Joyce had told me on the front end that you were leaving in a week, a month, a year, or ten years." I concluded by saying, "Notre Dame's loss would be the Atlantic Coast Conference's gain."

After careful consideration, he finally took the job.

I had been at Notre Dame one year, and the president, the vice president, and the athletic director who had hired me had all retired or moved on to other jobs. I had no idea who the new athletic director would be, but I knew it would not be me. I had no desire, and I knew that I was not a candidate. The person who came in would inherit me as the head football coach: a coach who didn't have a written contract, and who had just come off a losing season.

In any other circumstance, at any other school, I would have been concerned for my job. But I never worried, because of the faith I had in Notre Dame. I was doing everything I could to coach the football team. The rest was out of my control. As long as I did what I had been hired to do, everything else would work out. Father Edward Malloy was named president of Notre Dame and Father William Beauchamp became vice president, succeeding Father Joyce. The athletic director's job took a little longer to fill.

One day I received a call from Dick Rosenthal, a former All-American basketball star from Notre Dame who had started a successful bank in South Bend at the age of twenty-six. I knew Dick but did not socialize with him. So when he came to my office, I had no inkling that he might be our new athletic director. Dick was about to retire from the bank he had founded, so it was perfect timing. The thought that Notre Dame might hire a businessman as the athletic director had never entered my mind.

330 | LOU HOLTZ

"Lou, they've asked me to be athletic director. I don't want to accept the position if you and I can't get along."

I said, "Then take the job, because I'm sure you and I will get along just fine. We're working toward the same thing. We both want to see Notre Dame be successful."

He nodded. Then I said, "I'm sure there will be times when we disagree, but we won't ever have any long-term problems as long as we're both working for the same thing. We'll have some disappointments, but I'm sure we'll also have some great experiences. It won't be easy, but it will be fun."

Dick took the job, and he remains one of my best friends to this day—a tremendous person, a great leader, and a brilliant man.

The one person who did not retire or resign after my first year was a gentleman named Kevin Rooney, the director of admissions at Notre Dame. Kevin was appointed to his position just before I arrived, stayed the entire eleven years I coached there, and was reassigned soon after I left. During that time, he and I had many disagreements, so many in fact that I didn't talk to him the last eight years I was at Notre Dame.

I wasn't the only person who had trouble following Kevin's logic when it came to admissions. He obviously selected outstanding students to attend Notre Dame, as virtually all our football players graduated. In 1988, we were the only school in the history of football to win the national championship and graduate 100 percent of its seniors. Kevin selected good students, students who knew why they were in school, and who had a commitment to stay at Notre Dame through graduation. Emil Hoffman, the legendary chemistry professor at Notre Dame, was in charge of all freshmen while I was coaching there, and he and I had an annual bet: If he lost more freshmen due to grades, dropouts, or transfers than we lost football games, he paid. If we lost more football games than he lost returning freshmen, I paid. In the ten years we had this wager, our football team averaged 2.5 losses a year. And I lost that bet with Emil more often than I won it.

From an admissions standpoint, I understood the need to be tough and selective, and I never had a problem with the players Kevin accepted. I did, however, have a problem with the ones he didn't.

I believed that we had a great opportunity to create a dynasty at Notre Dame if we did nothing more than recruit from every Catholic high school in the country. This premise was based not on faith, but on the numbers. Year in and year out, the top twenty-five high school teams in the country included a dozen or more Catholic schools. By recruiting from those schools, I felt, we could get the kind of athletes we wanted and needed, and get young men who understood Notre Dame, who wanted to come, and who would receive great support from their families. Unfortunately, we had very little success in recruiting Catholic men into our program, which I did not understand.

Kevin felt that it was unfair to accept an athlete from a Catholic high school who finished lower in his class than a student who had not been accepted. As he told me, "We can't accept them all."

I didn't want them all, but I did want some who I felt were good students and good young men who would make a great addition to the football team and the student body. I didn't want athletes to be given special consideration if they were academically incapable of competing—that would have been unfair to the athlete and the university—but I did expect their athletic contribution to be taken into account. If a student applied to Notre Dame who had excellent grades and also could sing like Ella Fitzgerald, or had Picasso potential as a painter, or was a Miles Davis–type jazz trumpeter, or had Hamiltonian debating skills, those traits were taken into account, and rightly so. All I wanted was the same consideration given to athletes.

Too often, in my judgment, that did not happen. For example, I tried to recruit two excellent defensive linemen in Cleveland, one from Saint Ignatius and the other from Juliet Catholic. Both were men of great character and integrity, and both were intelligent, good students having scored over 1,000 on their college boards. But both were denied admission. I was never given an adequate explanation, but both of those players went to Michigan, where they succeeded both academically and athletically. Rather than have them helping our defense, which they both wanted to do, we had to play against them every year.

I remained loyal to Notre Dame, and neither Kevin nor I ever talked publicly about the admissions problems we encountered. A sign on my desk said it all: "Coaches coach, players play, administrators administrate, reporters report, admissions reject, and there shall be no overlap." From the day I arrived until the day I left, the truth of that sign remained constant.

There were several requirements the admissions office placed upon the football office that put us at a disadvantage. For example, we could not offer a scholarship to a young man until his transcript had been approved and Kevin had a personal interview with the prospect. If we could have brought prospects to campus in the summer, we would never have lost one. Notre Dame in July resembles paradise. January is a different story. South Bend always seemed to experience snow, wind, and flight delays on a recruiting weekend.

During the early nineties, schools changed their recruiting techniques. They urged, and in many cases got, the top prospects to commit to their schools before the athletes entered their senior year of high school. A coach would tell a young man he had a scholarship, but the school couldn't guarantee the offer would still be available in January. Place yourself in the position of the athlete. He wants to attend Notre Dame, but his second choice has offered him a scholarship. He won't receive a definite offer from Notre Dame until January, if his personal interview goes well.

Kevin worked with us to alleviate the problem, not eliminate it. He would have the prospect's guidance counselor send Notre Dame a transcript at the end of his junior year. The admissions office would then tell us "forget him," "looks favorable," or "possible." All prospects, even those rated favorable, had to show positive grades in their senior year, or they would not be accepted.

My frustration was natural, and it had nothing to do with Kevin personally. He had his job, and he did it well. He wasn't antifootball. He was trying to uphold the integrity of Notre Dame. However, the rare times he did change his mind and admit a student-athlete, these young men succeeded at Notre Dame. Take the case of Todd Lyght from Flint, Michigan. Todd struggled academically in his first year, but he did graduate in four years, and he started at cornerback for four years. He became captain of our football team and an All-

American, was selected in the first round of the NFL draft, and made a sizable contribution from his signing bonus to Notre Dame.

Todd succeeded because of the support he received from the Notre Dame family. I believed there were a lot more athletes like him who could have done well at the university if they had only been given the chance. I saw what the love and support of the priests, dorm rectors, students, faculty, coaches, and teammates could do to change a person's life positively. I witnessed firsthand how a person learned to be accountable for his actions and become a responsible young adult. Maybe I believed in the spirit of Notre Dame too much, but I don't think so. I witnessed the power of that spirit too many times.

As frustrating as the admissions madness could get, we hit the recruiting trail hard and undaunted. I still felt we could get the best and the brightest student-athletes in the country, because I believed we were giving these athletes a tremendous opportunity. As I explained to many families, coming to Notre Dame was not a four-year decision, it was a forty-year decision, one that would affect the way a student-athlete would spend the rest of his life. The education our athletes received, not just in the classroom but in the entire life experience of Notre Dame, was second to none. The contacts he would make through the student body would serve him well for the rest of his life. Plus, we were giving him a chance to come to the most beautiful campus in the world. The only drawback was the weather. The old joke said that Notre Dame wasn't supposed to be in South Bend. Father Sorin's original plan was to establish the school in San Diego, but when he and his fellow priests got to northern Indiana, they were snowed in, and had to set up camp until the weather broke. It never did.

Snow aside, we had great success signing such players as Ricky Watters, Rocket Ismail, Tony Brooks, Tommy Carter, Jerome Bettis, and many other outstanding athletes. All of these recruits fit our criteria for what a Notre Dame football player should be. They could run and make plays; they had football intelligence; they were physical; they wanted to play for Notre Dame; and they wanted to be students at our university.

We were building a solid foundation for the future. As for the present, I felt that we had a talented football team, perhaps no more talented than the one we had fielded in 1986, but more comfortable with our program than that first team had been. Terry Andrysiak would take over at quarterback, and while he didn't have the arm strength of Steve Beuerlein, I thought he was a better overall athlete. Tony Rice was an unknown, since he hadn't been allowed to be near the football team during his freshman year, including spring practice. Tim Brown was back, as was

Mark Green. Throw in Watters, Brooks, and some of the young players we had brought in, and, on paper at least, we looked like a pretty good team. I took little comfort in that. I had learned early in my career that you don't play football games on paper.

We opened at Michigan against a team ranked ninth in the nation in the preseason polls, and a coach, Bo Schembechler, who had never lost a season opener at home. We played a great football game. Our defense forced seven turnovers, four of which we converted into touchdowns. Tim Brown was unstoppable, and Mark Green and Anthony Johnson played great, mistake-free football. Before a crowd of 106,000, the largest in Michigan history, we won by a final score of 26–7.

We came home and rolled over Michigan State by a final of 31–8. Another big win over Purdue, and suddenly we were 3–0 and being talked about as contenders for the national championship. Morale was great, and our confidence was high. A week later, we traveled to Pittsburgh for what I hoped would be our fourth victory in a row.

When you play on the road, you must pack your quickness, discipline, defense, offense, and kicking game. We took none of these to Pittsburgh.

In Pitt Stadium, our team played the flattest and most uninspired first half of football I had seen since coming to Notre Dame. We trailed 27–0 at halftime, having been beaten on every side of the ball. To add insult to injury, on the final play of the first half, Pitt blitzed their outside linebackers and Terry Andrysiak went down for a sack. He didn't get up. When he finally righted himself, it was obvious he was injured. He couldn't move his left arm, and his shoulder hung awkwardly in his jersey. In the locker room we discovered that our senior starting quarterback had a broken collarbone. Terry would miss at least six weeks, and more likely eight. He was, for all practical purposes, out for the rest of the season.

I had to choose between Tony Rice, our first-year sophomore I had worked so hard to get into Notre Dame, and Kent Graham, another outstanding athlete, who went on to have a fine NFL career. I decided to go with Tony, even though I had no idea what would happen. It was Tony's first time playing more than a mop-up role, and the first time he would be called upon to lead the offense. I knew he had plenty of physical skills, but until an athlete is forced to perform under fire, you're never sure how he will respond.

It took two series for all of us to realize that Tony was a natural. He made good decisions, and showed the kind of poise I expected out of a four-year starter, not someone taking the reins for the first time. Tony led the offense on three second-half scoring drives, which pulled us within a touchdown and two-point conversion with less than a minute to play. Our special team did a great job of fielding the onside kick, but we ran out of time and downs on the Pitt forty-two-yard line.

The final score was 30–22, a hard loss, but one in which we learned a lot about what kind of football team we had, and discovered an offensive leader in Tony Rice, a man who would become one of the all-time greats in Notre Dame history.

We won our next five games with Tony taking snaps, and Tim Brown proved to be the best player in college football. Where we had come so close to winning in 1986, we won decisively in 1987, defeating Air Force, USC, Navy, Boston College, and Alabama by a combined total of 186–73. With two games remaining, we found ourselves ranked seventh in the country. The national championship was a long shot, but if we beat Penn State and Miami in our final two games and won a bowl game, anything could happen.

Unfortunately, I made a mistake at State College that cost us any shot at that championship. During what was as cold and windy a day as I can remember inside Beaver Stadium at Penn State, we played a tough back-and-forth game all afternoon despite temperatures in the teens and winds that gusted up to forty miles an hour. With the game tied just before halftime, we drove the ball to the four-yard line, and had time for a couple of plays. Instead of kicking a field goal to give us a three-point lead, I put Kent Graham in to throw the ball. Tony had a strong arm but was an inconsistent passer. Kent could throw the ball, and I wanted him to know I believed in him and that he was an important part of our team.

As I gave Kent the play, I looked him in the eye and said, "We've got three points on the board, so don't take them off." This was like telling a baseball pitcher, "Don't throw it high and inside." When the last thought you give an athlete is negative, negative things usually happen. The pitcher throws the high-inside fastball because that's the pitch he has on the brain; the golfer hits his ball left into the hazard because his caddie said, "Don't go left"; and the quarterback throws an interception because that's what he's thinking about. Rather than telling Kent, "Make a good decision, and let your talent handle the rest," I left him pondering a negative. As a result, he threw an interception, and we went into halftime with the score tied.

Penn State took the lead 21–14 early in the second half, and that was how it stayed until late in the game. We had plenty of opportunities to score, plenty of receivers open on play-action passes, but the wind made it virtually impossible to complete a pass that afternoon. When we finally scored late in the game, we were forced to go for the two-point conversion for the win.

We missed the conversion, and lost the game 21–20, a loss I blame on myself. Had we kicked the field goal before halftime, we wouldn't have needed the two-point conversion. The athletes played their hearts out, and I felt terrible for having made such a critical and ill-timed mistake. It wasn't Kent's mistake, it was mine.

But I didn't have time to beat up myself or anybody else for our loss. The following week we played Miami, a 9–0 football team ranked second in the country, in the Orange Bowl. I probably overreacted to the loss at Penn State and took the approach that we had to throw the football to beat Miami, but I'm not sure any game plan would have worked. Miami was as talented as any college team I had ever seen, and they proved it.

We tried to throw the ball against them to loosen up their defense. Instead, they sacked our quarterback six times, and held us to only 87 yards in the air. That was 5 yards more than we gained on the ground. We never got closer to the goal line than the Miami twenty-six. On the other side of the ball, Miami quarterback Steve Walsh threw for 196 yards, and their running backs, Melvin Bratton and Leonard Conley, gained another 207 on the ground. The final was 24–0, but it looked and felt a lot worse than that. For the first time all year, we had been beaten on both sides of the ball for sixty consecutive minutes. And I left Miami feeling that this team still had a long way to go.

Before traveling to Miami, Notre Dame accepted a bid to the Cotton Bowl, the first New

Year's Day game for an Irish team in seven seasons. Accepting that bid took a little of the sting out of losing our final two regular-season games. Plus, it was my first trip to the Cotton Bowl. I had been to every other major bowl game, including the Rose Bowl when I was at Ohio State, but had never taken a team to Dallas. We would play Texas A&M, the champions of the Southwest Conference. (Even though we were cochampions of the Southwest Conference at Arkansas in 1979, we didn't get the bid because of the way the conference decided tiebreakers.)

I really wanted to win that Cotton Bowl game. Losing the final two games of the season had left a bitter taste in my mouth. I wanted to validate that Notre Dame was, indeed, back. Also, Tim Brown was from Dallas. I could think of no better homecoming than for the Heisman Trophy winner to win a New Year's Day bowl game in his hometown.

The team didn't respond as I had hoped. The players didn't seem as interested in winning the game as they did in simply being there. They viewed the bowl game as a reward, not a challenge. We worked hard, but we didn't accomplish much. Once we got there, some of the players appeared to be more focused on enjoying themselves, taking in the sights and sounds of the city, than winning.

When the game finally got under way, Tim Brown had an outstanding first half, and we went up 10–0. They scored a field goal, and then we got caught in man-to-man coverage without a free safety, something I don't believe in playing when you have a team backed up. I've always said you shouldn't give them something they haven't earned, and man coverage allows that. Late in the first half, we got caught in that very coverage, and A&M's quarterback hit a receiver on a slant pattern. Seventy yards later, the game was tied at 10.

In the second half, we never got the ground game established, and had a hard time stopping their offense. Even though we threw the ball well, being unable to gain yardage on the ground had been a weakness of our team all year. This game was no different. We gained only 76 yards in the second half and lost the game by a final score of 35–10.

I felt devastated. This was a terrible loss, and a terrible way to end a season where, at one time, we had been 8–1 and ranked seventh in the nation. I left the field not knowing what to say to the team. There wasn't much I could say. I told them that for the rest of their lives, they had to learn to handle success and adversity in the same way, and that all they could do was answer the question, "What are we going to do now?"

I found little to feel good about in that locker room. Most of the players seemed unfazed by the loss. The seniors appeared disappointed, but none of them looked as though they felt as sick as I did. Then I saw Chris Zorich. He was a freshman substitute middle guard, a player who hadn't played a single down all day. He had come to Notre Dame from a broken home in a crime-infested neighborhood where he had to fight his way home from school on a daily basis, and from a high school where you were more likely to become a drug dealer than a college All-American. Chris thought he would be a great linebacker. I knew he might make a passable middle guard. He didn't like the idea of moving positions, and got into a fair number of fights during practice (something I didn't tolerate). But no one worked harder on the practice field or in the library than Chris. He wasn't blessed with outstanding speed or size, but he did have the fortitude to do whatever it took to reach his goals.

That afternoon in Dallas, with the sting of the loss burning inside me, I looked up and down the rows of players, searching for a bright spot. I found one in Chris Zorich. He sat in front of his locker with his face in his hands, his shoulders heaving. It took a second for me to realize he was sobbing. A player who hadn't broken a sweat after warm-ups, who had stood on the sidelines and encouraged his team all afternoon, was distraught to the point of tears by our loss. That was the kind of player we needed at Notre Dame. Before I left the locker room, I remember looking at Chris and saying to myself, "This guy has got to be on the field. And if possible, I need to find forty more just like him."

After the game, I met with the coaches and talked about recruiting. I was adamant in my directive. We had to find players who were as self-less and committed to the idea and ideals of Notre Dame football as Chris Zorich. I expected us to recruit attitude over athleticism, and an aptitude for hard work over natural ability. I could not stand what I had seen during the Cotton Bowl. And I told our staff that we would not let that happen again. I accepted the blame for our loss, as a coach should. Before you start blaming others, look at yourself. You will find you must look no further for the cause of the problem. I asked our coaches and players to do the same.

The next morning I flew to Japan, where I would coach in the Japan Bowl against a team of all-stars coached by Jackie Sherrill of Texas A&M, the head coach I had just faced in the Cotton Bowl. The flight took fourteen hours, and I didn't sleep a wink. I kept replaying the final three games of the season over in my mind. We had turned a losing team into a winning team in one year. Now, we had to turn a good team into a great team.

For most of the flight, I made lists of the things we needed to do to reach that goal. The lists included all the fundamentals we had to improve, like carrying the football properly, blocking and tackling more effectively, and protecting the ball. We weren't going to play foolishly, and we weren't going to tolerate players who did their own thing. We had to eliminate missed assignments. The one thing I wanted out of all future Notre Dame teams was smart, disciplined play. Teams might beat us, but we were not going to beat ourselves. Finally, I wrote a model profile for the type of player who would play for Notre Dame from that point forward: someone who was motivated and who wanted to do something with his life, who wanted to represent Notre Dame and its values on and off the field, and who stood up and led in everything he did.

Beth and three of our children went with me to Japan, which was great. Liz had started at Notre Dame, Kevin was a senior, and Skip had taken a graduate assistant-coaching job at Florida State, so it was a good trip for everyone, except me. Even after trying to purge all my disappointment by writing my lists, I couldn't shake the frustration of our Cotton Bowl loss.

Then, in our first night at the Okinawa Prince Hotel, I saw something that changed my outlook. I woke up at 5 A.M. hearing noises outside our hotel room. It sounded like a military exercise.

Men were shouting and chanting in unison, and although I don't speak Japanese, I could tell these were disciplined responses to commands. When I looked out the window, I saw dozens of construction workers, hard-hat guys, lined up in perfect formation. They shouted in unison again, and began calisthenics. No one missed a beat or a repetition. I watched them exercise for a half hour, realizing that these construction workers, hourly laborers, had committed themselves to this program, not because it made them better masons, carpenters, or electricians, but because it made them better individuals, and brought them closer together as company men.

That's when it hit me: If the Japanese could get a group of construction workers who cared enough about their company to perform calisthenics every morning at five o'clock, we ought to be able to find a group of athletes who cared enough about Notre Dame to work harder than ever, and to settle for nothing less than perfection.

13

PERFECTION IS POSSIBLE IF YOU ACCEPT NOTHING LESS

With the trophy that declared me 1988 Coach of the Year, a proud moment. I had learned, from Coach Hayes, that a team goes through four stages: learn how to compete; learn how to win; learn how to handle winning; then and only then are they ready to win championships.

When I first went to Ohio State as an assistant, the team had come off a mediocre season, and the prospects for the upcoming year were questionable. We started twelve sophomores (freshmen weren't eligible at the time), young men who had never played a down of Division I football. I had three sophomores in our defensive backfield, none of whom had ever played his position prior to the previous spring. We were as green as any team in the country. No one would have been shocked if we lost two, three, or even four games against more experienced opponents.

Coach Hayes didn't see it that way. From the moment we began winter workouts, he talked about winning the Big Ten championship and the Rose Bowl. He spoke of these things, not as pipe dreams, but as goals we should reach. He left no doubt that he would be disappointed if we lost one game. He demanded nothing less than perfection, even though many of our athletes were still learning the basics of college football. This wasn't a ploy: Coach Hayes believed that if you wanted to achieve perfection, you had to demand it. "Inexperience" in his eyes was an excuse put forth by those who knew they were going to lose.

A couple of years later, after I had been at William and Mary for two seasons and had become close friends with Coach Hayes, I realized that his philosophy of demanding perfection wasn't accidental or unique. He had learned it from studying history. Besides having been a captain of a ship in the U.S. Navy during World War II, Coach Hayes was as well read as anyone I've ever known. He could recount the strategies and tactics of major battles from every war the United States had ever fought, and could tell you what the commanders were thinking when they made their decisions. He knew, for example, that the 101st Airborne was an "inexperienced" combat unit before it was dropped into Normandy to cut off German gunners on D-day. He knew that most of the Fifth Army Ranger Battalion hadn't seen combat before launching the most ambitious military raid in history, one that would ultimately free five hundred American prisoners of war at Cabanatuan in the Philippines. He would tell you that these men did not become heroes because of their prior experience. They had no prior experience. They became heroes because they did what was necessary to achieve the impossible. Coach Hayes did his best to instill that mind-set into his football players.

One night I was visiting him in Columbus. He had invited me up to offer me a job as his defensive coordinator with the promise that I would succeed him as head coach when he retired. I was still at William and Mary at the time and the offer sounded great, except that I wasn't sure Coach Hayes could guarantee that I would replace him. "I'll make sure they hire you," he said. "If they won't agree to it in writing, I'll retire in the middle of the summer when they've got no choice but to promote you." It was a great offer, and one I thought long and hard about accepting. But in the end, I didn't feel confident that Coach Hayes could pull off the ascension strategy he had outlined, and I had no idea how much longer he would coach. Plus, I was happy in Williamsburg.

The night he made the offer we talked football until three o'clock in the morning. When I finally retired, I collapsed, fully clothed, on the bed. Five minutes later, I heard a knock on the door. When I opened it, Coach Hayes stood there holding three books: an autobiography of Winston Churchill, a biography of Abraham Lincoln, and a book on the great military battles of history.

"I thought you'd need something to read yourself to sleep," he said.

It took a lot of effort not to fall asleep standing up talking to him. I thumbed through the books, though, because I knew he would want to discuss them at the breakfast table.

I never came close to equaling Coach Hayes's knowledge of history, but I did learn a lot about the tactics he employed to build teams of over-achievers. I learned that a team goes through four stages: first, they have to learn how to compete; then they have to learn how to win; after that, they have to learn how to handle winning; then and only then are they ready to win championships. My first year at Notre Dame, we learned to compete again. In so doing, we rid the program of negativity and personal agendas, and focused everyone on competing as a team. In my second year, we learned how to win, and how to handle winning. Unfortunately, we had to handle losing as well. Now, it was time for stage four. This team was ready to learn how to win championships.

On February 10, 1988, I called a team meeting where I laid out an ambitious objective. I wanted the team to settle for nothing less than perfection: perfection in themselves; perfection in their goals; perfection in their preparation; perfection in their character; and finally, perfection on the field. I wanted them to think about their competition, not in terms of the teammates they had to beat out for starting jobs, or the opposing teams we would face in the fall: I wanted each player's opponent to be "perfection." Once each athlete on our team learned how to beat Old Man Perfect, everything else would take care of itself.

I felt so passionately about this objective that I gave one of the most important and heartfelt speeches I've ever given. I told them, "There are going to be some changes, but I can assure you they are going to be positive changes. We are going to practice strict loyalty to one another. We are going to be loyal to the University of Notre Dame, the administration, the coaches, and teammates. We are not going to make negative comments about anybody on this football team. We cannot be a close-knit team without showing respect and concern for one another.

"This loyalty will extend to coaches as well. You aren't going to complain and moan about them, and you aren't going to talk among yourselves about them. By the same token, the coaches are not going to deride you, ridicule you, or question your courage. The coaches will show you how to become the best football players possible. They will tell you what you are doing wrong and in what areas you need to improve. If you have a problem with someone, get it straight. Remember, if you can't say something good about someone, don't say anything. This is a good philosophy to practice the rest of your life."

Then I asked a question that most of the players hadn't thought of before. "Do any of you know why men die for their country?"

There were some curious looks. Nobody knew where I was headed.

"The first reason is discipline," I said. "Why does the military conduct its close-order drill, although it carries no military significance whatsoever? Because it stresses discipline. The second reason is the history of the regiment, the great tradition, and great successes." I didn't go into lengthy detail, but examples of this are legend. Rangers greet their brothers with "Hoo-ah" not because of military significance, but because of the history and tradition of the rangers. The cavalry still has buglers, even though the necessity to communicate commands through bugle went out with Colonel Custer.

"However," I continued, "the most important reason why men die for their country is their love for their fellow man. One soldier I saw interviewed related a most revealing story. He was wounded in combat and was convalescing in a hospital when he discovered that his fellow soldiers were going on a dangerous mission. He escaped from the hospital and went with them. Then, while participating in this mission, he was wounded again. When interviewed, he said, 'You work with people and live with them, and you soon realize that your survival depends on one another.' Whether it be a military battle or Notre Dame football, we can enjoy success only when we realize that we must be able to count on one another."

That theme would be repeated hundreds of times throughout the course of our season. Those athletes had to understand that if they were playing for personal glory, they were in the wrong place. Championship teams play for things larger than themselves—the history and tradition of the institution, the quest for perfection, or the love of their teammates and coaches. I wanted every member of this team to internalize all of those motivators.

"I firmly believe that if you really look at this school, you realize that it has been blessed," I said. "The people who attend this school are blessed. Father Sorin said it best in 1842 when he said, 'I've raised Our Lady aloft so that men will know without asking why we have succeeded here. All they have to do is look high on the Golden Dome and they'll find their answer.' When we do what is right, we bring glory and honor to Notre Dame. When we win in football, we help this university. This school is special. There is a mystique about it. And you are special for being here as students at Notre Dame."

Then I outlined the rules, and what I expected. I told the players that they wouldn't drink during the season, and if they did, they didn't have the discipline necessary to be on this team, and that their social lives would be nonexistent. "Our practices must be more productive, and our retention greater," I said. "We cannot waste any time on the field, and we must insist upon improvement. I don't believe we made the kinds of improvements as a football team last year that we have to make this year.

"I don't know if anything is more important than self-discipline. We have scientists who go

358 | LOU HOLTZ

into space and scientists who go to the depth of the oceans. It's ironic that we can conquer space and sea, but many times we cannot conquer ourselves. Until we learn to have self-discipline, we cannot control our own destiny. Self-discipline is the greatest asset an individual can possess.

"I also think perseverance will be an important part of our success this year. We must overcome all adversity. The only reason for a person to exist is to be the best he can be. That requires discipline and perseverance. If you don't have the desire to be the best in every single phase of your life, you need to check your values.

"There are millions of people who live and die with Notre Dame football. There are an awful lot of Catholics and non-Catholics, Irishmen and non-Irishmen, successful and less-fortunate people, who follow the University of Notre Dame, and you should feel a sense of obligation to them. They follow Notre Dame football because it is synonymous with success."

Finally, I got to the specific expectations I had for our on-field performance.

"I'm here to win football games for the University of Notre Dame," I said. "Not some of our games, and not most of our games; I'm here to win all of our games. Every one of them. We aren't here to come close. We are here to win every single football game we ever play at the University of Notre Dame from this point forward.

"I want you to be the best, the very best, in all areas of your life. I want you to be the best student you can be. I want you to be the best person you can be. I want you to be the best football player you can be. To play at Notre Dame is to seek perfection. I want to tell you something: either we are going to reach perfection, or we're going to come so close that the average person won't know the difference. To strive for perfection means you've got to be totally dedicated. It can't be an occasional thing—it's got to be a total dedication in everything you do. If you don't have total dedication to perfection in your life, then I believe your attitude toward life is flawed.

"Perfection at Notre Dame will be demanded, and expected. I don't ever expect to lose another football game as long as I'm at Notre Dame, and I sure don't expect to lose one this year. I expect to see a perfect football team, because that's going to be the criterion we use to evaluate it. A loss is absolutely disastrous. You cannot give me one reason in the world why we should ever lose another football game at Notre Dame, and we aren't going to. Less than perfection is a personal embarrassment to me, to you, and to this university. For us to represent the University of Notre Dame with less than perfection is totally inconsistent with our goals, our objectives, and our beliefs.

"Don't expect us to lower our standards to satisfy people who are looking for mediocrity, because this won't happen. Mistakes are a thing of the past. We are going to expect perfection, and we are going to get it. I'm sure that we have some people in this room right now who are glad to hear this and are saying, 'We want to be the best. We want to strive for perfection. Tell us what we have to do, because we're willing to pay the price.' On the other hand, there may be some people in this room who will say we can't do it. Well, I don't care who questions our ability to succeed—as long as they aren't members of this team.

"Congratulations again on the fine start you have made in the winter program. This is our first step toward perfection."

Our coaching staff believed this philosophy, and we hammered that theme home through spring practice, summer workouts, and into the fall. The quest for perfection tends to focus the mind and sharpen the senses. It's a little like the guy who clips the wire to disable a bomb. Cutting a wire might be something he has done a thousand times in the past, but when the consequences of failure include being blown to smithereens, you tend to devote yourself completely to the task. Our football team wasn't disarming explosives, but I wanted the players to feel that same sense of urgency. I wanted them to know that perfection didn't allow for an "off day."

The same was true for the coaches. We had made some key changes to our coaching staff after the 1987 season. Barry Alvarez was elevated to defensive coordinator, and it immediately became apparent to me that Barry Alvarez was a special person, coach, and leader. Joe Moore was hired as the offensive-line coach. Joe came highly recommended. Jackie Sherrill, who coached winning teams at Pittsburgh, Texas A&M, and Mississippi State, told me I should hire Joe, who had been his offensive-line coach at Pittsburgh. Other coaches gave Joe high marks as well, and when I met him, he immediately impressed me. He was a big man with a weathered face and eyes that always appeared to have bags under them. His voice rumbled as if it came from the bottom of a coal mine. Everything about Joe reminded me of a Parris Island drill instructor. He was perfect for what we were trying to achieve.

We also hired Chuck Heater to coach our defensive secondary. A former defensive back for the New Orleans Saints, Chuck had been the defensive-backfield coach at Ohio State and Wisconsin. He was smart, hardworking, motivated, and tough as a week-old pork chop—again, a perfect addition to our staff.

Finally, I brought in my defensive-line coach from Minnesota, John Palermo, to coach the defensive tackles. We had lost all our defensive front-four starters after the 1987 season, so I brought in John to train Chris Zorich, Jeff Alm, George Williams, and the rest of our interior defenders. I knew that you won championships by stopping your opponents. To do that, we had to shut down some impressive running games, which meant controlling the line of scrimmage. John was the best in the business at finding, training, and motivating athletes to get that job done.

We also had a lot of questions about players in key skill positions. I knew Tony Rice could run the ball, but could he throw it effectively enough to win? Could Ricky Watters catch the ball? We had a new punter, Jim Sexton, who was a walk-on. Could he make a critical kick under pressure? I had no idea, but I had faith that all these players could and would step up to the task. Before the season was over, we would have twenty-one players who would make their first start in a college football game. But I never allowed any of them to use inexperience as a crutch. They knew that perfection was the standard. They simply had to be perfect in their first start at Notre Dame at positions many had never played before in their lives.

The one thing we had going for us was that we had student-athletes who wanted to be nowhere else in the world than the University of Notre Dame. For most of them, Notre Dame was their first and only choice. That went for the entire student body. We were the only school in the country that lost more football games than students. Our athletes were exactly where they wanted to be, doing what they wanted to do. The only remaining question was, could they achieve perfection?

The first drive of our first game answered a lot of those questions: we drove the ball 70 yards in one minute and seventeen seconds against a very good Michigan football team. We led 10–0 at the end of the first quarter. Our walk-on field-goal kicker, Reggie Ho, would kick four field goals that night, the last one coming with just over a minute to go in the game to seal our first victory of the year, and our first over a top-ten-ranked team.

After that, we did not have a close game until we traveled to Pittsburgh. We had lost three straight games to Pitt, and playing in their stadium was tough. They had a great quarterback named Darnell Dickerson, and we lost two key members of our offensive line to injury. Chris Zorich recovered a fumble early, and we scored to go ahead. We recovered another fumble in their end zone to prevent them from scoring late in the second quarter and took a 17–14 lead into the locker room at halftime. Then in the fourth quarter, Tony Rice showed me the depth of his leadership skills when he drove the team 53 yards for a touchdown to give us a 30–20 lead, which was how the game would end. That brought us to the

Miami game, the biggest game in college football that season.

We had lost to Miami three consecutive years by an embarrassing combined score of 133–20. The 1988 Hurricanes were the number-one-ranked team in the country, and billed as the best Miami team yet. Their quarterback, Steve Walsh, picked apart defenses with his high-powered arm and great instincts. I said at the time that Walsh was the best quarterback Miami had fielded, including his predecessors Jim Kelly, Bernie Kosar, and Vinny Testaverde. They also had backs like Cleveland Gary and receivers like Andre Brown and Leonard Conley. Plus, Miami would be coming off an open week, while we were battered and bruised from our game against Pittsburgh. All the factors were in their favor; but I knew we were going to win.

Our talent matched Miami's, but our players weren't as heralded, because they were young and hadn't had great 1987 seasons. Rocket Ismail was as good an all-purpose receiver and kick returner as there was in college football. Our senior team captain, running back Mark Green, was a leader and a winner in every respect, and Tony Rice continued to improve at quarterback every week.

I knew this would be our biggest challenge to date, and a test of my "perfection" strategy. As a result, I began preparations for the Miami game before we left the Pittsburgh locker room. After congratulating them on the big win, I told them that Miami was a great football team, but that we could beat them if we did certain things. "You have to believe in your coaches and do exactly what they tell you," I said. "You also have to believe in the spirit of Notre Dame. There have been plenty of other games where Notre Dame teams have played number-one-ranked teams and won. You have to believe that it will happen again. If you don't have faith, it won't happen. But if you do have faith and confidence, it will happen again."

The next day, I called another team meeting and tried to calm the team down and give their confidence another boost. "Miami is an extremely disciplined football team," I said. "You can talk about the extracurricular things and the way their players have talked in the past"—at the time Miami players were notorious for their antics and trash-talking—"but from the time the ball is snapped until the whistle blows, they are as disciplined and fundamentally sound as any team I've seen. They play with great emotion and confidence, a tribute to the staff.

"We can beat them," I said. "We are a much better football team than we were a year ago, though we might not look impressive to our opponents. We do the things to win that don't show up on the statistic sheet."

Then I told them that I had played my last football game in 1957, so there was no way I could help any of them on the field. All I asked was that they do three things: "One, just relax," I said. "We don't play for six more days. I called the NCAA, but they can't make Miami come up here until next Saturday, so there's no reason to get all pumped up now, and have all that adrenaline gone by kickoff. If you make a fist and hold it for two hours, you can't pick up a stick, so there's no reason for anyone to be tense now.

"Second, we want you to go through your relaxation techniques every night before bed." We had preached these techniques all year, having the athletes lie in their beds for several minutes, quietly visualizing themselves making great plays.

"And third, I want every single one of you to have faith that we will be successful. Never doubt it. I don't have proof that we can win—if we had proof, there would be no reason for faith—but just have that abiding faith that if you listen to your coaches, and do what they say, we can and will win this football game."

Early in the week I called Bo Schembechler. I called Bo quite a bit to talk about various things. He and I were close friends and remain so to this day. This call was about Miami. The Hurricanes had come back to beat Michigan in a close game the week after we had beaten Michigan. I wanted to know what Bo thought of Miami, and what he thought about our chances of winning.

"They are an outstanding football team," he said. "No weaknesses."

"You've played them and us. You think we can beat them?"

He thought for a second before saying, "Yes, you can beat them, but you've got to play a flawless football game."

We did just that. Offensively, defensively, and on special teams, we played as fine a football game as we could play. We rushed forty-nine times for 113 yards, and completed ten passes for 218 yards. Unfortunately, Miami rushed for 73 yards and passed for 424. The game seesawed back and forth all afternoon, and Steve Walsh was as prolific as I had feared he would be.

We scored first on a twelve-play drive capped by Tony Rice's 7-yard run. Walsh came back and hit Andre Brown for a touchdown early in the second quarter to tie the score. Tony answered with two great plays, a 57-yard throw and catch to Rocket Ismail, and a 9-yard touchdown pass to Braxton Banks. Then Pat Terrell, one of our outstanding defensive backs, intercepted a Walsh pass and ran it in for another touchdown.

Five minutes later, Walsh had orchestrated two flawless drives resulting in touchdowns to tie the game again. We scored another touchdown and a field goal in the third quarter, but were shut out in the fourth. Miami scored a field goal on their first possession of the final quarter, and drove deep into territory twice more.

With seven minutes to go in the game Walsh hit Cleveland Gary on fourth and seven from the eleven-yard line. Gary came close to the end zone before our strong safety, George Streeter, hit him and forced a fumble. Mike Stonebreaker, our All-American linebacker who would finish the season as the fourth-ranked defensive player in all of college football, recovered the fumble.

That might have been the ball game if our offense had been able to sustain a drive. But we gave the ball back to Miami when Tony Rice fumbled on the fourteen-yard line with a minute and twenty-five seconds left. Thirty-five seconds later, Walsh found Brown in the end zone. The score was 31–30 with forty-five seconds left. Miami had to go for two to win the game.

Walsh dropped into the pocket and looked one receiver off before firing a shot into the end zone intended for Leonard Conley. But Pat Terrell stepped up and batted the pass away.

Notre Dame defeated Miami for the first time in four years, and beat the number-one-ranked team in the nation for the first time in eleven seasons. It was Steve Walsh's first loss in seventeen starts as Miami's quarterback. And it was one of the greatest college football games I've ever had the privilege of coaching.

After our victory over Miami, our team truly believed that perfection was not only possible, but highly probable, even likely. They never got cocky, we made sure of that, but they exuded the kind of confidence I had been hoping for all season. After the game, I immediately refocused the athletes on the upcoming Air Force game. With their wishbone offense, Air Force could demoralize a team with a pounding ground attack.

Fortunately, our athletes did not have a letdown. We beat Air Force, Navy, Rice, and Penn State and entered the final game of the regular season ranked number one in the nation. Our final opponent was Southern Cal, the number-two-ranked team in the country. It was the first time in this historic rivalry dating back to 1928 that Notre Dame and USC would play as the number-one- and number-two-ranked teams.

The game was at the Los Angeles Memorial Coliseum, which meant we were traveling. I called Miami's head coach, Jimmy Johnson, and talked to him about traveling to California, and how he had prepared his top-ranked teams for the rigors of cross-country travel as well as the media spectacle that went along with being ranked number one. Calls like this were a common practice among coaches. Jimmy was helpful, as were all my friends in the coaching community. One of the big misconceptions about college football is the belief that coaches have the same vitriolic dislike for one another that some fans have for the opposing teams. Nothing could be further from the truth. I talked to other coaches throughout my career, and didn't think twice when other coaches called me. Sure, we were opponents on game days, and I wanted to beat Jimmy, and Bo Schembechler, Bill Walsh, and Bobby Bowden, as much as anyone, but when the games were over, we remained friends. What I didn't know when I talked to Jimmy that afternoon was that a reporter was in his office. The reporter heard only Jimmy's end of the conversation, but that was all he needed to hear. It didn't take long for the story of our conversation to hit the newswires, which provided even more of a distraction. Not that Jimmy and I revealed the secrets to the college football Rosetta stone that afternoon; but as the coach of one of the only unbeaten teams in the country, everything I did got scrutinized. If I went to the bathroom three times a day instead of two, people tried to read something into it, like I might be more nervous than usual, instead of checking to see how many Cokes I had after lunch. My call to Jimmy was no big deal for the two of us. That didn't stop the press from talking about it for the rest of the weekend.

Unfortunately, the call would become a blip on the radar later in the week, as I was, once again, forced to do something that sent my critics over the edge. Twenty-four hours before our biggest game of the year—one of the biggest games in the history of Notre Dame football—I was forced to suspend two of our best players.

Throughout the year, I had told our athletes that perfection required discipline, perseverance, and faith, but discipline above all else. That had been one of the tenets I had written in my notes during my flight to Japan after our disappointing Cotton Bowl loss, and it was something I believed in my bones. Without discipline, nothing else mattered. With few exceptions, the players responded. Our practice sessions were tough and hard-hitting (they had to be, given the number of players we had playing new positions throughout the year), and the players sacrificed all semblance of a social life. If not every day, at least every other day, I reinforced the need to abide by all the team rules, with no exceptions. Doing the little things right, including obeying all the rules all the time, was another of the items I had written on my list during my fourteen-hour flight.

Promptness was Rule Number One. I told our players from day one that being on time was a basic bare-minimum requirement to play for Notre Dame. "If you are late, you are telling the rest of this team that you are more important than them, the coaches, and time itself," I said. "Tardiness is a loud and clear message that you think everyone else's time is worthless, and the world should revolve around your schedule. Well, gentlemen, the world doesn't work that way, and Notre Dame football is certainly not going to work that way."

Because the USC game fell on Thanksgiving Saturday, our schedule was tight and different from the usual. We practiced on Tuesday, had a Thanksgiving meal together on Thursday, went through a short practice session, and flew to Los Angeles Thursday night. Friday, we met for a pregame dinner and our final meeting before the athletes suited up for the game.

All went well until the Friday night meal and meeting. I arrived exactly on time, as was my custom, so that I could close the door behind me. The team managers came in to tell me who was late. In this case, it was two stars of our backfield, Ricky Watters and Tony Brooks, good men who had a blind spot when it came to being on time. I knew immediately that they would not be playing on Saturday.

This was not a first-time offense for either of them. Even so, if Tony and Ricky had delivered a legitimate excuse, I probably would have kept them out of the starting lineup, but I doubt I would have sent them home. After all, I had gotten caught in Sunset Strip traffic once and missed an assignment. Coach Hayes had chewed me out in front of everyone in the hotel, but he hadn't sent me home. Unfortunately, Tony and Ricky had been warned. They had been late for several meetings, sometimes five minutes, sometimes ten, once or twice twenty minutes or longer. "If you're late again, one more time, you're not playing," I told each of them.

Tony and Ricky had lost track of time wandering through a shopping mall. They had tried to call, but hadn't been able to reach me.

I did not immediately announce my intention to suspend Ricky and Tony, although I knew that would be the outcome. I wanted to talk it over with our coaches and some key members of the team before laying down the verdict. Not that these conversations would change my mind—I knew they were going home—but I wanted to gauge the staff and players to see how traumatic this decision was going to be.

The team was watching **The Untouchables** in the common area before bed. Mike Green, the head manager, summoned our senior leaders, Andy Heck, Wes Pritchett, Frank Stams, Tim Grunhard, Mark Green, Ned Bolcar, Tony Rice, George Streeter, Corny Southall, Flash Gordon, Pat Terrell, and Stan Smagala, to my makeshift office. I lit up a pipe, and told these team leaders that Tony and Ricky had missed the team meal. Then I said, "What do you think we should do about it?"

Andy Heck was the first to speak. "I feel real strongly about it," he said. "I think we should send them home."

Wes Pritchett agreed enthusiastically. Then Frank Stams and Mark Green said they agreed as well. Soon, it was unanimous. I hadn't said a word, and the team had come to the same conclusion I had arrived at earlier. The only modifier was that some of the players wanted to throw them off the team altogether.

Corny Southall stood up and said, "We've come a long way. We're not going to let this stop us."

This made me happier than anything that had happened in weeks, and took a little bit of the sting away from the hard news I had to deliver to Tony and Ricky. This team had, indeed, achieved Level Four: they knew how to be champions.

Tony and Ricky were not thrilled when I told them I was sending them home. In fact, they did what I expected: they asked for a second chance. "Look, I'm simply enforcing the choice you made," I said. "I told you that if you were late again, you were not going to play. You promised me you would be on time. You didn't keep your word, but I'm going to keep mine."

I believe that if you aren't prepared to keep your word, you shouldn't give it. If I had said to Tony and Ricky, "If you're late again, there will be dire consequences," then there might have been some leeway in what happened to them (although given the team's attitude, I doubt the decision would have been any different). But I had been very specific about the consequences of being late. Knowing what they knew, they should have done whatever it took to be on time, even if it meant staying by my side for the entire weekend. Not keeping their word left me no choice. Had I not followed through, I would have lost all credibility. Potentially losing a football game was minor compared to losing credibility and respect. That was what I wanted Tony, Ricky, and everyone else on our team to take away from this incident.

Certainly, I felt compassion for those guys. They had worked hard to be where they were. They were fine young men with good parents, but that had nothing to do with their actions that afternoon. Their problem was immaturity. Actions have consequences. In this case, the action of being late earned those two players an early ticket home to South Bend.

I allowed the seniors to tell the rest of the team about the decision. There was not a peep of dissension. Tony Rice called a meeting of the backs and receivers and told them, "We were going to win with them, and we're going to win without them." Then Tony went to coach Pete Cordelli and said, "Coach, we're going to win no matter what."

We won 27–10 in a game that was never that close. Mark Green stepped up and had a great game at tailback, and our defense shut down their high-powered offense, led by Rodney Peete. Every player elevated his game, and we played almost flawless football. When the clock ran out in the fourth quarter, for the first time in eighteen years, Notre Dame finished the regular season as the number-one-ranked team in the nation, with a flawless record of 11–0.

It all would have been for nothing if we hadn't come together one more time on January 2 in Sun Devil Stadium in Tempe, Arizona, and beaten West Virginia in the Fiesta Bowl. West Virginia was ranked second in the nation and was undefeated. If they could beat us, they had a legitimate claim to the national championship.

The tone was set on the first series of downs. Facing a third and long, West Virginia's quarterback, Major Harris, did what he'd done all season long—he rolled out and looked to run for the first down. Our All-American linebacker Michael Stonebreaker tripped him up behind the line, and Jeff Alm, our 260-pound tackle, finished off the tackle, landing hard on Harris's shoulder. He limped off the field holding his left shoulder, and the game was never close after that.

We won 34–21, with Tony Rice rushing for 75 yards and completing seven of eleven passes for 213 yards. Throughout the course of the season, Tony had competed against the top three Heisman contenders of the year—Rodney Peete of USC, Steve Walsh of Miami, and Major Harris of West Virginia—and he had beaten them all. But the Fiesta Bowl proved to be the best statistical game of Tony's collegiate career. It was also his greatest moment as a leader at Notre Dame.

The 1988 Notre Dame football team was the undisputed champion of Division I-A college football, a title those players earned, and one the school deserved.

Afterward I said, "I've underestimated this team in a lot of ways. If you ask me, 'Is this a great football team?' I'd have to say, 'Yes,' because nobody proved otherwise."

Then someone asked if I had one word to describe this team, what would I use.

That one was easy.

"Perfect."

14

ALL YOU CAN DO IS ALL YOU CAN DO

Leading the team out of Notre Dame Tunnel. The 1988 Notre Dame football team was the undisputed champion of Division I-A college football, a title those players earned and one the school deserved.

There is a simple but poignant prayer that I repeat to myself quite often. It's called the Serenity Prayer, and it's one of the most ancient and oft-quoted prayers in the world, dating back to A.D. 500, when it was supposedly penned by a Christian martyr named Boethius. You've probably heard it or read it. Alcoholics Anonymous made it famous in twentieth-century America when AA founder Bill Wilson incorporated it into the organization's 12-step plan. It goes:

Lord grant me
The Serenity to accept the things I cannot change,
The Courage to change the things I can,
And the wisdom to know the difference;

Living one day at a time;
Accepting hardship as a pathway to peace;
Taking, as Jesus did, this sinful world as it is,
Not as I would have it:

Trusting that You will make all things right
If I surrender to Your will;
That I may be reasonably happy in this life
And supremely happy with You forever in the next.

Like a lot of people, I've struggled with the things I cannot control. It's natural to become frustrated when things affect you that are beyond your control. That's why praying for serenity is so important. In coaching, it was difficult to remain serene when the actions or inactions of others led to outcomes I thought were wrong. I didn't believe that my dismissal from Arkansas was justified, or even explainable. I had changed the things I could at that university; we had won football games; attendance and donations were up; and I was fired. Accepting this with a serene and trusting heart was difficult. Thankfully for me, God knew best, and things worked out better than I ever could have imagined.

At Notre Dame, our teams responded exceptionally well to our style of coaching and we won a lot of football games (one hundred to be exact) and one national championship, finished second in the nation twice, and were in the top-twenty teams in college football every season but two. During my first season at Notre Dame, our Friday home-game luncheons, a tradition started by the Quarterback Club when Ara Parseghian was coach, attracted between 100 and 150 people, and the pep rallies were attended by about two thousand fans. By my fourth year, the luncheon had to be moved to Joyce Auditorium because we had three thousand people for sit-down lunches, and the pep rallies were moved to the basketball coliseum, which sat ten thousand. We were forced to shut the doors at 5 P.M. for 7 P.M. pep rallies, and people actually camped out to get seats. The only exception to this was the 1988 Miami game, when we held the pep rally outdoors. Twenty-five thousand people attended.

Also, in our eleven years in South Bend, our family grew as close as we had ever been, and I grew stronger and more devoted in my faith. These are all things on which I can look back with great pride. Not all those successes were within my control, but many of the football-related decisions were mine. I was head football coach, so I led the program.

The things I could not control, and things I sometimes had problems with, included the polls, which sometimes ranked our teams higher than we deserved, and sometimes denied our athletes the championships I felt they had rightfully earned. In 1987, for example, a reporter from **Sports Illustrated** told me the magazine was considering putting us in its preseason top twenty-five.

This was typical, and, in my view wrong. Because Notre Dame had such a huge national following, ranking it high in the polls boosted magazine sales. I always said that if Notre Dame had a mediocre team, it would be ranked in the top twenty. If it had a decent team, it would be in the top fifteen. If it was good, it was top ten. And if it was a legitimate top-twenty team, it would be ranked in the preseason top five. In 1987, I told the **Sports Illustrated** reporter that the magazine would lose all credibility if it put us in its top twenty-five. "The only way you could lose more credibility," I said, "would be if you put me on the cover of your swimsuit issue."

A year later, I think poll voters kept us out of the number one spot longer than we deserved because the "experts" said we were still one year away from greatness. It wasn't until we defeated two number-one-ranked teams (Miami and USC) that we were begrudgingly elevated to the top spot. And we were still considered underdogs against West Virginia in the Fiesta Bowl. It took a perfect 12–0 record for us to earn that national championship. Once there, we stayed number one in every preseason 1989 poll, and remained in the top spot for fifteen weeks, the longest such streak in Notre Dame history.

Coach Vince Lombardi had it right when he said, "Winning is a habit, and, unfortunately, so is losing." A lot of people asked me how you come back from a national championship and keep your team up every week the following year. The answer is simple: Winners win. We didn't change anything in our approach. The 1989 team worked just as hard as the 1988 team; the players demanded the same level of excellence out of themselves and their teammates, executed the fundamentals, limited their mistakes, and approached each down as a battle they expected to win.

When we lost to Miami in 1989, breaking a twenty-three-game winning streak, we dropped out of the top spot for the first time. That was fair. Colorado was undefeated and a great football team. We had a loss, and even though we beat the ACC champion (Virginia), the Big Ten champion (Michigan), the Pac-10 champion (Southern Cal), and three more bowl-bound teams (Penn State, Air Force, and Michigan State), Colorado deserved the number one ranking at the end of the regular season. I figured our destiny was in our own hands when we accepted the Orange Bowl bid to play Colorado.

When we beat the number-one-ranked team by a score of 21–6, I felt as though our team deserved to be number one, and I wasn't bashful about expressing that view. Minutes after our win I said, "I can honestly say, right now, that we have the best record—no other team has twelve wins—and the toughest schedule. I don't know how you can decide on anybody else being number one. That's my personal opinion, unless you want to say who's the best team on November twenty-fifth [the day after we lost to Miami]. We were number one for eleven weeks, and the one week we were out of the number one spot we came back to beat the number-one-ranked team by fifteen points. I know people will say head-to-head, and that's fair. But on that particular day, you did not see a typical Notre Dame team. When you play nine bowl teams, those kinds of things are going to happen. We have the best record against the toughest schedule. Case closed."

But the case wasn't closed. Miami was voted number one, and we finished the year ranked second. That irked me because I felt we had done what we'd had to do. The 1989 Notre Dame team was perhaps the best team I had ever coached. We had done what we could to win the championship, but those voting on such matters saw it differently. That was frustrating because it was out of my control. It was one of those times when I needed to pray for serenity.

The same thing happened in 1993. Our team won eleven football games and lost only one, again playing the toughest schedule in college football. When we beat Texas A&M 24–21 in the Cotton Bowl, I thought we had the best team in the nation. The logic that had kept us out of the top spot in 1989 had been that we had lost head-to-head against Miami, so Miami should be number one. In 1993, we beat Florida State head-to-head and finished the year with the same won-lost record as the Seminoles, but poll voters put us at number two and FSU at number one. At the time, I felt that this was due to a backlash from the NBC contract that Notre Dame had signed to have all our home football games nationally televised. No other school had such an arrangement, so this may have caused some negative feelings among the media and the coaches, both the voting groups at the time. I had nothing to do with the contract, and didn't even know about it until it was all but completed, and our players certainly had no role in the negotiations. It was unfair in my view to penalize our athletes because of a television deal our administration had entered with a network. But, there was nothing I could do about it, and if we couldn't win the national title, I was happy that my old friend Bobby Bowden could.

From my earliest years at Notre Dame, I spoke out against the polling system as it was structured at the time. I thought that it did not reward teams for playing tough schedules, as too many voters based their decisions strictly on won-lost records. To prove my point, I compared the schedules of many of the top football schools with those same schedules a decade before. As I suspected, I found that many schools were canceling games with top-ranked teams and playing schools that were far below them in size and ability. This made sense because if you wanted to be the top team in the country, you had to win all your games. If you had an open date, were you going to schedule Miami or Our Sisters of Mercy? I couldn't fault the coaches and administrators who dropped the tough games, but I did think that the polling system was unfair to the teams who continued to play hard schedules.

For eleven years we played the toughest schedule we could find, just as Father Joyce had promised me we would. In 1992, Dick Rosenthal informed me that Penn State had asked us to release them from their contract in the 1993 and 1994 seasons because they wanted to join the Big Ten. I told Dick, "The Penn State game is good for college athletics, but I understand their situation. Who can we get to replace them?"

Dick said, "How about Florida State?"

At the time FSU was the number-one-ranked team in the nation. I said, "Great. Let's do it."

Because of the strength of our scheduling, I felt that Notre Dame should have won at least one and possibly two more national titles on my watch. But I didn't control the polling process, so I had to accept the outcome. We had done all we could do, and our coaches and players had done all they could. If the outcome of a process we did not control did not go our way, we had to accept what we did not control. In hindsight, I made a mistake by saying Notre Dame deserved to be national champions prior to voting. I simply should have said, "Que sera, sera—whatever will be, will be."

I also had no control over what was and was not written about Notre Dame and about me. I have to say that 99 percent of the reporters who covered me throughout my career were fair and honest people who did a good job. Sometimes I didn't like what was said or written, but there were very few instances when I thought a reporter behaved maliciously. As a result, my relationship with the press was always forthright and open.

The one noteworthy exception came in 1987 when a writer for **Sports Illustrated** named Doug Looney approached me about doing a book. I was skeptical, as was Notre Dame, and we said no. **A Season on the Brink,** a less-than-flattering book about Bobby Knight, had just been released, and we were reluctant to go the independent author route. Furthermore, Simon and Schuster had purchased the rights to a book that would end up being titled **The Fighting Spirit: A Championship Season at Notre Dame,** written by me with the help of our outstanding sports information director, John Heisler. We had no idea when we started that the book would be about a national championship season. All we were hoping to do was chronicle the inner workings of a Notre Dame football season. So John and I taped all the team meetings and kept a running log of my thoughts throughout the season. The fact that we won the national championship that year was a bonus.

Midway through the season, word filtered back to me that Looney's book would not be flattering. Several former players called me to express their concerns. Those who had met with Looney felt he had prodded them into saying things that could be taken out of context. For example, one player said he was asked about drug use. He said, "I never saw any." When Looney pressed two or three more times, he finally said, "There were probably some players who used, but I didn't know about it, and I don't know anybody on the team who did." Of course, the quote that made it into the book was, "There were probably some players who used."

Looney's book came out in 1989 and was titled **Under the Tarnished Dome**. I never read it and never commented on it, despite getting calls from everyone from newspaper reporters to Ted Koppel of the ABC show **Nightline.** I was busy coaching another very good Notre Dame football team. The last thing I needed was to get embroiled in a point-by-point debate on a book I hadn't read, written by a person with a personal agenda, with quotes and attributions I knew to be suspect. As my old friend Mark McCormack, the founder of the sports management conglomerate

IMG, used to say, "Don't ever wrestle with a pig. You both get muddy, but the pig likes it."

Dick Rosenthal also gave me good advice on how to handle the situation. "The book is coming out and there's nothing we can do about it," he said. "If there is any truth in there, it might hurt us. If it's not true, it will probably help us. Either way, there's nothing we can do about it now, so let's work on the things we can control."

Despite an initial media splash, **Under the Tarnished Dome** had no impact whatsoever. It soon fizzled, while our book, **The Fighting Spirit,** became a **New York Times** bestseller. And our team won twelve games playing the toughest schedule in all of college football.

There have been other times when I've had to close my eyes and remember the words to the Serenity Prayer. On occasion, columnists have accused me of skirting NCAA rules, leaving the impression that I would do anything, including cheating, to win. Some have gone so far as to imply that I intentionally broke the rules to win, and then left the schools to pick up the pieces after the NCAA found out. These charges have been particularly hurtful given the history of the programs I inherited and the things we accomplished during my tenure. Arkansas was never reported to the NCAA for any infraction during my seven years. We played in the Southwest Conference, where boosters from certain schools paid athletes to attend their institutions. We never paid a player or a parent, never intentionally violated a rule; there were no recruiting inducements, no cars, no job offers, no ticket scandals; and we never engaged in anything remotely resembling a cover-up. Not one assistant coach or former player has ever made a single accusation that we violated NCAA rules during my entire coaching career. Yes, we made mistakes, but never intentionally.

There were some things that were indeed violations, but they were either honest mistakes or decisions made by people who did not report to me or consult me, and I never asked them to intercede on behalf of an athlete. Nevertheless, the accusations hurt, and I was wounded every time I had to answer such charges. Then I remembered that "accepting hardship as a pathway to peace" was a blessing I should cherish. It wasn't always easy, but it was always better than letting criticism and name-calling drag me down.

Throughout my life, I have striven to be the best I can be at whatever I have done. As many of my golf partners will attest, those efforts haven't always been successful, but lack of success has never stopped me from giving it my all. That practice has earned me a reputation for being intense. In fact, one of the commercials I shot recently—one of the only television ads I've ever done—spoofed that intensity by having me grab and shake an unsuspecting motorist at a gas station. The ad was funny because, like all good humor, it was rooted in truth. I am intense because I am totally committed to whatever task is in front of me. Whether it is trying to hit a seven-iron over a bunker to a closely tucked pin, or organizing my thoughts to write this book, I give every task my very best. And in the end, all that can be asked of a person is the best he or she has. If your best is not enough to produce the outcome you desire, you can rest comfortably in the knowledge that you have given all you have, and are a better person for the effort.

I told every athlete I coached that the only thing I expected from him was the best he had to give. I pushed men beyond what they thought they were capable of, because I knew that their best was buried deep inside them, but I never asked anyone to do anything I believed he could not do. Consequently, no one asked me for anything other than my best.

In eleven seasons at Notre Dame, we were booed one time. Oddly enough, it didn't come during 1986, the only losing season we had, or in 1994, when we lost a core group of athletes and had a so-so rebuilding record. No, the only time I heard catcalls from the Notre Dame faithful came in 1992, a year when we won ten football games and finished the season ranked fourth in the country.

The reason was simple, and in many respects understandable. We were playing Michigan at home, and, with the game tied and time running out, we called a couple of offensive plays that, in hindsight, appeared to be too conservative for the situation. The fans thought we were playing for the tie. That was unacceptable. Losing was something the Notre Dame fans could accept as long as they knew we had given it everything we had. Playing not to lose was not the Notre Dame way, and the fans let me know it. Of course, I was not playing for the tie—I never did in three and a half decades of coaching—but I understood the fans' reaction. All they wanted was the best we had.

The results weren't always what we wanted, but I felt we gave it our best effort.

I gave the University of Notre Dame my best, but the university gave me much more in return. The honor of coaching a day at Notre Dame can never be repaid. When Father Beauchamp gave me the equivalent of a lifetime contract at Notre Dame—his word that I could coach at the university until retirement—I felt as blessed as any man on earth. I knew I could stay at Notre Dame until the day I was ready to leave.

That day came in 1996.

We had just come off a disappointing 1995 season. We'd lost a lot of fine athletes to graduation in 1994, and I had lost a number of great assistant coaches to head-coaching jobs, including my son Skip, who had worked for me as an offensive coordinator and receiver coach. Skip took the job as head coach at the University of Connecticut with my blessing. Prior to assuming his coaching responsibilities he did a huge favor for me by tricking me into interviewing a young receiver coach from Colorado State named Urban Meyer. I didn't know who Urban Meyer was, nor did I have any interest in talking to him. So Skip asked me to lunch at the National Football Coaches Convention, and when I showed up he said, "Dad, I'd like to introduce you to Urban Meyer." I wasn't thrilled about the way Skip had me meet Urban, but I was pleased once I hired Urban to coach our receivers. He went on to win Coach of the Year honors as the head coach at Utah, and was the hands-down choice for the head-coaching job at the University of Florida when the job came open in 2005.

I also lost staff members and friends like George Stewart, who moved on to a successful career in the NFL, and Rick Minter, my defensive coordinator, who took the head-coaching job in Cincinnati. Then, at the end of the 1994 season, Dick Rosenthal, a man who had become one of my all-time best friends, retired as the athletic director of Notre Dame. His replacement, Mike Wadsworth, was a sharp Canadian lawyer who had played defensive tackle at Notre Dame during the Ara Parseghian era, and who had gone on to be the Canadian ambassador to Ireland before assuming the reins as athletic director.

I had a professional relationship with Mike Wadsworth, but it was not the same kind of relationship I'd had with Dick. While I spoke to Dick almost every day about one thing or another, I did not speak to Mike Wadsworth at all. He wanted me to go through his assistant, George Kell. This was a different approach, much more bureaucratic, but Mike had worked for the Canadian Department of Foreign Affairs, so that was to be expected. I didn't mind going through George as long as the lines of communication worked. But as the 1995 season wore on, I realized that I was getting tired, many of the friends I had made during my time at Notre Dame had either retired or moved on to other jobs, and the expectations of the job were beginning to wear on me. Frank Leahy and Ara Parseghian had both coached Notre Dame for eleven years, the same length of time I did.

Rather than let any negativity seep into my psyche, I decided that 1996 would be my last year at Notre Dame. I wanted to retire having given the University of Notre Dame my very best. But I also wanted to retire before I broke Knute Rockne's record as the school's all-time winningest coach. Even an undefeated 1996 season would leave me a few wins shy of Rockne, which was how I thought it should be. Some records should never be broken, and in my mind, Rockne's was one of them. I probably wouldn't have come close if Rockne had not been killed in an airplane crash in the prime of his career. It didn't seem right that I hang around to break a record just because I coached more games than Rockne. So I told Father Beauchamp that I intended to retire.

The only thing I'm sorry about was how the transition took place. We were 8–2 in 1996 and ranked number ten in the country when my retirement became official. I had asked Mike Wadsworth not to name my replacement until the end of the season, because I had seen what had happened to Gerry Faust when I had been named head coach before his tenure expired. Focus shifted away from winning the remaining games on the schedule and toward who the next coach would be, with players and assistant coaches worried about their futures. Mike named Bob Davie, my defensive coordinator, as the new head coach the Monday before our last game with the University of Southern California. I didn't think that was right, but it was Mike's call. A week later, the turmoil I had feared with the naming of a new coach became a reality, and we played a flat and uninspired game against Southern Cal.

In my final two home games as head coach at the University of Notre Dame, we beat Pittsburgh 60–6 and Rutgers 62–0. I had been asked by the administration to say a few words to the crowd after the final home game. We led by 35 points at halftime and by 62 at the end of the third quarter, so I had plenty of time to think of what I planned to say.

Unfortunately, the memories of my time there were too many to mention, and my emotions were so high that I was afraid I couldn't get through the few things I hoped to say. I remembered that first phone call from Father Joyce inviting me to be the new head coach at Notre Dame; the first-season struggles through numerous heartbreaking losses; the great players and great men who had taught me as much as I had taught them—people like Jerome Bettis, whose team won the Super Bowl after the 2005 season and was one of the most popular players in the history of the Pittsburgh Steelers franchise.

I also thought about the summer of 1987, when Notre Dame hosted the Special Olympics. Six thousand athletes traveled to South Bend to compete. All had special needs, but not one of them had a bitter attitude. My job at the Games was to provide hugs to every athlete who came across the finish line at lane four. No matter where the athletes finished, I hugged them and said, "Congratulations. I'm proud of you, and I love you." The joy on the faces of those athletes was as clear to me nine years after the fact as it was during the Games. I found myself near tears as the memory of those Special Olympians flashed through my mind. Talk about people who gave it their all! For the rest of my life, I will never forget what I learned from that experience.

When our final home game of the 1996 season ended, I refused to let the players take a victory lap on my behalf. We still had to travel to Los Angeles for the Southern Cal game, and I didn't want the players to lose focus. Still, I became choked up as I spoke to the crowd. Officially, we had 59,054 people in the stadium—a sellout crowd—but there had to be more than 60,000 people there when I walked to a makeshift podium to make my final remarks.

Most of what I said is a blur. It was all I could do not to break down (which I later did at my postgame press conference—a first for me as a coach). What I do remember saying is: "If you have never been a part of Notre Dame and are asked to explain it, you can't. There are no words to describe what we have here. But once you've been a part of the Notre Dame family, no explanation is necessary. I will always cherish the fact that I had the opportunity to be a representative of Our Lady's school, both on and off the field. To a Catholic, no man could ask for a more important role in life."

Later that afternoon, I bristled at questions about my "legacy." Legacies were for others to decide. I wanted to be known as a man who did all he could for the University of Notre Dame.

All I could do was all I could do. If history treats me kindly, I will be happy, and if future generations forget about my efforts, I will be content with that as well. Notre Dame got the best I had. Hopefully, it was enough. If not, it was still my best.

Beth and I will be buried at Notre Dame. Father Beauchamp helped us pick out plots on a beautiful hillside overlooking Our Lady on the Golden Dome. Granted, the site is more beautiful standing upright aboveground than it will be from our final resting places. But at least we will be there, where Our Lady can watch over us for eternity.

15

EVERYONE NEEDS SOMETHING TO LOOK FORWARD TO

I didn't plan on ever coaching again, but I soon warmed to the idea of ending my career at the same school where I had penned my original 108 goals for life. After all, everyone needs something to look forward to. **(Courtesy of the University of South Carolina Media Relations)**

When I retired from Notre Dame, my plan was to spend time in my home in Orlando, play a lot of golf, plant a garden with my wife, throw an occasional fishing line in a lake, travel abroad to places like Scotland and Ireland, and enjoy my family. We were grandparents, and I looked forward to spoiling my grandchildren. By this time I was one of the most sought-after motivational speakers in the country, I had written two bestselling books, and I had just signed a contract with CBS to work with Jim Nantz on the network's college pregame show. I figured I would give a few speeches a year, spend about fifteen days a season doing television, and set out establishing a new routine in Florida.

We had owned a home in Orlando since 1979, starting out in Arnold Palmer's Bay Hill Club Community, then moving to Bay Hill Village, where Payne Stewart was our neighbor. When Arnold Palmer and Mark McCormack started Isleworth, an upscale golf community in Windermere where Tiger Woods, Mark O'Meara, and John Cook live now, we joined there and bought a lot with every intention of building a home. Then

Lake Nona, a competing golf development near the Orlando airport, offered us a corporate membership and a great deal on a lot. We took them up on it, and built a home near the clubhouse. This was where I hoped to spend the rest of my life.

Coaching was the furthest thing from my mind. I figured that once you had been at Notre Dame, the only place left to go was heaven. When I announced my retirement, Bob Davie, who would succeed me at Notre Dame, approached me and said, "Coach, I can help you with the Maryland job if you're interested. I know those people fairly well, and I'll be happy to make some calls for you."

I laughed out loud and said, "Bob, I'm retiring. If I wanted to stay in coaching, I'd stay here."

I figured my coaching days were over. It was time to move on with the rest of my life. I had no idea how quickly things would change.

During our final year in South Bend, Beth had experienced some problems with her throat, so much so that she lost her voice. The doctor she visited took a culture. He said he didn't find anything. It was probably strained vocal cords from screaming at the games, he said. This puzzled me, although I didn't make much of it. Beth was the calmest person in Notre Dame Stadium on game days. She would have been more likely to put on a uniform and field a couple of punts than lose her voice screaming at a football game. Still, I figured the doctor knew what he was doing. It was a sore throat. She would be fine.

But the problem didn't get better. In fact, when we moved to Orlando it got worse. I still didn't worry, because Beth wasn't worried. The pollen in central Florida can wreak havoc on even the strongest throats. A month or two of rest, and she should be as good as new. I didn't think twice when she went to another doctor. Maybe he could give her some lozenges.

That afternoon, in early March on a Tuesday, Beth called me. She was crying.

"What's wrong?" I asked.

I'll never forget her exact words. "The doctor says I have throat cancer," she said. "He's not sure it's curable."

Nothing can prepare you for this kind of news. No matter how many times you hear about friends who have been diagnosed with cancer, when the word comes from a family member, your brain freezes. The phone felt like it weighed a hundred pounds, and my shoulders didn't feel as though they could support my head. More than anything, I wanted to reach through the phone line so I could hug and kiss my wife. Instead, I said, "Come home." I couldn't believe it, because Beth was not a smoker; but she had been an X-ray technician.

After I hung up, I called the developer who had sold us our house. Within fifteen minutes, we had come to terms on the one-acre lot next door. Then I called our builder and told him we would be adding an addition. I not only wanted Beth to believe she was going to live; I wanted her to wake up in the mornings with something to look forward to. I wanted her to have a project to take her mind off of her illness. She loved building and renovating our homes. Within an hour of getting the news that she had cancer, I had arranged for us to almost double the size of our house.

When she got home, I did my best to console her. Then we sat down in the kitchen and talked through what we had to do next. Beth's father had passed away a few years before, so Beth's mother was living with us, which turned out to be a blessing. After the initial emotions, we started making lists. The first item was to find the best doctor for a second opinion.

Thankfully, I was in a financial position to seek out the best doctors in the land. But even if I had been less well off, I would have sold everything I owned and borrowed the rest to make sure Beth had the best care possible. I know of no one who ever asked "How much is this going to cost?" as he was being wheeled in for lifesaving surgery.

We settled on Dr. Bruce Pearson at the Mayo Clinic, the best in the business in every respect. He did not sugarcoat the diagnosis. Beth had stage-four throat cancer. He recommended surgery but did not recommend radiation treatments, because of the devastating effect they have on your body. Regardless of the direction we chose, the doctor said, she had less than a 10 percent chance of survival.

I firmly believe that God took me out of coaching to be with my wife during her illness. I was only fifty-nine years old in 1996, an age when some men get their first head-coaching jobs, not retire from their last one. Yet, I knew in my heart that retiring from Notre Dame was the right thing. Now, I believe that this was God's way of putting me in the right place at the right time to take care of Beth during her greatest time of need. For thirty-six years, she had taken care of me. It was time for me to take care of her.

The surgery lasted fourteen hours. Doctors had to remove the tumors in segments and run biopsies throughout the procedure. It was grueling, not just on the patient, but on our family as well. Luanne, Skip, Kevin, Liz, and I were all praying, as were my daughters-in-law and sons-in-law and our grandchildren. They were stronger than I could ever have hoped, and their strength helped me. I knew we had a long, tough road ahead, and I needed all the support I could get.

I read every book I could find on how to act when your spouse has cancer. Some of the tips were useful, especially the ones on what to expect physically and emotionally from a cancer patient.

Beth would be very sick, outwardly sicker in fact from the treatment than from the disease. She would probably go through many more emotional swings than I was used to seeing. As a spouse, my role was to be supportive and upbeat, and provide her with the kind of loving environment every person, sick or well, craves.

Beth did indeed have a tough time physically. After surgery we decided to get radiation treatments even though Dr. Pearson had said he didn't think they were necessary. Even with the side effects, Beth decided it was critical to follow up the surgery with radiation. She received eighty-six radiation treatments in six weeks. Each treatment left her sick and drained. She had difficulty moving and speaking. Her weight went from 129 pounds to 89 pounds. She was helpless. And in many respects, so was I.

The people at CBS could not have been more supportive. Sean McManus, the president of CBS Sports, went out of his way to make sure we had everything he and the network could provide. I must admit, I wasn't very good on television that first year. My mind was always with Beth, and my demeanor and delivery on camera lacked the kind of upbeat pizzazz the show deserved. Thankfully, I was sitting next to Jim Nantz, one of the most naturally gifted sports broadcasters in history, and one of the nicest and most genuine people in the business. Craig James was the third person on

the set, and like Jim, he was a talented and personable young man. We had great chemistry.

Every weekend I would fly to New York for the
show while a car and a chauffeur drove Beth and
her mother from Orlando to Gainesville, Florida,
for Beth's treatments. My good friend Harvey
Mackay helped arrange transportation when I
was away, and my friend Steve Spurrier, who was
the head coach at the University of Florida at the
time, and his wife Jerri, kept tabs on Beth when
she was in Gainesville. I was with her for as many
treatments as my work schedule allowed.

Nor did I miss an opportunity during that
time to go to my knees and pray. What I didn't
realize was that millions of people were praying
for her as well. Not a day had gone by in the last
twenty-five years of marriage when Beth did not
spend at least an hour alone in prayer. Her faith
was as strong as that of anyone I had ever met.
Now it was my turn. Even though the odds were
against her, I felt that Beth had a good chance
of survival for three reasons. First, she had great
faith. Second, she had a fantastic attitude. I was
furious when I realized that her first doctor had
misdiagnosed her and missed an aggressive form
of cancer. But Beth would not allow any of us to
be angry or negative. She said, "I'm going to need
all my strength to get better. I don't want to waste
any energy blaming someone else for where we
are." Finally, I felt confident because of the qual-

ity care we found at the Mayo Clinic. The doctors and nurses worked as long and hard as any group of health-care specialists I had ever seen. Without them, I feel certain, Beth would not be with us today.

Beth responded remarkably well to the treatments, and while she wasn't completely out of the woods, we spent most of 1998 believing she was on the road to recovery.

My second year at CBS was better, but I still wasn't as good as I had hoped I would be. Jim Nantz had moved on to **The NFL Today,** but my new studio partner, Tim Brando, was talented, and I was starting to enjoy television even though every question directed my way was immediately followed by Vinny Devito, our producer, counting down in my earpiece: "Five...four...three...two..."

I was also working for U.S. Filter, a six-billion-dollar natural resource filtration company headed by Dick Heckmann, one of the most talented businessmen I know. He had offered me a vice-presidential position with U.S. Filter. I had told him I couldn't accept his offer, but I would work on special projects for the company.

Toward the end of my second year of television, I got a call from Dr. Mike Magee, the athletic director at the University of South Carolina. Mike and I were contemporaries. He had been an offensive tackle at Duke while I was playing at

Kent State. That's where the similarities ended. Dr. Magee had been a first-team All-American for the Blue Devils, and the 1959 Outland Trophy recipient as the nation's top lineman. The only national award I was in line for at Kent State was "smallest college football player not to be injured for life in a game."

Mike did not call to reminisce about the good old days. He wanted to talk to me about coming to South Carolina. My first reaction was to turn him down. Between Beth's recovery, my speaking commitments, television, and U.S. Filter, my schedule was already overbooked. I told Beth, "I'm not retired, I'm retarded."

A schedule like I had was stupid. But the desire to coach—or more aptly, to get back into teaching—kept coming back. When I retired from Notre Dame I thought I was tired of coaching. In fact, I was tired of maintaining. After ten winning seasons, nine bowl appearances, a national championship, and a decade of being ranked in the top twenty, I felt as though I had done all I could do, so it was the right time for me to retire. My mistake was confusing my unwillingness to maintain the status quo (even though the status quo at Notre Dame was pretty high) with a desire to get out of coaching altogether. I was in my early sixties, and I still believed I had enough energy to go back and coach a few more years, and enough enthusiasm for teaching to influence another group of student-athletes. There is a rule of life that you are either growing or dying. Grass is either growing or dying and so is a person, a marriage, and a business. The minute we try to maintain, we start dying. When I left Notre Dame, I wasn't tired of coaching, I was tired of maintaining and I wasn't smart enough to know the difference.

Beth saw it. She knew that I had to get out. She also knew, as I did, that everyone needs four things in life:

- First, you have to have something to do. Stories of healthy individuals who die within a few years of retirement are too numerous to list. It's also true that prisoners serving life sentences sleep for twelve to fourteen hours a day because they have nothing in their lives that compels them to get out of bed.
- The second thing you have to have is someone to love. We are put on earth to love other people. Those who don't have anyone exist without happiness.
- Third, you have to have something to believe in. I've always said that not believing in a god is not an option for humans. You might not believe in the Heavenly Father, as I do, but everyone has a god. It might be the quest for power or material gains; it might be a cause—environmentalism,

conservationism, global socialism, or one of countless other isms; or it might be the search for peace—but everyone has a god.

- Finally, you have to have something to look forward to. In his famous book **Man's Search for Meaning,** Dr. Viktor Frankl, a Holocaust survivor, made some interesting clinical observations in the midst of the horrors of Auschwitz. Dr. Frankl noticed that prisoners who had nothing to live for and nothing to look forward to died quickly of starvation, fatigue, or abuse at the hands of their captors. But those who survived shared one thing in common: they all had something to look forward to. Often the survivors lived for the thought of rejoining a relative, or escaping to another country. Sometimes they hung on in the hopes of exacting revenge on the Nazis. But whatever the reason, those who survived the greatest atrocity in history were those who had something to look forward to.

By late 1998, I had someone to love, and something to do, and plenty to believe in. What I didn't have was something to look forward to. Beth saw this, and said, "Why don't you at least talk to Dr. Magee? It can't hurt."

She was right, so I entered into discussions with Mike about coming back to South Carolina.

I wasn't sure where the discussions would lead, but I soon warmed to the idea of ending my career at the same school where I had penned my original 108 goals for life. South Carolina had unbelievable fan support, and it would be a challenge to compete in the Southeastern Conference. I trusted Dr. Magee. He was very intelligent and personable, and I would enjoy working with him.

I was informed the program was in shambles. In 1998, the Gamecocks won their opening game and then lost ten straight. Even worse, they had eighteen wins, thirty-seven losses, and one tie in conference games since entering the Southeastern Conference. They had won a single bowl game in the 108-year history of Gamecock football. This did not discourage me. I had taken similarly disheveled programs and been successful. I thought we could do it again.

My main concern—other than Beth—was knowing I would stay only a few years. My health was good, my energy level excellent, but I did not want to make a commitment longer than three years. Some schools aren't interested in talking to a coach who can make only a three-year commitment. And most quality assistant coaches don't want to work for someone they know will be leaving in a few years. So I told Dr. John Palms, the school president, and Dr. Magee that I would promise to stay for only three years and I would consider the job only if the university agreed to replace me with a member of my staff when I retired.

"We'll work hard, win games, go to bowl games, but I'm not going to stay forever," I said. "And I can't have assistants running off after a couple of years because they think I'm going to leave. If they know there will be continuity once I retire, I can recruit quality assistants and quality players." In addition, I knew I could retire with peace of mind because the assistants would not be out of a job when I left.

Mike gave me his word that this would be the case, but he could not put it into writing. To me, this was a deal killer. I'd seen a lot of verbal agreements expire when one of the parties lost his job, retired, or had a convenient memory lapse. For me to commit to South Carolina, I needed written assurance that one of my assistants would take my place when I retired.

Both Dr. Palms and Mike Magee said, "I can give you my word, but I can't put it in writing."

Again I told them I didn't think I could come without this in writing. They flew to Connecticut, interviewed Skip, and told me they were comfortable with his replacing me, provided we went to bowl games. Again I said, "No, not without this in writing."

After we went back and forth for a while, Beth finally settled things by saying, "I've been praying hard about the future, and I think you should take the job at South Carolina." Within twenty-four hours I had accepted the job. In no time I assembled an excellent staff. In addition to Skip, I hired Charlie Strong from Notre Dame (now the defensive coordinator at the University of Florida) and a number of other talented assistants. I told Skip and Charlie that our offensive and defensive schemes would complement each other. I wasn't interested in statistics. I was concerned only with wins. I have seen coordinators jeopardize a team's chance of winning by calling a pass when a conservative run would secure the win.

Some members of the board of trustees were aware of the agreement Dr. Palms and Mike Magee had made with Skip and me. I was not concerned so much about Skip's future, since he can coach (and is proving this as the head coach at East Carolina), as for our staff when I left. If I was going to build continuity in a program, I wanted it to continue after I left.

The press conference announcing my hiring was held in the stadium in front of six thousand enthusiastic people. I told them I would do everything in my power to turn the program around, and that there was no reason why South Carolina could not have a winning football team. The team's attendance already averaged over eighty-one thousand people a game, number eleven in the country, and our stadium seated only eighty thousand.

When practice started I realized that I might have been overly optimistic in my press conference. The team had a long way to go. We had some talent, but no chance to win. Our defense was pretty good. Offensively we had more problems then solutions. We had four good offensive linemen and lost two of them with injuries in fall camp. We had one quarterback on scholarship, and he injured his knee in our fourth game. In the backfield we started three freshmen who, if you told them to block a man, thought it was a suggestion.

They worked hard and wanted to win, but deep down inside I don't feel they trusted me or my assistants. Then the Monday before our game with Georgia, trouble struck. Skip caught a severe gastric infection, causing him to be hospitalized for most of the week. He didn't completely recover for a month.

A few weeks later, I got news that made me forget about Skip's illness. During a routine exam, Beth's doctor found elevated blood-count levels. A few tests later, we got the worst news any cancer survivor can receive: the disease was back. She had to have another round of surgery, this time to remove her adrenal gland. To say that this took my mind off of football would be an understatement. I questioned myself every day. Was coming to South Carolina the right thing? Had the hectic pace of taking on another football team and moving to another school somehow contributed to Beth's relapse? Had I so looked forward to the challenge of another program that I had failed my wife?

As if grappling with these questions were not tough enough, while I was on a recruiting trip, flying in a private plane between Georgia, Florida, and South Carolina, the pilots dropped me off at Lady Island Airport. They said, "Coach, we are going to fly eleven miles to Hilton Head to get gas and we will come back to get you." During the eleven-mile flight the plane crashed. One school pilot was killed instantly. The other died later.

Then, in early November as we were getting ready to play the University of Florida, my mother passed away. By Christmas I was referring to 1999 as our "lost year." Still, I never doubted our ability to win. We were down, but not yet out.

When you are in a hole, rule number one is to stop digging. We were so low we had to stand on our tiptoes to touch the bottom. We had two choices: stay down or pick ourselves up. The first pick-me-up for me came on December 12, when Dr. Pearson told us that he thought Beth would one day be cancer free.

I wasn't the only one who had confidence in her. Dr. Pearson told me, "You know, we don't have many good-news stories on the twelfth floor at the Mayo Clinic. By the time a patient gets here, things are already pretty bleak. But I think your wife is going to be one of the few."

Thankfully, his prognosis was accurate.

As for the football team, we finished the year without a single win, 0–11. It was the first time South Carolina had gone a full season without a win since 1897, a year when they only played three games, and two of those were against the same team. We also owned the longest winless streak in college football, having lost twenty-one consecutive games. More troubling than any of that, however, was the feeling I had that this team lacked trust in me, and in each other.

That changed in the summer.

On a Monday evening around six o'clock, in the heat of summer workouts, I got word that two of the players from the previous team had been arrested for selling drugs. I was stunned. I also found out these players had been suspected of being dealers.

By seven, I was standing in the middle of a team meeting saying to every player in the room, "I want to know why you didn't tell me. You knew it. Why didn't I know it? How can you distrust me so much that you would keep something like this from me?"

After a few moments of silence one of the players stood up and said, "Coach, I trust you, and I trust the assistants. But I don't trust some of the players in this room. We've got guys on this team who lie, and who just aren't trustworthy."

Then another player stood up and said, "I agree with him." These players were highly respected by their teammates, and soon most of our team stood up and voiced similar complaints about their teammates. I listened intently, knowing that this would make or break our team. As it turned out, it was just what we needed.

After everyone spoke, I emphasized what I'd told all my players over the years: "Men, this is why we have three rules: Do right, do your best, and show people you care. When our teammates ask the questions: Can I trust you? Are you committed to excellence? Do you care about me? the answer will always be yes. When this happens, we won't be having these discussions."

I followed up the speech by passing out sheets of paper to every player. "I want every one of you to write down everything you do not like about yourself. Everything. Be as honest with yourself as you have ever been."

After several minutes of silence as the players wrote themselves notes, I said, "Your comments will remain confidential. Now go home. We will meet back here tomorrow. Bring your papers with you, and between now and then, I want you to think about what you've written."

The next afternoon, we met at the practice field. We dug a hole, put all the papers in there without reading them, burned them, and covered up the ashes. That morning I had a blank tombstone delivered, and we placed it over the ashes.

"From this moment forward, everything you wrote down on your list, the things that you don't like about yourself, and the things that have kept us apart as a team, are history. They are buried, and they will never be brought up again. We have a new covenant starting today."

We also implemented an idea I received from Pete Carroll. At ten thirty at night in our empty stadium, we had a tug-of-war between the offense and the defense. After some huffing and puffing I stopped and said, "Men, we can't win if we pull against each other. The only chance we have is when we pull together and for each other." I felt they got the message.

During fall camp we would meet every night with the sole purpose of having our players get to know one another. During each meeting I would have five or six players stand up and tell stories of their life experiences. The players got closer to one another as they learned about everyone's background. We also hit them where they lived. Before the 2000 season, I asked every player who lived off campus to move back into the athletic dorm. Virtually everyone complied. Now they were spending time together before practice, during practice, and after practice. When camp began, we took everyone's car keys away. The entire team rode the bus together to and from practice. Most thought this was an awful idea, but it brought us closer together.

When we won our first game of the 2000 season, against New Mexico State, the student body at South Carolina charged the field and tore down the goalposts. A week later we played ninth-ranked Georgia at home and beat them 21–10. The goalposts came down again. Then we beat Mississippi State at Starkville to go 3–0. It was the first time a South Carolina team had won three straight games to start a season since 1990, two years before the school joined the Southeastern Conference.

By November, we had completed the second greatest turnaround in NCAA history, winning seven games and losing four in the regular season after losing twenty-one in a row. We went on to beat Ohio State in the Outback Bowl, the first bowl victory for a South Carolina team in six years and only the second in the history of the school.

A year later, we bettered our won-lost record by one, and contended for the conference championship late into the season before losing to Tennessee and Florida. Then we beat Ohio State again on New Year's Day and finished the season ranked twelfth in the country. It was the school's second-highest ranking ever, and the first time in history that South Carolina had gone to back-to-back bowl games, let alone won them.

I would later be asked what I did to turn the South Carolina program around. "What's the magic touch?" was a question I got a lot. The simple answer was: "There is no magic touch. Hard work, discipline, and perseverance win more often than they lose."

It's just that simple. The only thing I did outside of those three things—and spreading the offense and defense to take advantage of our quickness—was give the athletes at South Carolina something to look forward to.

With that, they had everything they needed to win.

I was ready to leave after my third year, as I had fulfilled my promise to South Carolina. But Dr. Magee prevailed upon me to stay. Why did I? I don't know except that I learned to love the state, the school, the students, and the most loyal and best fans in the world. They all deserve a championship, and I not only hope this happens, but believe it will happen under Steve Spurrier. Recruiting was going well. We finished seventh and eighth in the country in back-to-back recruiting seasons, and the future looked solid. The expectations of the fans went quickly from wanting to win a few games, to wanting to win a bowl game, to wanting to compete for the national championship.

Following the 2002 season, Dr. John Palms resigned as president of South Carolina after ten years of excellent leadership. He was a man of integrity and a friend. He was replaced by Dr. Andrew Sorenson. When the president that hired you leaves, the environment changes. Word started getting back to me that a member of my staff might or might not replace me, and the decision would be up to the president.

I made his decision easy by having two seasons that were mediocre at best. We went into our last four games with a record of 5–2, but failed to qualify for a bowl. We lost very close games both years to Georgia and Tennessee, but they were still losses. These disappointing seasons were nobody's fault but mine. I was as tough as I have ever been during fall camp, and early in the season we were an excellent team. But as the season went on, I didn't work our team hard enough, and we lost our physical toughness. By the time we got to Clemson we were a poor team, and we embarrassed ourselves with our performance. After the 2003 season it was obvious to me that I would coach only one more year, and my replacement would not come from our staff.

This hurt me deeply because Skip and I had been misled. After the 2002 season, Skip was offered a lucrative head-coaching position at a fine school. He declined it after consulting with Dr. Magee. He was assured that he had a future at South Carolina after I left. That proved to be erroneous.

My last season was one of ups and downs. We were up when we defeated teams like Alabama and Arkansas. We were down after losing to Georgia and Ole Miss, both losses coming on almost the last play of the game. Still, we were bowl eligible; it was only a question of which bowl we would play in after our last game against our archrival, Clemson.

Sadly, my last game at South Carolina, and my last game as a head coach, ended with a loss and an ugly bench-clearing brawl. Late in the game we were losing, and a scuffle broke out during a possession change. As our defense and Clemson's offense went onto the field during the possession change, players on both teams thought the benches were clearing for a fight. They weren't, but soon both sides were engaged in a full-scale fight. In my entire career I had never had a player ejected for fighting. Now I had a whole team involved.

The scene prompted appropriate outrage from writers, commentators, administrators, and fans from both schools. It was embarrassing, and unacceptable in every respect. Because of those actions, our administration decided that South Carolina would not go to a bowl game.

That made my last game memorable for all the wrong reasons. My last action as a coach, however, was to introduce Steve Spurrier to the team. If there was a bright spot, it was in passing the torch to a first-class individual like Steve.

South Carolina is fortunate to have a coach the caliber of Steve Spurrier. Any intelligent person would say I would rather have Steve Spurrier be the coach of my Gamecocks than an assistant coach from Holtz's staff. I agree. Do you think Steve Spurrier would have come to the University of South Carolina if we hadn't built a competitive team that could win in the Southeastern Conference? I doubt it.

EPILOGUE

I love golf, my pipe, and reflecting on the many blessings of my life.

On November 22, 2004, I returned to my home in Orlando—embarrassingly big now that Beth's addition is complete—having accumulated 249 victories as a head coach, placing me eighth on the all-time win list in major-college football history. When I am introduced to an audience, the speaker will normally say that I am the only coach in NCAA history to take six different teams to a bowl, and always by the second year at the latest, despite never inheriting a winning team; the only coach in NCAA history to win five bowl games with different teams; and the only coach in NCAA history to take four different teams to top-twenty final rankings. While he is saying these things, I think about the sacrifices my family, former players, and assistant coaches made in order to make these things happen. It is so true that when you receive recognition, someone gave you the opportunity to do so.

At every institution where I've coached I've been blessed with great athletes and coaches. The question I'm most frequently asked is "Who was your favorite player that you ever coached?" I reply, "Which is your favorite child?"

When you coach as many fine athletes as I have over the years, you can't pick a favorite. I can recall almost every athlete who played for me at every school, and I remember something good and worthy about each and every one of them. In hindsight, it seems that the athletes from whom I demanded the most are the ones who seem most appreciative years later: not just those who made All-American, but the walk-ons, the men who weren't talented or gifted, who were willing to subjugate their personal welfare for the benefit of the team. Those are the men who remain my friends today, and they are the ones I remember most vividly when I think about my days in football.

I've received plenty of awards in my life. I like to think of these as tributes to the players, coaches, administrators, alumni, and my friends, because without them I would have had nothing.

When I reflect these days, it's rarely about the plays we called or the games we won. I almost always think about the people I've been able to meet and the friends I've been able to make. I've met popes, presidents, and kings, and made friends who will remain close to me for the rest of my life.

Beth and I were fortunate enough to go to the White House for the first time for dinner with President Reagan when we were at the University of Arkansas. I splurged and hired a limousine, and the evening was everything I had hoped it would be. At our dinner table were Chief Justice Warren Burger, Olivia Newton-John, and others. Beth and I aren't much for dancing, so we left the White House around midnight. I asked the chauffeur to drive us around the Capitol, the Lincoln Memorial, the Supreme Court, and other historical buildings. I had seen them previously, but I was feeling very patriotic and, as always, proud to be an American. However, I had a headache, so our first stop was at a drugstore five blocks from the White House. I had no sooner gotten out of the car than the driver locked the limo for safety. Once inside the drugstore I saw a man with a gun sticking out of his pocket. Then I noticed a huddle of drug addicts and homeless people standing near the corner. And these were the impressive ones!

Just one hour earlier I was socializing with the president of the United States, members of the Supreme Court, senators, movie stars, and entertainers. Five blocks away from the White House, it was hard to believe I was still in America. It was a sobering moment, one I have never forgotten and one that taught me that the people I met at the White House, despite all their accomplishments, are no more important then the ones I met in the drugstore. I was sorry I didn't exhibit the same respect and friendliness to the armed homeless man that I did to those I met at dinner. I made a promise to myself that night, one I've tried to keep for the past quarter century: I do everything I can to treat all strangers as celebrities. The truth of the matter is they are.

President Reagan invited us back to the White House a second time after we won the national championship. When the president was an actor, he played the famous Notre Dame player George Gipp in the movie **Knute Rockne, All American,** so he wanted his last official act as president to be congratulating the Notre Dame team on its undefeated season. I also met and became good friends with President George H. W. Bush and his lovely wife, Barbara. When we attended a state dinner at the White House with President Bush (41) for the first time, I didn't realize what a caring person he was. I have spoken in the same program quite often with him, and have gotten to know him well, and I'm still struck by how genuine and thoughtful he is in everything he does. On the day I retired from coaching, for example, the first call I received was from President Bush.

I wasn't surprised when President Clinton called and invited us to attend a state dinner at the White House, but I was surprised when he added, "How about spending the night in the Lincoln Bedroom?" Prior to dinner, we attended a private party with President Clinton, Vice President Gore, the prime minister of Ireland, and their wives. After dinner we went to bed, and we were awakened the next morning by President Clinton with a tray of coffee. After a private tour of the White House by the president himself, we ended up in the Oval Office talking about leadership and problem solving. It was an amazing day with an amazing man, one I will never forget.

But perhaps the most awe-inspiring person I've had the chance to meet in my life was Pope John Paul II. I have been a Catholic all my life, so when I got the opportunity to visit the Vatican and have a special tour of the grounds by Archbishop Mischenko, I thought I had died and gone to heaven. Meeting the Holy Father made everything else I've done in life seem insignificant.

The thing I've come to realize about famous and powerful people from all professions is that they are, at their core, nice folks. I have played with many great golfers including Arnold Palmer. His attitude is not "Here I am," but "There you are." This isn't a show for Arnold; it's how he behaves with everyone. That's why he's universally recognized as "the King." He has never let his celebrity get in the way of his manners.

In the early nineties, Skip had returned to Notre Dame as an assistant coach for me. His next-door neighbor was Dan Reuttiger, a former walk-on at Notre Dame. Everyone called him "Rudy." He came to our home and gave me a proposed movie script titled **Rudy**. It was the life story of his struggle to enroll at Notre Dame and play football for the Irish; even though he played only thirty seconds in a game, he was carried off the field by his teammates. He asked me to read it and give him my impression. Reading it was not one of my top priorities, so I set it aside. Eventually, Skip called and informed me that Rudy needed to know right away my reaction to the movie script. I read it that day and was impressed. When Rudy was informed of my approval, he went immediately to see Dr. Beauchamp, vice president of Notre Dame, to receive the university's approval to film it on campus. Later, Rudy told me that Notre Dame approved the script within a couple of hours of my endorsement. That approval came one day before Rudy's Hollywood contract was to expire. Fortunately for millions of happy viewers, the movie became a reality because Rudy had friends that helped him. Rudy will be the first one to tell you that despite his persistence, it was the assistance of friends like Skip, Roger Valdiserri, and others that got his story on the screen.

The story of Rudy is the story of life. If you have a dream, chase it. And if you want friends in life, be one to others.

I don't think about the wins and losses these days, so I hope no one remembers them when they think of me after I'm gone. I want the great games to be remembered for the players who played in them, not for the short, skinny man who paced the sidelines. I don't want to be known for the successes I had as a coach, or as a public speaker, because success dies. Significance—helping others to better their lives through word and deed—lasts forever.

The only thing I hope is that when I die, someone says, "That Lou Holtz was significant to a lot of people." It is the best thing that can be said of a person. I hope it will be said of me.

ACKNOWLEDGMENTS

An individual should have six friends so his wife doesn't have to hire pallbearers. I have been blessed to have some very special friends at every school I have coached. However, there have been certain friendships that have lasted for years regardless of where I coached or the amount of success we enjoyed: my high school buddies of fifty years, Bill Roush, best man in my wedding, Jack Goodwin, Bob Dorsey, Tim Sheerer, Ron Friess, and Nevitt Stockdale; my college roommate John Konstantinos; Skip Strzelecki and Mike Nolan with St. Andrew Products; Mike Leep, Ara Parseghian, George Thomas, Father Joyce, Father Hesburgh, Frank Eck, Jay Jordan, Vince Naimoli, and Terry McGlinn of Notre Dame; Joe Ford, Warren and Jack Stephens, and Frank Broyles of Arkansas; Sid Hartman and Harvey Mackay from Minnesota; and Joe Wells III and Frank "Digger" Dawson from East Liverpool. The three people who I consider the brothers I never had are Harvey Mackay, Skip Strzelecki, and Digger Dawson.

And, of course, my good friends and golfing buddies at Lake Nona.

I could write a book about each one of the above-mentioned people, but that would be impossible. There is no way I could write a book on my life and not let you know how special these people have been to me.

It's important for me to tell you how proud I am of all four of our children. Neither time nor space allows me to tell you about the numerous things that each has accomplished or how each one has influenced my life in a positive manner. However, let me tell you where each one of them is at the present time of his or her life and please forgive me if I feel it's worth repeating their accomplishments.

Luanne, age forty-four, graduated from Centenary College and married her husband, Terry Altenbaumer, twenty-three years ago. Terry is a graduate of the University of Arkansas and a chemical engineer. They live in Houston and have a beautiful daughter, Lindsay, who will enter college this fall.

Skip Louis Jr., age forty-two, graduated from Notre Dame, where he lettered in football. Fourteen years ago, he married Jennifer Fitzgerald, a graduate of Florida State University. They have three talented children: Trey (Louis III), age twelve; Chad, age ten; and Hailey, age seven. Skip is presently the head football coach at East Carolina, where he is doing a fantastic job. They now live in Greeneville, North Carolina. Someday I will be known only as Skip's dad.

Kevin, age forty, is a graduate of Notre Dame and also Notre Dame's law school. He married Kelly McLaughlin seven years ago. She is a graduate of the University of Mississippi. Kevin is a public defender and lives in Daytona Beach, Florida, with his family. Kevin worked for five years for the Dallas Cowboys and has three Super Bowl rings; however, he is proudest of his wife and two children, Katherine (the great), age four, and Aaron, age two.

Our youngest child is Elizabeth, age thirty-seven, who graduated from the University of Notre Dame. She is married to Mike Messaglia, a graduate of Notre Dame and Notre Dame's law school. He is a managing partner in Indianapolis for the law firm of Krieg DeVault. They have been married for twelve years and have three beautiful children, Zachary, age eight; Beth, age six; and Jacob, age three.

Because our family is spread all over the country, we get together for a week in July. The location varies annually, but the schedule does not. In the morning we play golf, the afternoon is devoted to children's activities, the evening to family participation (putt-putt golf, amusement park, etc.). At 9 P.M. a babysitter takes the children upstairs and we have a family meeting until

11 P.M. My children will often stay up most of the night discussing the ideas we addressed. We have a set agenda: the first night is devoted to our family business, the second night to our foundation, the third night focuses on their religious progress, the fourth night deals with goals for the coming year and their greatest accomplishments this past year, and the fifth night is dedicated to any problems they or their friends might have that we can help as a family. This is one of the best things we do as a family. It gives our grandchildren the chance to get to know their aunts, uncles, and cousins. For the many years we have done this, attendance is 100 percent.

My father died of a heart attack in January 1977 at age sixty-six, two months after I resigned from the New York Jets.

My mother had a stroke in 1982, which left her paralyzed and unable to speak for seventeen years. She died in November 1999, the Friday before we played Florida.

My younger sister, Vicky, a special person, died in February 2006 at age fifty-nine from a brain aneurysm.

My older sister, Shirley, lives in Indiana.

Just like in football, writing an autobiography is a team effort where success requires a 110 percent effort from everyone involved. The book you are holding required some extraordinary efforts from a lot of unsung heroes. Among them were my editors and friends at William Morrow, Mauro DiPreta and Joelle Yudin; my agent, Sandy Montag at IMG; my friends Harry and Bernie at the Washington Speaker's Bureau; Dick Heckmann at K-2; my collaborator, Steve Eubanks; and my administrative assistants, Rita Ricard and Laurel Lamb.

I also want to offer a special note of thanks to those not mentioned by name, the friends, family members, teachers, athletic directors, players, alumni, sports information directors, and assistant coaches who helped make this book worth writing and helped make my life story something people might want to read. All successful lives are shaped through the help of others. I am no exception. These people, too numerous to mention but too important to be forgotten, helped me in ways I cannot begin to describe. For that I will be eternally thankful.

And, finally, I have to thank my wife, Beth, who spent tireless hours helping with this book, as she has with every other project I have undertaken. No matter what else I might accomplish, life with her will always be my greatest victory.

APPENDIX

Lou Holtz retired from coaching in 2004 after six seasons at the University of South Carolina, and thirty-three years as a head coach. In that time he won one national championship (Notre Dame), 249 games (ninth in college football history), received three national Coach of the Year honors, and is the only coach in NCAA football history to lead six different schools to bowl games. He is also the only coach to lead four different schools to season-ending top-twenty rankings.

In 2005, Holtz joined ESPN as a college football analyst. He is still one of the most sought-after motivational speakers in America.

His collegiate head-coaching record is as follows:

SEASON	SCHOOL	RECORD	BOWL/OPPONENT/RESULT/RANKING
1969	William & Mary	3–7–0	NA
1970	William & Mary	5–7–0	Tangerine/Toledo/L 12–40/NA
1971	William & Mary	5–6–0	NA
1972	N.C. State	8–3–1	Peach/W. Virginia/W 49–13/#17
1973	N.C. State	9–3–0	Liberty/Kansas/W 31–18/#16
1974	N.C. State	9–2–1	Bluebonnet/Houston/ T 31–31/#11
1975	N.C. State	7–4–1	Peach/W. Virginia/L 10–13/NA
1977	Arkansas	11–1–0	Orange/Oklahoma/W 31–6/#3
1978	Arkansas	9–2–1	Fiesta/UCLA/T 10–10/#11
1979	Arkansas	10–2–0	Sugar/Alabama/L 9–24/#8
1980	Arkansas	7–5–0	Hall of Fame/Tulane/ W 34–15/NA
1981	Arkansas	8–4–0	Gator/North Carolina/ L 27–31/NA

SEASON	SCHOOL	RECORD	BOWL/OPPONENT/RESULT/RANKING
1982	Arkansas	9–2–1	Bluebonnet/Florida/W 28–21/#9
1983	Arkansas	6–5–0	NA
1984	Minnesota	4–7–0	NA
1985	Minnesota	6–5–0	Independence/Clemson/W 20–13/NA
1986	Notre Dame	5–6–0	NA
1987	Notre Dame	8–4–0	Cotton/Texas A&M/L 10–35/#17
1988	Notre Dame	12–0–0	Fiesta/W. Virginia/W 34–21/#1
1989	Notre Dame	12–1–0	Orange/Colorado/W 21–6/#2
1990	Notre Dame	9–3–0	Orange/Colorado/L 9–10/#6
1991	Notre Dame	10–3–0	Sugar/Florida/W 39–28/#13
1992	Notre Dame	10–1–1	Cotton/Texas A&M/W 28–3/#4
1993	Notre Dame	11–1–0	Cotton/Texas A&M/W 24–21/#2

SEASON	SCHOOL	RECORD	BOWL/OPPONENT/ RESULT/RANKING
1994	Notre Dame	6–5–1	Fiesta/Colorado/L 24–41/NA
1995	Notre Dame	9–3–0	Orange/Fl. State/L 26–31/#11
1996	Notre Dame	8–3–0	#19
1999	South Carolina	0–11–0	NA
2000	South Carolina	8–4–0	Outback/Ohio St./W 24–7/#19
2001	South Carolina	9–3–1	Outback/Ohio St./ W 31–28/#13
2002	South Carolina	5–7–0	NA
2003	South Carolina	5–7–0	NA
2004	South Carolina	6–5–0	NA

About the Author

After nearly three decades on the sidelines, Lou Holtz retired from coaching and now shares his strategies for success with Fortune 500 companies, groups, and organizations. He is the author of two bestsellers, **The Fighting Spirit and Winning Every Day**. He lives in Florida.

Visit www.AuthorTracker.com for exclusive information on your favorite HarperCollins author.